Edwin

Shirley Eldridge

A catalogue record for this book is available from the National Library of Australia

Copyright © 2020 Shirley Eldridge
All rights reserved.
ISBN-13: 978-1-922343-10-9

Linellen Press
265 Boomerang Road
Oldbury, Western Australia
www.linellenpress.com.au

Author Notes

Although *Edwin – Flamboyant Australian Pioneer* is a work of historical fiction, every person named existed in the context in which they appear.

The events are real, although not necessarily occurring at the time of year or in the specific order reported.

Most dialogue has been created.

Unless nominated otherwise, all indented quotations have been taken from the Rockhampton Bulletin, or the Morning Bulletin, Rockhampton.

Variations in spelling are deliberate e.g. the ship, *Deutschland* was often spelled *Deutchland* in newspapers of the day. Because it was a German ship, the spelling should contain the letter 's'. If it were a Dutch ship it would not contain an 's'.

All decisions have been made for the purpose of readability.

Contents

Author Notes iii
Contents v
1861-1864 - Arrival 1
1865 - Settling in 16
1866–1868 - Progress 23
1869-1871 - Family 29
1872–1874 - Expansion 37
1875-1879 - Growth and Adversity 46
1879-1880 - Welcome the Fraser Family 58
1881-1882 - Foray into Local Government 69
1883 - The Salvage 79
1884 - Another Foray into Politics 91
1885-1886 - Edwin Misbehaves 105
1887 - Court Matters 120
1888 - Edwin takes the reins 137
1889 - Brewing 155
1890 - More Fraud 163
1891-1892 - Difficult times 172
1893 - Romance 182
1894 - Tough Times 197
1895 - Tougher times 202
1896 - Ned, Ned, you should have stayed in bed. 205
1897-1898 - Jessie's brother, Donald 212
1899 224
1900-1905 - Post Edwin Macaree 249

1914-1918 - Post War Years with Jim and Jessie Macaree 271
The 1930s 281
Cremorne, the Hub. 283
Bibliography and References 290
Acknowledgements 291
About the Author 292

1861–1864

Arrival

They stood shoulder to shoulder, holding the rail on the deck of the clipper as the captain manoeuvred the ship up the mud-tainted Fitzroy.

Edwin pointed to the mangroves being cleared from the banks of the river. 'I hear they catch mud crabs in there, Jane. You'll love them.'

'Oh, Edwin.' Trust him to think about food at a time like this. So much to take in, she thought, staring at the unfamiliar surrounds. Her mind flashed back to their wedding in London the previous year. That night he'd made a promise of an exciting time ahead. Never could she have imagined they'd find themselves halfway around the world beginning a new life in this strange country.

The clipper docked at the timber wharves of the small settlement on the south side of the river. The rocks further upstream had prompted both the name and the location of Rockhampton just a few years prior.

Once the ship moored, Edwin left Jane and sought out the captain who'd become a friend, shook his hand, and thanked him. Jane, meanwhile, heart thumping, gazed ashore at the drab and dusty foliage on the native trees, far less green than those she'd left behind, and wondered what was next.

Edwin steadied her as they climbed ashore. Not only was he concerned about her sea-legs, but, glancing sideways at her skirt, wondered how she was coping with the claustrophobic steamy heat in all the paraphernalia she wore beneath it, including the metal crinoline. Her once-white gloves had taken on a hue resembling the river. He'd experienced the murderous tropics along with its humidity in South America, and even a couple of times before in Australia during his years at sea with the British Merchant Navy.

Jane hesitated, swaying a little when her feet hit the crude timber wharf. Edwin led her along to firmer earth consisting of thick, powdery dust that was so violated by the maelstrom of events that it created its own brown fog. She looked about with disgust and felt repulsed when the polluted air stuck to the perspiration on her exposed bits. Anchored to the spot, her head swivelled from left to right as she drank in the sights: drays, carriages, horses, clusters of passengers, men working hoists, stacked, unloaded cargo. The associated noises accosted her senses even more.

Wharf Fitzroy River 1864, courtesy Qld State Library

'Oh, Edwin.' Descriptive words escaped her. She clutched his arm, not sure if she would fall or be swept away by the activities. They'd stopped off in New Zealand and again in Sydney on their trip out from England, but nothing had prepared her for this climate or this chaos. Her excitement had transformed into fear. She turned and looked up into Edwin's face. His deeply set, incredibly piercing eyes, shaded by his bushy eyebrows and complimented by his auburn hair poking out from under his hat like an exploding kapok mattress, expressed concern for her.

He took command. 'Come,' he said enthusiastically. 'Look at us. We're actually doing it Jane – just as I promised.'

She had faith in his decisions because of his worldly knowledge acquired from his experience during his years of seafaring, so she managed a lopsided smile that signalled she was coping.

He'd noticed his two-piece sea chest along with Jane's luggage in a net as it hit the dirt. With Jane at his side, he strode over, passed the gangers some coins, and arranged for storage. They left the wharf together, with Edwin carrying the hand luggage. The main street of the settlement was just a short walk, but when he saw that it would cost £1 for a meal and a bed at the only hotel offering accommodation, he said to Jane, 'The fencing work is near the Crescent Lagoon. We may as well get directions and walk there now. We shall

Edwin's sea-chest

start in the morning without having to walk far to work.'

After receiving directions, they began walking, and walking, and walking, the six miles feeling like sixty to Jane, with Edwin's last 7s 6d[1] jingling in his pocket.

Initial relief struck when cloud cover dropped the temperature. This was followed by a sprinkling of rain. Jane had relinquished all concern for her appearance. Her gloves were off. Was this a sign of things to come, she wondered, plodding along in her impractical high-laced leather footwear on the dirt track cut out by horses and drays heading southwest. Exciting this was not, and dusk was falling.

After a prolonged silence, Edwin pointed, *'What light through yonder window breaks?'* It emanated from beneath a couple of sheets of corrugated iron in a small clearing.

Tired and exasperated with his never-ending Shakespearean quotes, never mind the miles trodden, Jane retorted, 'Oh, Edwin, for goodness sake.'

Hearing their approach, Barrington Jenkyns scrambled from his crude shelter. After general introductions and explanations, Barrington took pity on Jane.

'Here, climb in,' he offered, indicating his lean-to.

'That's decent of you,' Edwin said, shaking his hand and taking an instant liking to the man, who appeared a couple of decades older than him.

The men sat in the drizzle, happy to cool off, exchanging pleasantries while Jane extricated herself from her iron petticoat and collapsed from exhaustion under the shelter.

'Call me Mac,' Edwin said, his back against a tree trunk. 'I believe the fencing work is around here somewhere.'

'Join me in the morning and I'll show you. Towards the

---

[1] **Imperial Currency, pounds shillings and pence (£sd)** 12 pence (d) = 1 shilling (s) 20 shillings = £1(£1=$2) eg £1.2s. 2d. 2 (shillings also 2/-) **Decimal Currency conversion: £1= $2**

Agricultural Lands. Charles Archer started up a couple of years ago out at Gracemere Station,' he said, indicating in the opposite direction over his shoulder with his thumb, 'With 8,000 sheep. Everything's grown since then. What's brought you here, Mac? The gold?'

'Well, yes and no. *All that glisters is not gold.* Discharged last year from the Navy. Then I married this fine woman.' He nodded towards the primitive shelter. 'Worked my way out here. Hoping to start a business. You?'

'Ah, that makes two of us. But I'm on my own. I've been here for a couple of years, but I'm expanding. Canoona's long over but there are plenty more opportunities.'

Edwin yawned and looked skyward. '*We are such stuff as dreams are made on, and our little life is rounded with a sleep.*'

'Ah, *The Tempest*. So you're a devotee of the "Swan of Avon" too?'

And so a friendship began, as they somehow fell asleep under the dark damp sky.

Jane accompanied Edwin to work and learned to hold the fence post centrally upright by wrapping her arms around it, her legs straddling the hole he'd dug with the crowbar. She watched him while he back-filled and compacted the soil around the post.

"We're doing 20 panels a day, Jane. That's great work,' he said.

She'd been forced to abandon her crinoline when she worked. Her hands became those of a navvy, and, even though she wore a straw hat tied with a scarf over her dark plaited hair, her skin was turning bronze and freckles appeared on her nose and cheeks. How her family back in England would gasp at her brazen appearance. She had plenty of time while she held the post to admire Edwin's tanned physique with his rolled-up sleeves and open shirt. His golden chest hair created a veritable forest.

With his first wages and a small loan, using his sea chest as security, Edwin purchased a large tent, surprised at its excessive cost. While he was erecting it away from where many others were camping, he inspected the stitching and design in detail. They settled within walking distance to their work. Some of the tent dwellers spoke little or no English, but Barrington Jenkyns, who was also from London, often shared an evening meal cooked by Jane over the open fire.

'We are so fortunate to eat beef like this, Mr Jenkyns,' Jane said, loading his tin plate with stew from a large cast-iron pot. 'And here we pay just a few pennies a pound for it.'

Both the simplicity and the complexity of living in a tent fascinated and tested Jane who, like Edwin, was accustomed to a solid roof overhead, separate rooms for different purposes and a degree of comfort. By far the most bothersome, and sometimes frightening things for Jane were the insects and bugs, not to mention the reptiles of all shapes and sizes. Flies, mosquitos, and sandflies, though, headed the list of frustrating creatures. Jane swung, swiped, slammed, and scratched, but to little avail, as lumps and rashes broke out on any uncovered flesh.

Closing the tent at night was essential, but, being November, it was suffocating. Staying outdoors on dusk was murder, and she could actually hear the attack coming. When the mosquito was silent she knew it was biting her somewhere as she waited for the inevitable sting.

The reptiles were the scariest of all, and it wasn't long before Jane learnt, through necessity, to kill a snake by jabbing the shovel behind its head – if she was close enough and courageous enough. Usually, though, the snake seemed as scared of her as she of it as it slithered off.

The lizards came in a variety of shapes and sizes. She soon became accustomed to the non-aggressive blue-tongued short grey lizards, but she was afraid of those huge frilled-neck lizards that ran helter-skelter. With their talon-like claws, they ran up trees as fast as they scooted along on the ground.

They'd agreed before setting out for Australia that they were prepared to face the hardships together in the shorter term to reach their goal of a life of luxury in the longer term. Edwin had sold her his dream well and she held the faith in spite of the suffering. They slept on a mattress stuffed with straw on a dirt floor on which Jane regularly sprinkled water and compacted the dirt to prevent the dust. Tea chests acted as tables and cupboards, logs as seating outside.

Edwin built a primitive-looking kiln. He hauled the timber and rock on his back to fire up the kiln. He purchased bags of lime, hauling them to the kiln on his back as well. He burnt the lime and sold it as mortar for building. In a small way this labour-intensive production supplemented their existence.

Over many days, weeks and months, working six days most weeks, a year passed by. They slaved and saved, living on the shared hope and optimism, and in desperate times, added pigweed to the diet.

'I wish we had our own horse and buggy,' Jane dreamed out loud, wiping sweat from her forehead with her apron, after a taxing trip back from Albrecht Feez's store in Quay Lane in the settlement, with supplies piled on the back of a shared dray.

'Ah my beautiful woman, you will have one before much longer. *The web of our life is of a mingled yarn, good and ill together.*'

'Oh, Edwin, there you go again.' This time Jane's voice held warmth and affection.

But Edwin was still contemplating the cost of tents. He'd registered his interest in acquiring a sewing machine when one came up for sale with merchant, Albrecht Feez. They were heavy-duty, but his experiences at sailmaking and repair in the Navy meant he understood well what was needed.

A small amount of back pay from the Navy had finally appeared at the Bank of New South Wales in East Street, but he'd decided to keep that to himself for now.

Returning home, he came upon Jane, small shovel in hand, raking back the coals she'd stacked on the camp oven containing the damper. With the aroma of fresh bread permeating the air, Edwin's mouth watered. He couldn't wait to pile treacle on hot clumps of it.

On Saturday afternoon, as sometimes was the case, Edwin made his way along the track to the Commercial Hotel down on Quay Street on the river.

'How's it going, Mac?' Barrington Jenkins made room for Edwin among the crowd.

With the week's two newspapers tucked under his arm and a beer in hand, Edwin said, 'I haven't read this week's papers yet. What's happening?'

'Well, they say the population's reached nearly 700. It must be time soon to buy some land.'

This too had been on Edwin's mind. Queensland had become its own colony, breaking away from New South Wales just a few years earlier, in 1859, with Her Majesty's new seat of government in Brisbane. In order to promote stability in the region, Crown Land had become available at absolute bargain prices. Archibald Archer, their Member of Parliament, recommended twenty-five pence per acre and conditions of purchase included occupancy and development.

'They are making it as easy as possible, that's to be sure,'

Edwin replied.

A voice across the room yelled, 'Mac, how about a song?'

Never shy, and never needing to be asked twice to perform, Edwin discarded the newspapers and made his way to the raised corner stage. Casting his eye around the room, he considered briefly before deciding this was definitely not a time for classical music. In his rich, deep baritone, he began:

What shall we do with a drunken sailor?
What shall we do with a drunken sailor?
What shall we do with a drunken sailor
Earlye in the morning.'

His feet tapped out a bit of the hornpipe before he raised both hands high to signal to his audience to join in the chorus, much to the delight of the publican, who saw more would-be-passers-by turn into the bar to be entertained.

'Way, hay up she rises,
Way, hay up she rises,
Way, hay up she rises,
Earlye in the morning.'

After several raucous verses, there was a rush to the bar. At 6 pm Edwin put his empty glass down and rose, intending to head home. Alexander MacKaskel, the publican sought him out and said, 'And any time you're looking for a job, Mac, just come and see me.' They shook hands.

It took almost four months for the trip out from England, so when Jane's full wardrobe and personal possessions finally arrived on a freighter it was time for celebrations. Sunday found them in the settlement where she wore her finest dress of sky blue over her crinoline, complimented by her straw and lace bonnet adorned with generous matching blue ribbons dangling. Attendance at the newly constructed Church of England church was a given. Edwin's hymn singing charmed the congregation. After the obligatory cup of tea following the service, a group of couples strolled along the river to the punt. The flat-bottomed boat was drawn by ropes and propelled by the boatman with a long pole across the river to the Pene's Gardens nestled just after the junction where Moore's Creek met the river.

'Good morning, M'sieur Pene.' Edwin doffed his top hat. 'I see the trees are maturing.'

Bernard Pene and his wife had arrived from France in 1858 to follow the gold at Canoona. Instead, they changed their minds and purchased land, fenced it in and cleared it, and speedily laid the ground out in shady walks, planting fruit trees, especially tropical ones, as well as flowers. The soil was rich enough to grow anything, so everything matured rapidly and luxuriously.

'Ah, M'sieur Macaree, Madame Macaree, yes indeed.' M Pene raised his hat and bowed. 'But do be careful of the pods from the Cascara.' He looked up, smiling. They were just inside the entrance, and the Cascara, yellow flowers trailing, was to their left. 'They will make you very ill,' he added.

'I promise we shall not eat from the forbidden fruit.' Edwin grinned. 'And I see you're ready to open the White Horse Inn,' he said, turning. Pene's new hotel complimented the gardens.

'You must come to the opening, M'sieur Macaree. We would be honoured to have you as a guest.' They turned and watched young couples, beautifully bedecked in their Sunday best, stroll by. 'There are so few places to take your sweetheart. We need a little romance in the air, non? We shall have tea and cake at the Inn soon too,' M'sieur Pene added.

The gardens were already incredibly popular.

'What is wrong with the Cascara, Edwin?' Jane asked when they moved on.

'Put it this way, my dear; you won't need to eat prunes for a very long time if you partake.'

'Oh, Edwin. Really.'

Edwin received a message from Albrecht Feez to call into his store.

He barged into the shop, booming, 'Ah, Colonel, my good friend, do you have news for me?'

'Come out to my office, Mac.' Seated behind his desk, Colonel Feez went on, 'We all know you have a great voice, and I hear you're interested in the performing arts?'

This wasn't the conversation Edwin was expecting, but his brain switched gears. He knew that the Colonel had a rich singing voice, and so he sang to him a few bars of *How should I your true love know*, from Hamlet.

The Colonel clapped.

'And I play King Lear and Othello, and could polish up on Macbeth.' Edwin's heart raced. He'd missed these cultural aspects of his life, which was now wildly out of kilter. Work and responsibility weighed him down so heavily that his feet dragged along the ground. 'What did you have in mind?'

The Colonel smiled broadly. Lighting up his pipe and leaning back, he said, 'We're developing a centre for performing arts. You know we do some amateur entertainment at the Courthouse. Mr Taaffe and Mr Milne are committed. Are you interested in being involved?'

Edwin jumped from his chair and paced, arms moving around in the air. '*All the world's a stage, and all the men and women merely players. They have their exits and their entrances; and one man in his time plays many parts.* I, Colonel, am ready for whatever part I am given,' he said dramatically, taking his seat again. Edwin promised he'd be at the meeting at the courthouse the following Wednesday night.

'Now to other business, Mac. I have two machines from a tentmaker who is moving into another venture.' A deal was slowly struck for the machines and accessories. The Colonel opened a cupboard and poured whisky into two tumblers and congratulated Edwin. He was ten years Edwin's senior and was an alderman on the Municipal Council. Edwin admired his negotiating prowess.

Edwin arrived back at the Crescent Lagoon full of spirit. 'We're going to stop the fencing, Jane.'

'And do what?'

The fencing was abandoned as he and Jane turned their efforts to the profitable pursuit of tent making. Edwin proved himself a great marketer of their goods, was fair in pricing, and the demand was never-ending.

'And now, Jane,' Edwin said, 'I'm going to buy some decent acres at Crocodile Creek. It's ridiculously cheap right now.' Crocodile Creek was just a few miles south of the Crescent Lagoon. 'But we have to work it too. With cattle.'

'So we'll keep making tents as well?'

'Yes, and I shall build us a home.'

Their tent and straw mattress were abandoned when they took up sleeping in a real bed under a real roof. Since coconut fibre was plentiful, Jane stuffed the new mattress cover with it. Happily and energetically she undertook the task of turning the cottage into a home. She continued to sew, using the veranda as a workplace in summer in order to catch a breeze and inside when the weather turned cool. She often chose to cook outside in summer so the interior wouldn't heat up by having to fire up the cast iron stove, although she welcomed its warmth in winter. She learnt to wield the axe, and there was certainly no shortage of timber.

Edwin purchased a herd of cattle. Jane learnt to milk the milking cow. Whatever would her friends back in England think? But there was nothing like warm fresh milk on a winter's morning.

Jane planted vegetables and flowers, although the beautiful English flowers like daffodils and poppies that she loved didn't blossom. They didn't even grow. The soil, though, seemed to be most agreeable to roses. The Penes supplied the seedlings, cuttings, and the advice.

'I'm so grateful we have the tank, and no longer have to haul water, Edwin. I had no idea the things I took for granted back home. Tell me – what do you miss the most?'

He didn't hesitate. 'The sea.'

Crocodile Creek's population continued to expand, and one evening, while Edwin was off wheeling and dealing – something Jane had become accustomed to – she lit a candle and sat on a chair Edwin had constructed with his clever hands, at a table Edwin had also built. She dipped the nib of her pen into the glass ink-well, wiped the excess away, and began her letter home, writing neatly in her copperplate style with light upstrokes, and heavy downstrokes, by the candlelight.

> *Dear Mama and Papa,*
>
> *Oh, how I miss you all. One day I shall ask you to visit. It will be important to visit in England's summertime as that is Rockhampton's winter and here it is kind. In summer the sun presses down like a hot iron, and it doesn't let up until the black clouds roll across in the afternoons and the rains pelt down. Then steam rises from the earth. My lovely leather shoes have grown mould. We must bathe every day.*

Yes, can you imagine? Truly, summer in the tropics is something to avoid.

And I miss London fashions. A fellow called Hemmant, and another called James Stewart from Scotland have opened a draper's shop and I am grateful for that.

Jane stopped writing and pondered her next sentence. She didn't want to admit how hard life was physically; hauling and cutting the heavy canvas for the tent-making, unloading supplies from the settlement, fighting off the vicious insects. She was ashamed of the state of her hands. She put the pen down and swiped the air as mosquitos buzzed, before inspecting her hands, rubbing one with the other. Lanolin helped a little, but the callouses were there to stay. Then, she thought, pondering again the hardships, there were the threats of spearing from the natives when they travelled back and forth from Crocodile to Rockhampton. How could she explain that in a letter?

The clip-clop of a horse broke into her thoughts. She wondered who the visitor was and went outside. Her hand flew to her mouth when she realised it was Edwin in the saddle.

'Just bought it, my dear Jane,' he explained, and with great ease reached down and pulled her light, lithe body up in front of him. He kissed the back of her neck. 'Next a wagon. Not long now.'

The Sabbath commanded great respect, always reserved for church attendance and gentler pursuits – never work. Although there were now a bowling alley, rifle gallery and many hotels in Rockhampton, they were closed on Sunday along with all the shops. Bernard Pene had changed the name of his property from White Horse Inn to Cremorne Gardens and Hotel, and Edwin and Jane were regular Sunday attendees.

'I wonder what this is?' Edwin had been exploring again in the Gardens. He pulled a small, shiny, green fruit from a tree quite a distance from the hotel, and bit carefully into it, immediately spitting it out again, and wiping his mouth. 'Ugg. Let's go and find M'sieur Pene and ask.'

'It looks a bit like an olive,' Jane commented.

When they found him, M'sieu Pene laughed. 'You cannot eat olives straight from the tree. You can eat the jujube, but you have picked a very green one. They turn yellow-ish when they are ready. Please come and have tea and cake with Madam Pene and me.' Bernard Pene was devoted to his wife and daughter, who was being home-schooled, even though Rockhampton now had a formal schoolhouse.

1865

Settling in

After four years in the colony, Jane and Edwin's first child, Edwin junior, was born.

'Hello, little Ned,' Edwin declared, picking him up and looking adoringly into his unfocused eyes for the first time. He kissed his wife on the cheek. 'And what a clever Ma you are.' He kissed Jane's forehead.

In his work shed, Edwin, ever capable with his hands, and with a growing collection of tools, which he himself created, had built a cradle on rockers.

Edwin's handmade tools. The top one is a spoke shave.

Baby Ned spent much of his time beside his mother while she worked the treadle of the sewing machine with her feet and guided the canvas with her hands.

Edwin was researching and seeking other forms of income. He often bought items cheaply from locals who were down on their luck or departing the area then re-sold them at a profit to new arrivals. His love of theatre consumed his spare time.

The School of Arts Committee had received a grant from the Government and the building was nearly complete. The rules were developed and ratified. The priority was the establishment of a library and reading room for the use of members and "… for the advancement of the community in literary, philosophic, and scientific subjects." Anyone who paid a subscription could be a member.

Edwin burst into the cottage one night. 'They are forming The Glee and Madrigal Society, Ma.'

'Oh, Edwin, that will be so much fun.'

They both attended the premiere performance at the new School of Arts. It was Jane's first opportunity to buy smart evening wear and appear at a formal event which attracted an elite audience. This included the Governor, Captain Pitt, members of the Ministry and of the Legislative Assembly as well as the Mayor, Mr Justice Lutwyche. The performance opened with Boieldieu's *Caliph of Bagdad*. Glees and solos including *Glorious Apollo* followed.

As they congregated in the foyer following the performance, Jane was surprised to see how many people came up and chatted with them. Edwin was certainly popular and well known.

'Well, my dear Jane,' Edwin, newspaper in hand, said two days later, 'They say the concert was well-received, but there was a general dissatisfaction that people with numbered seats didn't get to sit in them.'

'That sounds fair,' she replied absent-mindedly, key in hand, winding the new black marble clock Edwin had ordered from London. He enjoyed fine things and was acquiring more and more. A brown, leather grandfather chair sat in a corner beside his sea chest, the lower drawers of which had become the summer repository for winter blankets and clothes.

Edwin's clock

The tent-making business was booming. Edwin purchased more machines and employed two young men to whom Jane taught the skills required.

Edwin and Jane were on the road from Crocodile to town in the buggy to collect more supplies for their tent-making. Concerned about an aboriginal attack, Edwin decided to stop and clamber up a tree to check the heavily wooded area ahead.

'Keep low, Jane,' he said, tucking his pistol firmly in his belt. A minute or so later Jane heard a shot ring out followed by deep-throaty curses sprouting from Edwin's mouth.

Peeping up, she saw him struggling down the tree with blood seeping from a hole in his boot.

Swearing again, he added, 'What in the blazes! Come and help me, Jane. My elbow knocked the bolt on the pistol. I've shot myself in the foot.'

'Oh, no.' Distressed, Jane scrambled down from the buggy and offered her shoulder when his foot touched the ground.

He yelped. 'Drat it. I'm going to have to climb into the buggy somehow.'

There was nothing Jane could do to pull him up, but once he hauled himself in he handed her the reins. 'Straight to the hospital, Ma.' He muttered all the way there. Staff ran out and assisted him into a wheelchair. He began cursing again when his boot was unceremoniously cut off. 'Tarnation, do we need to do that?'

'Edwin, enough of that,' Jane scolded before she was escorted from the room.

Dr Callaghan stood back while Edwin's sock was cut off. 'Well, Mac, you've done a good job of that lot,' he said, looking at the angle of the shot which ran much of the length of his foot. 'I can't suture that.' The doctor asked for a hypodermic syringe filled with morphine and, using it said, 'This will allow me a better look.' Lifting a flap of flesh, Dr Callaghan saw that the bone was exposed.

A nurse recommended to Jane that she go home as they were going to admit Edwin. She needed to collect the canvas and get back to Ned who was being cared for by a maid. She had no major concerns for Edwin, realising it was a painful inconvenience for him, but he would be fine. How the hospital staff would cope with his inability to move and his swearing was another.

Next day, Jane organised a worker to oversee the sewing

of tents before heading into town, taking little Ned and the maid with her this time. She found a noisy Edwin surrounded by friends.

'They're keeping me here a bit longer,' he said as she handed over a bag of personal items. His heavily bandaged foot sat atop a pillow. 'Can you ask Colonel Feez to call in when he has time?'

The Colonel arrived just before lunch with a bottle of whisky hidden in his Gladstone bag. 'Here's my advice to you, Mac,' he said, pouring it into glass tumblers. 'Buy a town property while you recuperate. You'll be off your feet for a long time from what I'm hearing.'

'Why should I do that, Colonel?'

'There's a place almost opposite my store in Quay Lane for sale. With just a few modifications it would make a great boarding house. You could earn money while you stay there yourself, and you'll be just down the road from the hospital. Now, if you are short of funds we can do a deal.'

Edwin was silent. He desperately needed a project to keep him busy and he knew the property in question. He also wanted to use his hands. Somehow this might work if he borrowed a wheelchair. Jane was capable of managing their tent-making. He'd ask Barrington Jenkyns to keep an eye on things. He'd have to borrow more money, but he was confident he could ensure the boarding house was profitable. He found himself, while deep in his thoughts, staring at the framed photo of a young Queen Victoria on the wall opposite his bed when a smile spread across his face. He swung his attention back to the Colonel. 'Brilliant, Colonel, brilliant.'

Never one to let a good idea rest, Edwin did the deal and moved in after he was discharged. He still couldn't weight-bear on his foot, and the loose flap of skin was a constant reminder of his accident. He supervised renovations, fiddling at carpentry at a low bench as he stayed off his foot. He then placed the following advertisement in the newspaper:

> E. MACAREE'S SHAKESPEARE BOARDING HOUSE, LITTLE QUAY STREET, (Nearly opposite Mr. Feez's Store). Good Stabling for Horses. E. MACAREE has opened the above Boarding House in consequence of a long illness from being accidentally shot. He trusts his friends from the country will pay him a visit.

And so they did and the Boarding House prospered. With his network from the Glee and Madrigal Society in regular attendance, Edwin organised a concert and placed yet another advertisement.

> TO THE LOVERS OF SHAKESPEARE: MR. MACAREE, the Shakespearian Delineator, will give an Entertainment at the MASONIC HALL, on MONDAY NEXT, June 18, assisted by MR. H. RUSSELL, MR. VINING, and MRS. RICHARDSON.
> To the Benevolent. — E. MACAREE is just recovering from a long illness, having been accidentally shot. Being a resident of Rockhampton he trusts the public will support him.
> Patron: His Worship the Mayor, Captain White
>
> HAMLET! Hamlet ... Mr. Macaree. Horatio ... Mr. Russell. Ghost ... Mr. Vining. Overture. Songs by Company.
> MACBETH! Macbeth ... Mr. Macaree. Macduff ... Mr. Russell. Combat. Song — Interval.
> Toll's Speech— G. V. Brooke's style ...
> Mr. Macaree. Song. OTHELLO, THE MOOR OF VENICE!

Othello ... Mr. Macaree. Desdemona ... Mrs. Richardson
Admission— Front seats, 3s; back seats, 2s.
Tickets to be had at Mr. O. Gerber's, Skardon's Masonic Hall, Argus Office, and Shakespeare Boarding House, Little Quay Street.
Doors open at half-past seven; commence at Eight.

The concert was such a success a second followed, with different performers and different acts.

1866–1868

Progress

Jane maintained the tent-making business, and in June 1866 when Edwin was still organising concerts, a couple of local men found significant gold in Crocodile Creek. As a consequence, the population of Crocodile exploded to more than 3000. Hotels and shops popped up. Because of the necessity for speed, they were shabbily built, but it meant the miners didn't have to travel into town. Hundreds of Chinese were attracted to the new high yielding goldfields and pegged some of the best claims. Many of them were successful in their finds, making the Europeans jealous. They considered the Chinese intruders.

Mr John Jardine was appointed Gold Commissioner. Part of his role was to protect the Chinese population.

With all the action, Edwin, still limping, made his return to Crocodile on the daily coach for 2s 6d. He was stunned at the changes that had occurred in his absence. Mr Christian Jagerndorff had opened a general store and Mr Dibdin built himself an office where he purchased the gold, initially for himself, but then as an agent for the Bank of New South Wales.

Edwin watched and listened as the animosity between the white population and the Chinese escalated.

One evening, with young Ned in his lap, Edwin said, 'It's an *ill wind which blows no man to good*. There's going to be trouble, Ma. I can sense it.'

Early in the New Year of 1867, Edwin's prediction was realised. A riot broke out. Edwin summarised the newspaper report that evening while Jane knitted: 'It was not easy to know who did what to whom, but the outcome was a serious tomahawk attack on a European.' Edwin paused. 'That's not acceptable.' He shook his head and summarised again. 'And in retaliation, they burnt 30 tents and humpies belonging to the Chinese. And that's not defendable either.' Edwin rubbed Ned's head gently. 'What is this place coming to?'

'Is it safe here, Edwin?'

'Well, the police were called, they made arrests, but they couldn't identify which of the Chinese were involved. No-one was seriously injured, thank heavens. Mostly fistfights.' Little Ned was squirming, so Edwin put him on the floor to play with a wooden horse he'd carved for him. 'We're far enough away from the gold-mining, Ma.'

Nonetheless, Jane felt uncomfortable.

The following night Edwin carried home more tales. One of the primitive pubs in Crocodile was owned by a Chinaman who was married to a white woman. When the rioters arrived to attack, she deftly placed a drink in their hands and saved the establishment. 'Clever woman,' Edwin exclaimed.

Edwin developed a reputation for fairness in Crocodile by not profiteering and by decently treating those who worked for him with both the cattle and the tent-making.

'Do keep clear of the lower part of town if you want to stay safe,' he told his workers.

'You mean Chinatown,' one of them said. 'Full of gambling dens, and you can smoke opium, and buy a woman.'

Edwin was anything but naive. 'Just stay safe,' he recommended.

Uncovering the gold was hard work necessitating the removal

of massive boulders to make a find. Eventually, they called the place Bouldercombe. More hotels, a billiard room, music hall, and other forms of entertainments sprang up. Not only was there huge demand for new tents, but there was a large market for the sale of second-hand ones as the miners progressed to better forms of accommodation or moved on.

Edwin saw the potential for large-scale money-making in buying and selling all types of second-hand goods, from cast iron cookware to sturdy boots. People with only a few resources entering the goldfields needed to borrow money and buy cheap goods.

Edwin visited Colonel Feez to discuss this business opportunity.

'You need to apply for a pawn-broking licence,' he advised Edwin after listening to his ideas. 'Keep it legal – and you're better off here in Rockhampton in the main street,' Colonel Feez added. 'Crocodile isn't the only area booming. There are wider and bigger opportunities.'

Edwin trusted his advice. After all, the Colonel's own businesses were hugely successful.

'And, Mac,' he said, breaking out the whisky bottle, 'this is where the future is. Goldfields don't last forever.' They clinked their glasses together. 'Prost!'

Edwin acquired his pawn-broking licence and opened a shop in East Street with a residence nearby. Jane and little Ned moved to Rockhampton. Edwin kept the lucrative tent-making business going in Crocodile, and the cattle as well.

To promote his new venture, Edwin posted his first advertisement in the papers.

MONEY LENT! MONEY LENT!! MONEY LENT!!!
Cash advanced on Immigrants' Luggage, Gold, Silver, and all kinds of Jewellery, Guns, Revolvers, Tools, and

> *any other description of goods, or the same purchased by EDWIN MACAREE, Licenced Pawnbroker, East-street, Between the Bull and Mouth and Cricketers' Arms Hotels.*

This was the first of many pawn shop ads placed in the Rockhampton Bulletin and Edwin quickly developed a relationship with Mr Buzacott, its proprietor and editor.

It wasn't long before the first of several charges against Edwin and the pawnshop were brought before the Police Magistrate. On Friday, August 16, 1867, Edwin was charged with receiving a silk glass mantle valued at £3 10s purported to be the property of Annie Dalrymple of the Denham Hotel. She claimed it was stolen. Edwin declared he was happy to give it to her for 10s 6d which was what he advanced on the item. The Bench, though, was of the opinion that Annie's description did not match that of the mantle Edwin produced in court and so Edwin kept the mantle.

Edwin continued to bring the newspaper home regularly, and, from his leather chair, with his foot on the rocker of the cradle, rocked the newly born Emma while Ned, now two and a half, stacked blocks. Edwin summarised articles to Jane. 'See Charles Archer has a problem with ticks now he's added cattle and horses at his selection at Gracemere.'

'What does that mean?'

'Golden lads and girls all must, as chimney-sweepers, come to dust.'

'Edwin – I beg your pardon?'

'Ticks kill. Oh, and the new hospital has opened.'

Jane sighed. 'Yes, I know that. What other news is there?'

Edwin folded the paper. 'Did you know we're overcoming the shortage of cheap labour? They're bringing Kanakas in from Tanna in the New Hebrides.'

Again Jane sighed. 'I beg your pardon? Who?'

'Kanaka is the Polynesian word for man. And the New Hebrides is an island nation in the South Pacific. These are strong young men who sign up to come for three years to work. They can then choose to return home if they don't apply to stay on beyond that.'

'What a lovely idea. They are nothing like a slave?'

'No.'

But Edwin had heard rumours that a group of them had been kidnapped from their island home and brought to Rockhampton. However, the Captain who brought them in showed documents to Mr Buzacott, which seemed to refute the rumour. The men were provided with clothes and wages and a guarantee of return.

'Don't worry, Mac. I have an ear to the ground. I'll know about any abuses,' the newspaper proprietor said.

Now that Edwin was based in Rockhampton, he had greater opportunity to involve himself with seafaring and his love of the ocean again. He was in constant touch with the ships' captains when they came up the river. One such master was Captain Cornelius Norris who had built his own boat, *The Violet*, in Sydney at his father's boatbuilding yards. Captain Norris plied the trades on the seas off Queensland. When the Captain was in town, he and Edwin would meet up at the Commercial Hotel.

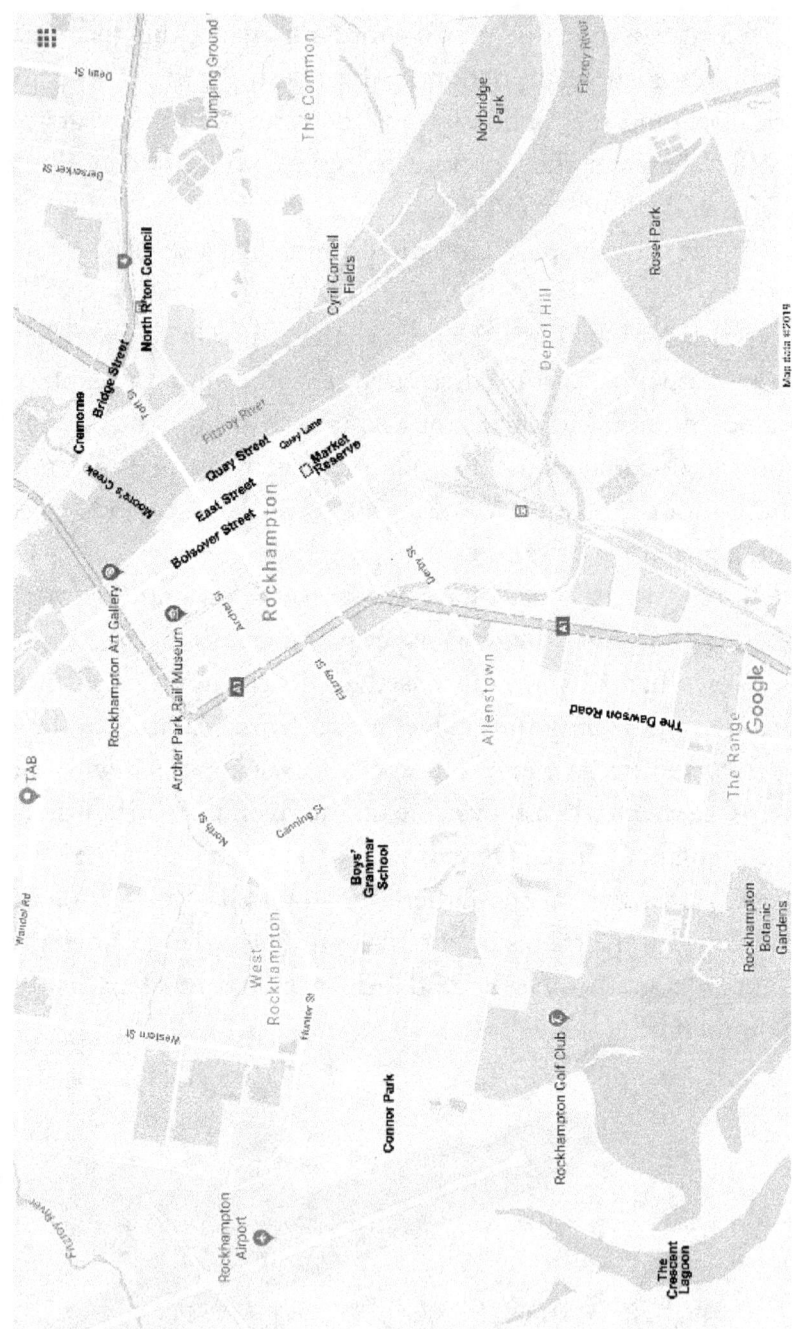

Map of Rockhampton.
Modified Google map to show locations in the 1800s

1869–1871

Family

In 1869, Edwin heard that the schooner *Jane Lockhart* had struck a reef off Heron Island, southeast of Rockhampton. The crew and passengers were all able to escape safely, albeit with just the clothes they were standing in. Captain Norris was placed in charge of the wreck and repositioned her so she could settle on the reef.

'Mac,' he said, 'most of her cargo can be recovered by raising her with airbags, then I can do some basic repairs and after that I can organise to tow her into port.'

With this information, Edwin and Albrecht Feez successfully bid at auction for the schooner and her cargo, paying a total of £82. The cargo included valuable equipment as well as ale, liqueurs, brandy, cutlery, and ironmongery. When the weather finally allowed a salvage attempt, a South Sea Island diver managed to bring up some eighty or ninety large iron pulley wheels, a quantity of machinery and the liquor. If the salvage crew hadn't run out of drinking water, Edwin reckoned they could have salvaged much more.

Nevertheless, he was pleased with the outcome. His businesses were thriving as they were moving towards a new decade. He ran a new ad.

> MONEY!
> Can be had on and after this date at 6d to the Pound interest. Deductions made for large sums at
> E. MACAREE'S LICENCED PAWNBROKER

EAST STREET.
N.B. Private Entrance Little East Street at the back.

Life for Jane on their selection had been peaceful, if not somewhat lonely. But in the East Street residence, she was on edge often, especially around one o'clock each day.

'Just feel that, Edwin,' she said one day as the glass in the cabinets and lamps rattled and the walls vibrated.

'Oh, they're now paying the council office boy to be powder monkey. He gets £20 a year to fire that time gun for us, Jane. We are supposed to be grateful. It's a carronade and sits right outside their chambers. Just be glad you don't live there,' he added with a laugh. 'And at least we know our watches and clocks are correct once a day.'

'Well, it wakes the children when they're sleeping,' Jane said, stroking her latest baby bump.

Time Gun (carronade)

She was even more unimpressed when Edwin came home to their East Street house and told her he was due to appear in court again.

'I'm being sued by Mr Bolger.' Seeing Jane's frown he added, 'It's one of the risks of the business, my lovely Ma. You know that. *Virtue is bold, and goodness never fearful.*'

Jane had occasionally helped out in the shop, so she had some idea of the risks of pawn-broking, which didn't really faze her. They were never big amounts.

'This time, though,' Edwin added, 'I have Rees Jones, the solicitor, to represent me. It's going before the District Judge.'

According to James Bolger's solicitor, £26 was advanced on goods deposited with Edwin. Some of them were sold with the permission of Bolger where Edwin kept the proceeds. Bolger claimed he eventually paid Edwin the balance owing on the deposited goods but claimed Edwin did not return his property. The goods were originally left for twelve months and £5 interest was proposed but was brought down to £4.10s, the rate being 17.5 percent. During the period, Bolger reclaimed some items and was charged £5. 10s. Edwin had sold some bullock bowes, cover dishes, a colonial oven, and other items. He hadn't sold the oil paintings valued at £20, but they were still hanging in the Catholic Church.

Bolger's solicitor continued to argue the case, pointing out how much his client was paid back on which items and when. It was agreed that £8 was paid to him by Mrs Macaree for 15 hides.

It was then Edwin's turn. He stated that Bolger asked him if he would stow goods. Edwin agreed to give him a loan on them and Edwin valued them individually and entered them in his book, making advances on each as he did so.

The book was produced. He'd advanced him £26 9s 2d. The established law for interest was 1s. 8d. in the pound per month. The Pawnbroker's Act would not allow him to keep them for more than three months. Bolger told Edwin he'd be taking some out in a week. The pawn ticket that Edwin issued was on a foolscap sheet, which he produced, as the items would not fit on the usual pawn ticket.

According to Edwin, several months passed before Bolger asked for some of his items. He took a chest of drawers with unidentified items inside along with several other pieces for which he did not pay. Bolger returned several times, always wanting to borrow money, but never offered to pay any. Item by item was gone through in the courtroom and there were many.

Finally, after both lawyers summed up, the judge, Mr Milford, found in favour of Edwin and awarded him costs, along with the costs of his three witnesses.

Edwin hurried home to celebrate. And there was even more to celebrate than he realised. When Edwin threw the door open, the midwife met him, nursing an infant. He opened his arms, took the baby and strode into the bedroom.

'My precious Ma.' He bent and kissed her forehead. 'Who have we here?'

'It's a boy, Edwin. Your turn to name him.'

'Hello, little James. My father was James, and my brother was James. I think we'll call you Jim.'

Jane now had a maid to help around the home and another to help with the children. She had ceased working in the pawnshop. Much to her horror, Edwin arrived home a few weeks later with a human skull. 'Oh, no, not around the children. What are you thinking?'

'I'm thinking phrenology. How can I give lessons without a model?'

'Lessons? Phrenology? And when were you planning to fit them in?'

'It's the study of the bumps and depressions of the skull. They demonstrate all kinds of traits and abilities. It's a science and it's helpful. Just you wait and see.'

He picked up baby Jim, felt the back of his still-forming skull and announced, 'He will be intelligent.'

'All our children are intelligent, Edwin.' She swept Jim from his arms possessively.

Before Edwin could teach Jane anything about phrenology, little Emma, now three, developed a fever. Jane was deeply concerned, because little Emma also had a sore throat, and her skin had a bluish tinge. Dr Callaghan was sent for.

'I'm sorry, Mrs Macaree, but this looks like a case of Diphtheria. You need to isolate her immediately and try to get the fever down.'

Jane was aghast at the diagnosis. She had baby Jim and five-year-old Ned taken from the home and cared for by one of the maids and a friend at the Crocodile homestead. She set up a sick room for Emma. Jane sat with her all night and was broken-hearted by Emma's struggle to breathe. When she tried to give her sips of water, Emma couldn't swallow.

Edwin stood in the doorway. He was helpless in such circumstances, rocking and fretting. He was able to take charge and control most situations, but this one eluded his abilities. Jane did not need any Shakespearian action from him, not that Shakespeare was in his mind or on his tongue.

'Go and get Dr Callaghan now,' she ordered.

Little Emma died that day in her mother's arms.

While Edwin sailed strongly through the business side of his life, building new premises on his recently purchased land in William Street on the Municipal Reserve, he drowned himself in Theatre, participating in the performance of *Paul Pry* put on by No 4 Company Q VRB officers, NCOs and Privates in the Theatre Royal to aid the Volunteer Band. After intermezzi Edwin danced a double hornpipe with Private Callaghan where his mended flappy foot was encased in a sock and shoe.

The next performance in which Edwin involved himself was one by The Great Clairvoyant, Miss Clara Baldwin, or, as she was otherwise known, the Doublesighted Lady. They played to a full house and yet again he danced the Sailor's Hornpipe during a variety evening at the School of Arts where *Only a Clod* and *The Unfortunate Housemaid* were played out by both professional and amateur entertainers.

Gradually Edwin's home life returned to some kind of routine. Jane stopped wearing black. The crinolines and full petticoats had disappeared and were replaced by the now fashionable bustle where Jane's silhouette was more apparent with much gathering of fabric at the back of her dress.

Edwin resumed reading sections of the newspaper to her in the evenings. 'The Lake's Creek Meat-Preserving Company has finished their preserving for the season, Jane. Hot weather apparently isn't conducive to the meat setting,' he said, glancing up. 'And I see John Jardine is going to grow tobacco and sugar on his new selection at Cawarral.' He leaned back in deep thought staring blankly at his newly acquired German twin ornaments on a wall shelf; a shepherd and shepherdess, which doubled as vases.

Edwin's Shepherd and Shepherdess vases

'No, Edwin,' Jane said, reading his thoughts. 'You just get yourself organised with the move into the new shop. Besides, Cawarral is in the opposite direction to our selection.'

'But it's nearer the ocean, Jane,' he snuck in.

The move to the new premises finally occurred and he posted this ad in the papers:

> E. MACAREE
> PAWNBROKER & General dealer Has REMOVED To
> his newly erected Stone Buildings
> WILLIAM STREET On the Market Reserve.
> Money Lent on all kinds of Real and Personal Property
> Dealer in Ship Chandlery and Importer Of all kinds of
> Canvass.

Edwin again found himself involved in a court case, but this time as a witness when the accused, Frank Beddek, was charged with pawning a saddle that did not belong to him. Edwin proved that the saddle produced was pawned with him by the prisoner, and he advanced Beddek £2 on it. When originally questioned over the matter by Detective Smyth, Edwin had immediately relinquished the saddle. The prisoner produced no defence. The jury retired, and after about fifteen minutes, returned with a verdict of guilty. A character reference was provided for Beddek, where the referee stated that Beddek had a wife and two children who were nearly destitute.

That evening, at home, Edwin told Jane, 'Regardless, the judge sentenced him to four months gaol and then to be released on a six-month good behaviour bond.'

'Thank goodness the Benevolent Society has formed. At least his wife and children won't starve while he's in jail. I wonder if I should become involved?' Jane put forth. Edwin was following, although not yet involved in the Separation Movement. A group of businessmen wanted to form a new colony in Central Queensland with Rockhampton as its capital. They were tired of decisions being made in Brisbane by those who knew nothing about Central Queensland and its needs.

'Did you read about Sir James Martin's speech?' Barrington Jenkyns asked Edwin.

'What's the Premier of New South Wales got to say?' Edwin asked.

'He was talking about the separation proposal. He said they just went through the Queensland set up in 1859. The cost of colonisation to the mother country was great, he claims, what with setting up a new place of Parliament. He said nothing could be gained by another.'

'Poppycock.'

'Absolute poppycock.'

1872–1874

Expansion

In the latter half of 1872, Edwin was elected to the General Committee of the Church of England. One of that committee's intentions was to lobby to extend the episcopate north of the See of Brisbane, meaning that Rockhampton would seek to build a cathedral with a Bishop installed.

'Let's see what the Brisbane power base has to say about that,' Edwin said to Barrington Jenkyns the next time he saw him.

And to round off the year, Jane and Edwin welcomed their third son, Peter.

'Did you hear what's happening?' Edwin said to Jane, nose in the newspaper again. 'Buzacott presented a petition to Parliament for a bridge across the river. Apparently very little was said in Parliament, and both sides seem not to care.' He glanced up over his glasses. 'But fortunately, the Committee is refusing to drop it.'

She heard the indignation in his tone. 'Now you've got enough on your plate, Edwin,' Jane scolded, feeding little Peter, who had been borne prematurely.

'How dare they not discuss it seriously? Is it any wonder we want our own colony?'

That night, Edwin was woken from his sleep at 3.15 am, by the sound of the fire bell. The alarm had been raised by two policemen on duty.

'Be careful, Edwin,' Jane called after him as he rushed out from their East Street house still buttoning his shirt, to see smoke rising from further along East Street. People were quickly flocking to the area of the fire on Mulligans Corner, in the premises of the grocers and tea merchants, Higson & Co. The timber construction fed the ravenous flames. With the strong breeze blowing, it was impossible to save the place and its contents. But one of the neighbours, Mrs Shaw, whose stock was mainly valuable canvas and fabrics, had her contents saved by volunteers who threw everything into the middle of the road.

By this time the volunteer fire brigade had arrived.

The strong breeze didn't let up and spectators were horrified to see the fire snake rapidly across the road via Mrs Shaw's rescued stock. Now it was threatening the Union Hotel.

The fire brigade dithered in disarray as the hose kept bursting. And the horse pulling the equipment was reluctant to cooperate. All attention was on preventing the fire from spreading from Mrs Shaw's property to Mr Bennett, the bootmaker, and Tin Foo's boarding house.

Volunteers, including Edwin, worked for hours to put it out. Covered in soot, Edwin came bounding through the front door of his home for a late breakfast still with energy to quote: *'And where two raging fires meet together, they do consume the thing that feeds their fury.'* Noticing how Jane was glaring at him, he meekly added, 'That was some fire.'

Just the next day, Jane was horrified to read in the Bulletin newspaper, left open on the table by Edwin, a section of a longer report:

> Mr Macaree was the first to catch the idea, and he, at great risk from the extreme heat, managed to fix a rope on to the corner of the building, and, all hands volunteering a pull, speedily brought the premises to the ground.
> All present worked with hearty will and so unusual at fires which have formerly occurred, we noticed a total absence of unnecessary destruction of property. As soon as the rookeries referred to were razed, it was at once seen that the fire had been cut off, and the breeze, which was still fresh, helped to rapidly consume the remaining portion of the buildings as they fell it. It is invidious to particularise any one for the way in which he helped to save property, but we must be pardoned if we mention that amongst the volunteers who were particularly noticeable for their endeavours to stop the ravages of the fire were the Rev Mr Leigh, Mr Budden, Mr Macaree, and sub-Inspector Isely.

The article went on to place values on the damage, but Jane didn't continue to read. When would her husband ever stop his daring and risky behaviour?

Jane discovered within a short time that it was no time soon. Word had spread some weeks earlier that the ship *Countess Russell* had dropped anchor in Keppel Bay with the immigrants on board suffering from an outbreak of typhoid. The ship was quarantined, but 25 deaths occurred. After finally dropping the surviving passengers, *Countess Russell* sailed south, picked up cargo and headed north again. During a gale she ran aground on Wreck Point, many miles south of Rockhampton. The crew all survived.

Edwin was with Cornelius Norris when he received word from the agents for the ship's captain that the wreck of the ship, together with all materials, boats, sails, and stores was to be auctioned.

'Here's a chance, Mac.'

'Edwin bid, and paid £207 for the donkey engine and condenser at auction. The major bidder later sold his interest in the balance of items to Edwin and Cornelius Norris.

'Edwin, you have responsibilities. Just take care,' Jane cautioned when Edwin said they were going off to Wreck Point to salvage what they could.

On Captain Norris' ketch *Violet* they made a formidable pair as they sailed south with a full rescue crew. On arrival they found the weather particularly unfavourable with a heavy surf rolling in. On the one fine day they experienced they rescued ten boatloads of cargo, but two lifeboats and a jolly boat were broken up in the rough seas following. They managed to fix a cable ashore and attach the end to a kedge anchor that was dropped into the water.

Edwin, while working in the rough conditions, was thrown against the heavy cable and was briefly knocked unconscious. He was swept away by a wave and landed on the beach severely bruised and battered but conscious again. One of the carpenters they'd employed was also swept away and also survived the experience.

With the *Violet* fully loaded, they headed back to Rockhampton, ready to sell the booty the following Monday, by auction, at the Queen's Wharf.

'Edwin, just look at you,' Jane exclaimed, hands on hips, when he arrived home. Bandaging his cuts she reprimanded him. 'You're nearly forty. You can't keep this up.'

'No, my dear, I can hear my body talking to me too. But as long as I *put my better foot before.*'

Exasperated, Jane shrugged.

Baby Peter began to cry. He was frail and sickly and

colicky. Jane dipped her little finger in honey and popped it in his mouth. She started to rock him in her arms while Edwin caught up on news from the Bulletin. 'And Rockhampton now has its first orphanage,' he said to no one in particular. 'And Antheline Thozet is making some great contributions to the Botanical Gardens. And I'll bet Bernard Pene is too.'

One month later, when all Edwin's injuries had healed, he was startled by Jane's cry early in the morning. Rushing out, he found her cradling little Peter, who had turned blue and was not breathing. It was far too late to get Dr Callaghan. Edwin, for once, was without words as he went about the house covering the mirrors.

In 1874 Edwin, with a multitude of business ventures to manage, decided to let the pawn-broking business lapse, although not the money lending. He posted the following notice in the Bulletin:

> *Wanted to be Known.*
> *MR MACAREE having let his shops in William Street, wishes it to be known that people wanting to see him on business can do so at the Old Shop on the 10th of May next from 10 to 3 o'clock, after which date he gives up taking in pledges, which part of the business Mr Jas McKean will continue for himself. No person will have anything to do with the management of E Macaree's business but himself – strictly private. No reasonable offer refused for the balance of his Stock, Jewellery, &c.*
> *EDWIN MACAREE*

'Colonel,' Edwin said, visiting Albrecht Feez's store, 'I think I'll try for more East Street land. What are your thoughts?'

'Can't go wrong, Mac. Look at how the place is growing.'

And so Edwin purchased land in East Street, for £12 14s 6d per foot frontage. He estimated that translated to £3300 per acre. While it was not in the heart of the business district, it was a developing area.

Edwin still held the property at Crocodile about seven miles from Rockhampton. He and Jane took the children there from time to time for a break.

'I'm planning to fence and stock more of the land, Jane. Come with me and have a rest.'

Jane jumped at the opportunity. She was still grieving the loss of Peter and craved a change. She gathered up the two boys. As well as the tent makers, who now worked in a dedicated building on the selection, Edwin had employed a German man and a South Sea Islander named Billy a few weeks earlier to excavate a dam and they, in turn, about ten days prior to Edwin's family's arrival, had hired a young German woman to cook for them.

One afternoon, Jane was pottering in the garden of their country home with Ned, nine, and Jim, four. She was being helped by an employee, George Otensen from Lifu in the South Pacific. The children were playing with small implements in the vegetable garden while Jane weeded her rose garden when a woman's scream shattered the idyllic peace. Jane jumped up, transfixed with terror, as the sound pierced her heart and froze her insides. The screaming didn't ease up. It was coming from a hut on their property about a quarter of a mile away.

George dropped his fork and ran towards the scream. He found the labourers' young cook on fire. He ripped off his hat and tried to knock the fire out. When it didn't work, he used his hands. They were severely burnt for his efforts. He ran into the hut and grabbed a blanket and finally put the fire out with it. He then carried the badly injured woman back into the hut.

Having left the children with the maid, Jane arrived. She grimaced when she saw the shocking burns. Language was limited, but it was obvious to Jane that, while cooking dinner over the open fire, the woman's skirt had caught fire. The iron crinoline she wore was still red hot and continued to scorch and burn the poor victim. Jane felt ill with the stench of the burning flesh but pulled her nausea into check. She knew she had to get the poor young woman out of the red hot metal petticoat and look more closely at the burns.

'What is your name?' Jane said.

'Anna,' she whispered, tears streaming. 'My father,' she said, indicating the older German man in the doorway.

He stood inspecting his fingernails and showed little concern for his daughter or her condition. Jane noted, however, that the South Sea Islander beside him was looking anxious, hopping from one foot to the other.

'George,' Anna said in a heavy accent to the worried-looking South Sea Islander, reaching out her badly burnt hand. 'Stay?'

Jane sent her man, also called George, back to her home for clean linen and a large bottle of salad oil with which to attend the burns. Anna's George knelt beside her.

Finally, armed with the materials, Jane ordered everyone out, got Anna out of the iron skirt and addressed the burns.

Edwin arrived on the scene. He poked his head into the hut. 'Her face isn't burnt,' he said to Jane.

'No. I've dressed the burns now.'

'Get the spring cart, George, as quickly as you can,' Edwin ordered his man.

Anna's George lifted her and placed her gently on it and Jane covered the exposed burns with more linen.

'Please, my head, my hair,' Anna begged her George to

help. He raised her head and pushed back her hair.

'Get her to the hospital,' Edwin said to both of the Georges.

'Nein, nein,' her father said. 'Mein Haus. Rockhampton,' he added.

Edwin was reluctant to argue with her father, so just nodded.

'She's in severe pain. Just make sure she's seen quickly.'

Jane raced back to her home and grabbed some medication. She met the cart on its way out and gave Anna weak brandy and water with twenty drops of laudanum in it to try to relieve her suffering. Anna was then driven away by her father and the two Georges. Edwin led them along the road for a distance so that they avoided the worst sections of road riddled with holes and bumps, hoping it might give Anna a degree of comfort.

He wished her well and headed back home.

It was later on the following day, while Edwin was doing business in Rockhampton, that he discovered that someone had eventually called a doctor to Anna who was lying in a humpy near the old Immigration Depot. He was furious that her father had such disregard for his daughter's life that he did not immediately transport her to the hospital.

Dr Thon, he heard, found her barely alive and noted that she was six months pregnant. With her limited speech, she had asked for the Rev Mr Hartley. Anna died shortly after from the burns.

Hearing of the pregnancy, and having observed her relationship with her George, Edwin grasped why her father had shown such disapproval and behaved so callously.

'That poor woman, Edwin.' Jane said when Edwin returned home and reported the outcome to her. 'I thought life out here in the country would be more peaceful.'

'It is the stars, the stars above us, govern our conditions.'

'Yes, indeed. Just so much hardship, so much pain, so much death.'

Over dinner consisting of homegrown beef, and vegetables from the garden, Edwin began to tell Jane about the new horse and buggy he'd purchased, along with all the accessories.

'The police confiscated it today. They think it is stolen goods.'

Jane stared at him in disbelief.

Yet another court case was held, with Edwin the sorry victim of a crime perpetrated by another.

Edwin had heard of a new way of keeping cattle out of the garden without worrying about timber fencing. The prickly pear had been introduced from South America, and it was guaranteed that the cattle wouldn't go anywhere near it. The plant provided a purple fruit that made great jam, although Jane hated dealing with the prickles on the fruit itself. Edwin's fences though were all post and rail.

After a few months had passed, Jane asked Edwin to move back to Rockhampton. In her late thirties, she was again with child. When the baby was born, she insisted on calling this girl child Emma, after the Emma she had lost.

1875–1879

Growth and Adversity

The town of Rockhampton grew to over 8,000. Seven hundred and twenty-five migrants arrived on the 131 ships that docked at the River Port in 1875. Three tailor shops, three hairdressers, and twenty-two hotels were among the town's services.

'Listen to this, Jane.' Edwin read from the newspaper. 'Last year there were 248 cases of drunkenness, with 128 convictions.' He chuckled. 'They should spend more time at the School of Arts, and less at all those hotels.'

Jane nodded absentmindedly.

Edwin had acquired a punt from Mrs Jewell for £10 to use on the river. He made sure there was a witness to the transaction. He hired the punt out for £1 per day but had a fee-paying arrangement with Mr Jewell for him to use the punt to transport timber for Edwin for use on his farm.

'Well, Jane,' Edwin said, 'I'm off to the Petty Debts Court today.'

'What have you done now?'

'It's an interpleader case first about the punt. I reckon I own it. The creditors are trying to collect on a debt owed on it, but it's a case of who owns the punt. I don't owe anyone anything. It's currently being held by the bailiff in the belief that it belongs to the Jewells.'

'Well then, it must be the Jewells who owe?'

'You'd think that but it's complicated. Morris sold it to the

Jewells. But he says they didn't finish paying for it. The Jewells gave me a receipt for my payment, so I've got proof of ownership. I'll let you know tonight.' Edwin picked up his hat and left.

And so the case proceeded. That night, Edwin came home and scooped up little Emma from her cradle, kissing the top of her head. 'Well, my wee one, there's the outcome. They think someone else owns the punt and they're suing them. The downside is, I might have to relinquish the punt if they're found guilty and can't pay.'

'You're calm about that outcome, Edwin.'

'Well, I've recouped more than my expenditure, Jane, whatever the findings.'

The 1875 Mango Season, as the locals called the end of the year, was in full swing, and so was the unrest.

North Rockhampton was considered a recreational resort, especially when there was entertainment at Pene's Cremorne Gardens and Hotel on weekends and celebration days. Jane and Edwin, with their children, still visited regularly. And then there was the Racecourse.

The South Sea Islanders were not only working on farms but were involved in industry, particularly meat preserving. Many of them had willingly signed up for a second three-year term, often at higher rates of pay. But with considerable numbers of Europeans migrating, and more new arrivals from the Pacific Islands there was now competition for jobs.

No restrictions existed on the consumption of alcohol. The bubble burst when a group of drunken sailors struck a South Sea Islander in the head at the racetrack. Naturally, other Islanders rushed to their countryman's aid, as did sailors and other Europeans to theirs. Mounted police drove them all away from the Racecourse but the riot escalated, and anything at hand became a weapon, including broken bottles and hunks of wood. It was estimated that there were about fifteen islanders and about 300 Europeans in the melee. Witnesses seemed to agree that the Europeans were the aggressors, and without police intervention, outcomes could have been much worse, as the Islanders fought like warriors, and demonstrated outstanding stone throwing skills.

'Did you hear, Jane, that a handful of sailors at that riot were convicted for being drunk, and just one Islander for being disorderly?' Edwin roared with laughter. 'Those Islanders are a tough bunch.'

'Rockhampton's like every other town now, Edwin. It's too rough and getting dangerous.'

'*We know what we are, but know not what we may be …*'

'What are you, or should I say, William Shakespeare, talking about now?'

'Maybe it's time to move a little way out of town and be and do something new?'

'Well, at least let me have this baby first,' Jane said rubbing the about-to-be-a-baby tummy.

It was a traumatic birth in that it all happened so quickly that there was no time to call the midwife. With the help of a maid, Jane gave birth to Mary, whom she named after her own mother. Jane, heartbroken, knew there was something very wrong, and Mary died just a few days later. The death certificate nominated the cause as convulsions.

Edwin was being sued by a Mrs Birmingham for £50 for malicious prosecution. Given the current circumstances, he kept this information from Jane, but he was confident, as the defendant, that he was in the right. He had Mr Real from the solicitor firm, Jones and Brown, to defend him.

Mr Milford, representing Mrs Birmingham claimed that

Edwin falsely and maliciously had her charged with fraudulently concealing the will of the late Mr Rogers where she was the beneficiary.

Mrs Birmingham had not seen Mr Rogers for several years prior to his death. She was aware that Mr Rogers owed Edwin £57 at the time of his death, with one year's interest at 10% owing.

Mrs Birmingham was in possession of the will, which she allowed Edwin to read at the time of Mr Rogers' death. He claimed the will would have to be probated, but regardless he held the deeds of the house as security over the debt and could sell Rogers' house, in which Mrs Birmingham currently resided, and take his debt from it.

When the property was under contract, Edwin requested the will from Mrs Birmingham in order to satisfy the purchaser. He said if there was any surplus he would give it to Mrs Birmingham.

Mrs Birmingham declined to give Edwin the will, and she claimed he then sprang from his chair and shook his fist in her face, using insulting language.

Edwin subsequently wrote to Mrs Birmingham informing her that if the will was not produced the matter would be placed in his solicitor's hands and the ensuing charges would be billed against the estate. However, Edwin sent a second letter, where he expressed a desire to let matters settle, as the only winners, he realised, would be the lawyers.

Edwin was one of the executors to the will, and he was the only creditor as far as Mrs Birmingham knew. Edwin had paid the funeral expenses because the late Mr Rogers had no money available.

Mrs Birmingham continually refused to give Edwin the will. She claimed she didn't trust him.

Finally Edwin instructed his solicitor to act. Several letters were sent demanding the will, with no response. When, eventually, Mrs Birmingham received a summons and appeared in the Police Court, she was locked up for three hours.

Charles Haynes, co-executor of Rogers' will, met three times with Edwin and Mrs Birmingham but he refused to probate the will as there was no money in the estate to pay for his services. But he believed Edwin would do the best he could for the estate as there seemed no intention to sacrifice the property.

After all this evidence was heard, the Judge found that Mrs Birmingham had failed to show that Edwin had acted maliciously.

Returning home from court, but mentioning nothing of it, Edwin sat in his armchair with the newspaper and looked up at Jane. 'We're finally getting our bridge across the river, Jane. They've budgeted £38,000 over 3 years for the build. It's going to be carried on iron cylinders and will combine lattice girders with wire ropes. Those girders will form the parapet. The abutment will be of stone.'

'What does all that mean?'

Edwin folded the newspaper and held it out to Jane so she could see the sketch.

'That should make it easier to go to Cremorne Gardens,' Jane said.

'Not to mention opening up more development.'

Jane looked into those deeply set eyes of his. 'Whatever do you have in mind now, Edwin?'

In response, Edwin simply ran his fingers through his great mop of hair.

While the bridge was under construction, and Jane still not fully recovered from Mary's death, Edwin applied for, and was successful in acquiring a selection of 1060 acres at Coorooman on Coorooman Creek, near Cawarral. Cawarral was located between Rockhampton and Emu Park, a popular coastal village.

Edwin set to and built a homestead, indentured and employed Islanders to work cattle, horses and crops on his selection. When his solicitor, Rees Rutland Jones was running for parliament, Edwin chaired the meeting at Cawarral for his friend.

Not only were there South Sea Islanders working as labourers, but many Chinese had chosen to stay after failures of some of the goldfields. The friction between the two groups created considerable unrest.

Rees Jones made it clear that he only supported the indenturing of Islanders for tropical agricultural purposes. He admitted that it was difficult, if not impossible, to legislate on the Chinese issue.

Edwin chose to spend much of his time at Coorooman. After he'd built the homestead on Coorooman Creek, which always flowed with fresh clean water, Jane often came and stayed. They planted fruit trees, including mangoes and citrus. The Islanders built fences and yards and moved the cattle from paddock to paddock. Edwin built a piggery for domestic use and bred horses.

Many of the farmers in the area were not satisfied with depending on cattle and wanted to grow crops. Edwin chaired another meeting in Cawarral to discuss agriculture, where some farmers decided to try growing sugar cane, and even tobacco. Edwin though planned to experiment with Canadian corn.

One Sunday night, with a storm raging, while Jane and the three children were in residence, they woke to a blinding flash, followed by an explosion. Edwin leapt up to find the sitting room alight.

'Out, out!' he yelled at them all, roughly ushering them to the door. Jane pushed the boys out and grabbed Emma's little hand. She was four years old, and still half asleep, but allowed herself to be dragged down the slope to the creek.

Edwin called to the Islanders who resided in huts nearby, but they were already up and alert. With buckets of water gathered from the tanks, the fire was quickly extinguished. Later, Edwin heard that the Emu Park Hotel had been unroofed during the same storm.

While repairs were being made, Jane returned to Rockhampton in the carriage, leaving Ned, who had turned twelve, with his father.

Occasionally, some of the local Aboriginal people camped on Edwin's land as they passed from one area to another, just as they'd done for centuries. They often brought freshly picked oysters with them. Edwin doled out sugar, tea and flour, but would always ask them to do something in return, such as collect and stack timber or load the dray. They also helped clear the roadway. It was usually an easy and comfortable relationship although there was one time he'd asked them to stack timber yet when he returned the job wasn't done. His diary explained how he negotiated.

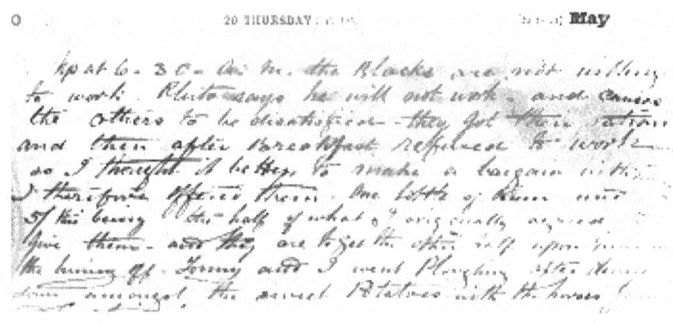

Edwin's diary entry, trying to bribe Blacks with rum

Up at 6.30 am. The Blacks are not willing to work – Pluto says he will not work and causes the others to be dissatisfied – they got their rations and then after Breakfast refused to work so I thought it better to make a bargain with them. I therefore offered them One bottle of Rum and 5/- this being the half of what I originally agreed to give them – and they are to get the other half upon finishing the burning off. Tommy and I went Ploughing after dinner down amongst the sweet Potatoes with the horses Jenny and Captain.

Ned was learning from his father how to manage cattle, and how to build and repair the fences and the machinery. Ned also enjoyed accompanying his father when he was buying or selling or negotiating in town. Edwin gave Ned his own horse and allowed him a good deal of freedom.

Early one evening, Edwin became concerned when Ned's horse found its way back to the stables minus Ned who'd been out alone checking fences. Edwin immediately ordered all hands out searching and calling. The search went on all through the night. It was not until morning that two Islanders found Ned lying unconscious on the hard ground. They carried him gently back to the homestead.

'Take a horse, and go and fetch Dr Callaghan and then my wife,' Edwin frantically ordered Charlie, one of his senior workers. The Islander women, who ran the homestead and looked after the men, tended Ned, cleaned him up, and gently applied damp linen to his head, murmuring soft words.

'Not good, Mac,' Dr Callaghan said when he arrived and tested Ned's responses and felt for breaks.

'Can't you do something?'

'We must wait. I note paralysis on the left side, and his jaw is broken. But the concussion is the greatest of all concerns.' Dr Callaghan frowned. 'I won't lie to you. He could make no recovery, some recovery, or full recovery.' Noticing that Jane had just arrived, he added, 'And let Mrs Macaree come in now.'

Edwin couldn't speak. He went past Jane with his head lowered and wandered down to the creek in denial. Soon Jane, having just heard the verdict from Dr Callaghan, joined him, an avalanche of tears cascading silently down her face.

They wrapped their arms around each other, maintaining the silence. Jane eventually climbed back up the creek bank, and began her bedside vigil.

Dr Callaghan called regularly and treated the paralysis with dry cupping. The special cups he used on Ned were heated before placing on him. They then created a suction which stimulated the blood flow. This in turn was believed to aid the symptoms of the paralysis.

Edwin's diary entry, trying to reduce Ned's paralysis with cupping

Edwin still speechless. Dr Callaghan call'd and pronounced his/Edwin's case to be concussion of the brain with Paralisis of the right side. Dry cupping and treat as before – The Dr went on to attend to a sprained foot of Mrs R Ross's.

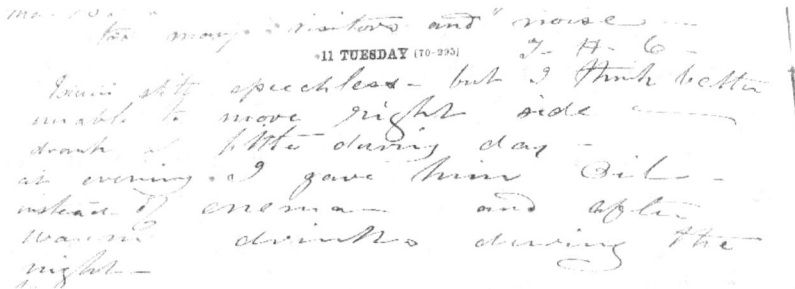

Edwin's diary entry, giving Ned oil instead of enema

Edwin still speechless – but I think better able to move right side. Drank a little during day – In evening I gave him oil instead of enema and after warm drinks during the night.

Day after day, Jane, and often Edwin, kept a bedside watch. For that Jane was eventually rewarded when, days later, Ned opened his eyes.

'Ned, can you hear me?' She squeezed his hand, hardly daring to breathe.

'Mmm.'

'Edwin!' she yelled, not letting go of Ned's hand.

'Ned, can you move your legs?'

Ned's right leg twitched and his toes curled. A panicked look crossed his face.

'No, no, that's very good. Now can you feel that?' His mother pinched the calf on his left leg.

A very concerned, 'Hmm?' came from Ned.

'It's alright. Dr Callaghan will come again. You've broken your jaw, that's why talking is so hard.'

Young Ned's right hand went to his face and his eyes reflected the pain of his touch. Edwin stood in the doorway, looking enormously relieved that he'd regained consciousness.

Jane had Jim and Emma escorted from Rockhampton to

Coorooman, and she began working with Ned under the instruction of Dr Callaghan. Edwin started each daily diary entry with: *Ned is still not talking*. But week by week and month by month Ned improved. His speech, when he was able to talk, was slurred, but in time, he made himself understood. Movement was not easy, and Ned listed and limped but eventually he was able to stagger about.

Then one day, the men loaded Ned into the back of the spring cart with Jane and the children up front with their picnic basket and blankets. They were being taken on an outing to the beach at Emu Park.

The cart followed Coorooman Creek upstream where the crossing was easy, unless it was flooding, which it wasn't. The only accessible road to Emu Park from Rockhampton ran through a neighbour's property before reaching Coorooman, and Mr Costello of Cawarral Station wanted to stop all traffic through his paddocks and force the Government to fix their original road, which had been there since 1870.

'Did you know, children, that Emu Park used to be known as Oopal? That's the Aboriginal word meaning place of emus,' Jane told them.

Coorooman was closer to Emu Park than to Rockhampton, and Edwin occasionally visited the Emu Park hotel. There were a few boarding houses to accommodate holidaying families, but Jane and her children were day-trippers on this outing. Jim and Emma scrambled over rocks and paddled through rock pools. Ned was limited to sitting on the rug but Jane was pleased to be out with him.

The mother of a holidaying family on the beach introduced herself to Jane. 'Mr Orr has just told us that he came across a crocodile nest at Deep Creek and he counted 45 eggs. Can you imagine? He cracked the shell of one of them, and the creature appeared quite lively.' She gave a shudder. 'He said the black fellows saw a big crocodile in the area.'

Jane shuddered too.

After packing up with the help of some of the women, Jane stopped and bought fish caught in the fish traps on her way home.

When she arrived back at Coorooman, she asked Edwin about Coorooman Creek. 'No, never, no crocodiles up this far. They've delivered timber up Cawarral Creek for Moore's Creek Bridge. You know where the junction of the two Emu Park roads is? Well, they got to within one and a half miles of there with the delivery. Saw no crocodiles.'

Jane had developed a fondness for Emu Park. For the first time, she was the one who initiated a property deal for the family. 'I think a cottage at Emu Park would be perfect,' she said. 'Perfect for escaping to in summer time. There's always a breeze.'

Edwin needed no encouragement, and the cottage was built on the hill in Phillip Street and registered with the Titles Office in Jane's name. Edwin expanded the deal by building a few more cottages for sale or for rent.

Because of the growth of Rockhampton into rural and farming lands, the Gogango Divisional Board was formed. It controlled all lands around the town of Rockhampton, but it was not independent.

1879–1880

Welcome the Fraser Family

'I see we have a new owner of the Frogmore wool scour over near Crocodile Creek,' Edwin announced to Jane. 'Old William Roope's health was poorly. I'm pleased he found a buyer.'

'Is the new owner anyone we know?' she asked.

'A fellow called William Fraser. He's brought his family out from Scotland according to the paper.'

A few weeks later, while Edwin and Jane were enjoying tea and cake at the Cremorne Gardens, in walked a tall, slender, straight-shouldered man with his wife and two young children.

Jane couldn't help noticing how well-groomed and dressed the group were.

Since Edwin and Jane knew most of the regular attendees, Edwin immediately rose and proffered his hand to the newcomer. He then bowed to his wife.

'I'm Edwin Macaree. I haven't seen you here before.'

'Och, Mr Macaree, I'm William Fraser, and this is my wife, Annie,' he said, having removed his hat as he turned to his wife.

'Do come and join us,' Edwin offered, turning and introducing Jane. The staff rushed to set more placings.

Jane smiled at Annie. 'And who are these delightful children?'

'This is Donald. He's five. And this is Jessie. She's six.'

'Oh, then Donald is the same age as Emma,' Jane said, touching Emma. 'How would you all like to play outside? Ned, would you mind watching everyone?' Ned was now fourteen.

Once the staff had poured tea, Edwin said to William, 'Where in Scotland are you from?'

'Well, we're originally from Dundee. The bairns were born there. I came out to join my uncle in Brisbane. I'm a tanner, and so is he.'

'But you didn't stay in Brisbane.'

'Noo. I lasted a year. I decided I wanted to try my hand as a butcher, so we moved to Toowoomba. But then I heard about the opportunity here with wool scouring. The tanning is complimentary, so I'm somewhat familiar with the whole process.'

'And how are you finding your new business?'

'Roope built it in '65, and I think he ran out of energy. So it really needs some upgrading. I've quite a job ahead of me.'

The men exchanged business information and ideas as the women moved closer together and chatted, agreeing that they'd meet at Cremorne as often as they could.

On their way home, Annie said to William, 'I've no idea what wool-scouring is. Will you take me one day and show it to me?'

A few days later, he fulfilled her request. Upon arrival, she said, 'You seem to employ a lot of people, William.' She was amazed at the vast number of men poking in the tanks with sticks.

'It's called pot-sticking. The tanks have a 400-gallon capacity and we add soap and other ingredients and keep moving the contents till the wool is clean.'

'Like linen bed sheets in the copper and stirring them till

they're clean.'

William nodded. 'Somewhat. Then, after a rinse, all the wool gets laid out on sheets to dry. But we must keep it clean and it canna get wet again. There's a strong market overseas for quality wool. And it's a big job sourcing supplies. I'll enter the quality product in agricultural shows down south. It will help me build a reputation for future sales.'

Annie was satisfied and relieved to escape the unpleasant smells.

After almost a year had passed, little Millicent Fraser was born. William, Annie, and their children met often with the Macarees at the Cremorne Gardens on Sundays after church. Millie, as she became known, stayed close by her mother in her wicker perambulator, clutching a tiny silver pole with a bell attached. Sunday was the nanny's day off.

While the women chatted and drank tea, Edwin said privately to William, 'I'm thinking of purchasing this property, William. What are your thoughts?'

'Property is your domain, Edwin. What do *you* think?' he asked in his broad Scottish accent.

'Well, I think Bernard Pene might be getting desperate. All he wants, poor fellow, is to take his daughter Josephine back to France.' Edwin reached into his pocket and pulled out a crumpled newspaper cutting. He passed it to William, saying, 'That was advertised a while ago. I haven't spoken to M'sieu Pene yet, but if the price is right …'

> *FOR SALE (privately), CREMORNE HOTEL, Gardens, Pleasure Grounds, Cottage, and Out-buildings. Also, Goodwill, Licence, Stock and Furniture of Hotel. Title Guaranteed. Apply to B. PENE.*

And so it came to be, after yet another visit to the Queensland National Bank, that Edwin Macaree was the second owner of the Cremorne Hotel and Gardens.

'Oh, Edwin, I think you've developed a Midas touch,' Jane said, hugging his toughened torso. This was one acquisition that particularly excited her. 'And we can move out of East Street, and into the Cremorne house.'

East Street was constantly abuzz with the noise of workers with laden bullock drays bringing supplies to the merchants, and with horses and carriages bringing the purchasers of the merchandise. The dusty whirlwind atmosphere kicked up a constant film of dust that settled on all surfaces including people. In the humidity the dust stuck, reminding Jane of her first experience of the climate on that afternoon after disembarking the ship.

The children were unable to play in the street due to the traffic.

'Think of the wonderful adventures the children can have with access to the Cremorne Gardens every day,' she said.

Edwin caught her enthusiasm. 'Well, the Cremorne property can only prosper more and more with the bridge now finished across the river to the north side,' he said. 'It might have taken an age to build, but with the Indian ironwork it's easy on the eye.'

They'd attended the official opening of the bridge back on New Year's Day. Two trees were planted on the north side of the bridge; one by Edwin's friend, William Patterson.

A group of influential town gentlemen, including Edwin, met to discuss forming the Central Queensland Meat Export Company. Queensland had a surplus of 64,000 tons of meat, whereas Victoria and South Australia had a deficit.

But it was a response to the needs of the mother country,

because of its large population, that they focussed. The risk factor of export was pointed out, but a couple of Queensland companies had experimented successfully with frozen meat.

Erection of a depot and the fitting out of a ship with refrigeration would have to occur. Constant reference was made to facts and figures in the ensuing prospectus. Edwin, convinced of the viability of the project, acquired 600 shares, and projections showed a profit of ten percent on investment could be expected.

Edwin was raising cattle on both his Crocodile selection and the Coorooman one. The Central Queensland Meat Export Company was located along the Lakes Creek Road, downstream on the northern side of the Fitzroy River, midway between both his selections.

Forever diversifying, Edwin was now dabbling in real estate, both buying and selling. He placed an advertisement:

> MONEY TO LEND,
> AT THE GOOD INTENT LOAN OFFICE, WILLIAM STREET,
> On every description of Property at a light interest, repayable by instalments; Pro Notes discounted; cash buyer of every description of Property.
> EDWIN MACAREE Established 1862.

The Rockhampton Grammar School, displaying an Ionic style of architecture, took only 13 months to build once the foundations were laid. Sitting on prime land on the Athelstane Range on the south side, it opened its doors to male students under the guidance of Headmaster, John Wheatcroft. The fortunate students and staff enjoyed magnificent views of the town below. Private apartments for the masters were also provided.

Edwin's newly acquired land nearby was advertised for sale, along with various other items. With his fingers firmly entrenched in this pie, Edwin placed several ads:

> EDWIN MACAREE,
> LICENCED AUCTIONEER, BROKER, VALUATOR, & MARKET AUCTION ROOMS AND LAND EXCHANGE,
> WILLIAM STREET, ROCKHAMPTON.
> Established 1862,
> Sales by auction.
> E. MACAREE'S SALE OF LAND BY Public Auction will take place THIS DAY, FRIDAY.
> Twenty Allotments of Land immediately adjoining the Rockhampton Grammar School on the Range, top of Archer Street, with Eastern Aspect. ...

(Here Edwin veers off-topic to advertise various other goods for auction.)

> Remember THIS DAY, FRIDAY, THE 4TH DAY OF NOVEMBER, AT 11 O'CLOCK A.M., AT THE MARKET AUCTION ROOMS, William Street.
> IT has been determined in solemn conclave that EDWIN MACAREE must sell the Twenty Allotments of Land (the very last remaining unsold block), with eastern aspect, immediately adjoining the Rockhampton Grammar School, on Athelstane Range, top of Archer Street, splendid soil, unrivalled position, suitable for Head Masters, Tutors, Parents who desire to be near their young, Gentlemen's Residences, &c. Terms to suit the purchasers, to be declared at sale

at the
MARKET AUCTION ROOMS, THIS DAY, FRIDAY NEXT, 4TH OF NOVEMBER
AT 11 o'clock sharp. God Save the Queen.

While Edwin was indulging heavily in all these activities, he divided his time between Cremorne and Coorooman. Jane chose Cremorne with the children where she had greater support from the many servants as well as more modern conveniences.

Sunday dinner at Cremorne in the middle of the day followed the English tradition that Edwin and Jane had experienced with their families back home. Tea, though, was at 6 pm. The whole family always gathered at 12 when cook prepared a roast. Edwin stood at the head of the table, vigorously sharpening his carving knife on the steel, then carved the meat, compliments of the Coorooman stock. He placed slices of beef on the warm plates placed in front of him, which Jane removed as he carved. She added the Yorkshire pudding with a crispy top. The serving dishes, piled with roasted vegetables, were passed around in matching dishes for the older children to help themselves. Last came the gravy boat.

Before sitting down in his carver chair, Edwin frowned at Emma. 'Elbows off the table.' She sighed and sat bolt upright, hands folded in her lap. No one ate until grace was said and their mother had picked up her knife and fork.

'Have you finished, Jim?' Edwin asked a while later. 'Then put your knife and fork together.' Mealtimes with their father always served as lessons in manners. The children were always silent, as was expected of them. When Edwin was absent, Jane was a tad more relaxed and they were allowed to mop up their left-over gravy with bread, after asking permission.

The midday main course was followed by a bread and butter pudding, or other similar dessert, eaten with a spoon and small fork.

With the family gathered around the table and having finished their meal, Edwin made an announcement. Ned was now sixteen, and had made a fair recovery from his accident four years prior. He still walked with a slight limp and was weak on one side. He was devoted to his father, and Edwin was teaching Ned everything he could. Jim was eleven years old, and was now attending the Grammar School.

'You know that I've been advertising the Hotel for its accommodation,' he said to his family. Pulling out the Bulletin advertisement he read:

CREMORNE TEMPERANCE HOTEL.
GOOD ACCOMMODATION for Boarders and Country Visitors.
House Paddock and Stabling for Horses. The Gardens are free to Boarders.
EDWIN MACAREE.

'Now, we need to consider the consequences of *too much of a good thing*.'

'Edwin, the children don't need a lesson in Shakespeare right now. Where are you going with this?'

'There is not enough of me to go around, Jane. I need to divest of something. So much management is required here, there and everywhere. I shall try to sell, or at least, lease Cremorne.'

Jane's face transformed; her jaw dropped and her eyes rounded.

Ned spoke up. 'But Father, what are Mother and the children to do?'

'Ned, my boy, *There is nothing either good or bad, but thinking makes it so.* We shall advertise and if there is a response, we, in turn, shall respond. Your mother shall choose the eventual outcome.'

Tongue in cheek, Jane said, 'With the advertising you provide to the Bulletin, you might have considered buying it as well.'

Edwin looked thoughtfully at his wife.

'No … don't you even think about it, Edwin Macaree,' she replied, unable to prevent the smile hovering around her mouth.

Edwin duly placed a simple ad:

> FOR SALE or TO LET. On easy terms, the CREMORNE HOTEL and GARDENS,
> the proprietor having to follow other pursuits.
> Apply at once to EDWIN MACAREE, Licensed Pawnbroker, &c. William Street.

In truth, Edwin was not fond of Cremorne, and regretted the purchase.

Edwin's diary entry expressing strong dislike for Cremorne

The family waited for a response to the ad, and relief rested warmly on Jane when nothing immediate eventuated. Thomas Lachlan became the licensee of the hotel, and that took some responsibility from Edwin.

The Cremorne Hotel and Gardens sat on the banks of Moore's Creek just a few yards from its confluence with the

Fitzroy River. Its address was 1 Bridge Street, and a weak and dilapidated bridge crossed the Moore's Creek adjacent to the premises. Edwin deemed it unsafe for travel, as did Captain Hunter. They called attention to its need for repairs to the Gogango Divisional Board who saw the creek not so much as a tributary of the Fitzroy but as a backwater from the Fitzroy. Edwin and Captain Hunter claimed that a quantity of earth had been removed from each side of the bridge which in turn endangered the supports. Of the timbers making up the bridge, sheer wear and tear had deteriorated the boards to such an extent as to pose a risk to those attempting to cross.

When the Board inspected the bridge, they also deemed it too dangerous for the public to cross and closed it rather than repair it.

Moore's Creek Bridge, from Cremorne, early 20th Century.

In the previous year, the initial meeting to set up the Gogango Divisional Board had met with zero interest. It was to come under the direction of the Rockhampton Council and was to cover all the districts surrounding the Municipality of

Rockhampton. Some months after that initial meeting a Board was finally appointed. A considerable time after its establishment, having faced the issue of Moore's Creek Bridge, the Board awarded a tender for carting and delivering gravel from the crossing of Moore's Creek on the North Yaamba Road to the bridge at Moore's Creek in order to resolve the undermining of the foundations at each end.

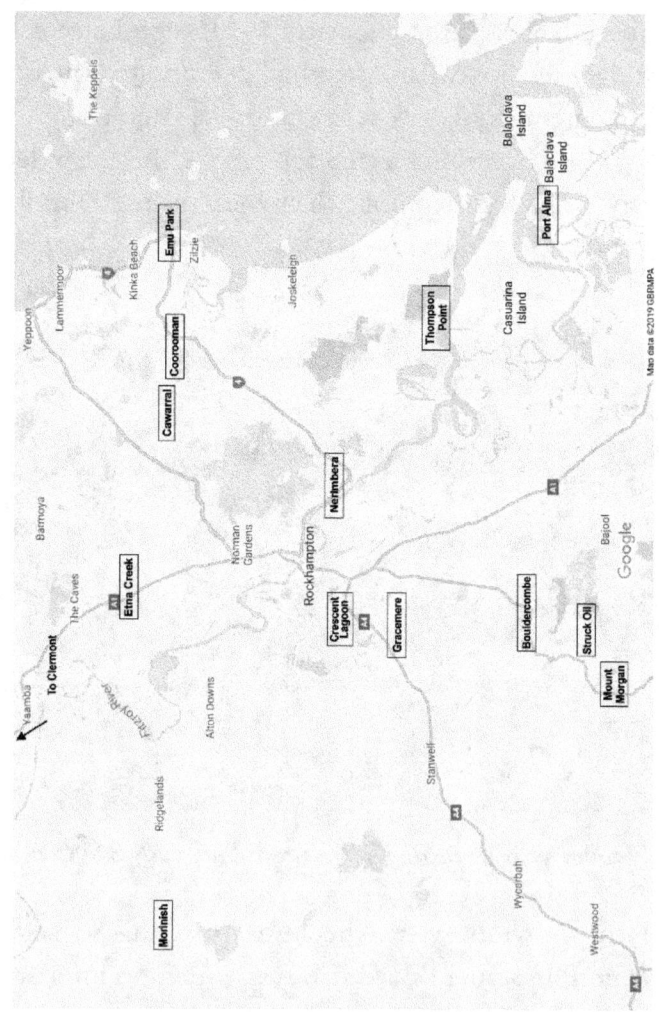

Map of district around Rockhampton
Modified Google map

1881–1882

Foray into Local Government

Edwin was heavily involved in his auctioneering work but still ran his Coorooman property with the help of Ned and the team of Islanders. Yet again Edwin, together with Messrs Osborne and Hayes this time, wrote to the Gogango Divisional Board, drawing attention to the injustice of forcing a road to Emu Park through their selections against their will. For twenty years, the old road had been adequate and disrupted only one owner, Mr Wright. The Chairman of the Divisional Board found the original road so choked up with vegetation that it was impossible to ride over and travelling stock could not make their way along it.

Edwin, frustrated, took the matter of his selection's invasion into his own hands, and advertised his intent with the following notice in the Bulletin:

> *Rockhampton, July 2nd 1881.*
> *I HEREBY give notice that I intend to apply at the Court of Petty Sessions to be held at Rockhampton on MONDAY, the 12th day of September ensuing, for a License to Erect two pairs of Swing Gates, according to law, on the road crossing my Selection No, 512, Coorooman Creek, near Cawarral.*
> *EDWIN MACAREE*

In December 1881, Edwin placed yet another ad in the same paper, this time for his auctioneering business.

Auction. See all
EDWIN MACAREE has received instructions from the owner to sell the south-east corner Lot of Land (splendid site, adjoining the Rockhampton Benevolent Asylum and immediately opposite the residence of J. Brown, Esq., J.P. in five lots.)

A grand chance to become a freeholder by time payments, equal to rent only. Go to, and examine the ground; it is pegged off in lots numbered, at the corner of Cambridge and Lennox Streets. Plans at Rooms.

Healthy sites, the very thing the doctor ordered, being Allotment 7 of Section 18, Town of Rockhampton. Title, RP. Act. after which Five Suburban Lots of 1 acre 2 roods each respectively on or near Limestone Creek, near to the famous Orchards of the Rev Mr Blanchard and John Maloney, Esq. Close to permanent water. Alluvial limestone formation. Good road; easy distance from town.

Secure one of these blocks of land, and take your time to pay; it will keep the girls and boys out of mischief to profitably till the soil.

A delightful Marine Residence, near Emu Park – Large House known as Mrs. Shaw's, with good fishing grounds and oyster beds and nearly 200 acres of Freehold Land fenced in; large stock yards and appointments. A fortune and health combined; on very easy terms to suit the purchaser.

Several other selections and town properties

To follow, time permitting, on

WEDNESDAY NEXT, 7TH DECEMBER AT ELEVEN O'CLOCK

MARKET AUCTION ROOMS AND LAND EXCHANGE,

William Street, Rockhampton. EDWIN MACAREEE Auctioneer &c.

Edwin followed this copiously worded ad with yet another, this time advertising 50 live pigs and other locally grown produce to be auctioned on Christmas Eve and concluded the ad with 'Who know him best trusts him most'.

Concerned for Ned's future wellbeing, Edwin wrote out a Deed of Grant, ensuring, should anything happen, that Ned would be taken care of, by leaving him land that he would inherit on his twenty-first birthday.

1881 deed of grant, leaving property to Ned

Rockhampton, October 20, 1881
Take Notice that this Deed of Grant No 24207 County of Livingstone. Parish of Nicholson Containing 54a 3r 33p Was put away by Me – Edwin Macaree - to be given to my son Edwin Macaree Junior upon His coming of Age. Signed ...

Early in 1882 Edwin, with support from Colonel Albrecht Feez and others, decided, instead of complaining constantly to Council, to nominate for Council himself. Edwin's first foray was into Number One Subdivision of the Gogango Divisional Board at Gracemere. There were only two nominations: John Murray and Edwin.

Henry Jones, Chairman of the Board, presided as Returning Officer. He pointed out that the usual deposit of £3, as required in the Act, was missing from Edwin's nomination which precluded his acceptance of the nomination.

Edwin, miffed by his own oversight, took himself off and nominated to serve as an alderman on the Municipal Council for the Archer Ward, as did William Caporn. This forced a poll to be taken. The poll was preceded by giving both nominees the opportunity to address the electorate in the Council Chambers.

Mr Caporn had the advantage of being known to the constituents, having been elected four times already.

Edwin took the floor.

> *'I'm just a young beginner in Council matters, but I intend, if elected, to have established, within one year, floating baths like those I've seen in my travels in Rio and in Oporto.*
>
> *'Even if I'm not elected I have some great ideas. The conservation of the river bank could be carried out in a system similar to what I've seen on the Mississippi and Missouri Rivers, by means of piles driven into the banks at short distances. A healthy promenade made of our local hardwoods, and lighted would be an asset.'*

Edwin concluded by saying that if defeated by Mr Caporn he would retire with good grace.

Mr Jones asked Edwin if he thought it was ethical for Edwin to sit in judgement over his own recent application for an extension to his lease connected with the Market Reserve.

'That, Mr Jones, is the unkindest cut of all. *I only wish to do what is good for the general public – pro bono publico. The leases, Mr Jones, should be put up for public competition when they expire. And that,'* Edwin held, *'should not exempt a man from sitting at the Council because he is a lessee.'*

Mr Shaw said, 'The money received for the rents has not been spent as first intended – for a market hall.'

'The idea of market buildings is premature, Mr Shaw. I'm rather inclined to the plan of erecting a number of buildings for the purposes of cold storage. Now that might not be payable but it would enhance domestic comfort.'

When another attempt to ask Edwin a question arose, the meeting was called to order. The Returning Officer asked Edwin if he considered he was doing the right thing as a lessee by occupying a seat on Council.

For once Edwin was verbally economic. 'Yes.'

When votes were finally counted the result was: W Caporn 225, and Edwin Macaree 66, with informal 2.

Edwin called in on Colonel Feez on his way home. 'Ah, don't give in, and don't give up, Mac,' he said. The Colonel was himself a Council Alderman representing a different ward. 'You have much to offer public life.'

Edwin returned home to Cremorne. 'I didn't stand a chance, Jane. They were out to knobble me. Petty jealousies,' he said, pouring himself a drink. But I shall *go wisely and go slowly. Those who rush stumble and fall.'*

William Fraser had been visiting the southern cities marketing his scoured wool. He arrived home on the *SS Derwent* to be met by his manager who told him there had been a fire at the wool-scour on the previous Saturday night.

As was the custom, a shift of men would sleep in the wool store at the wool scour to keep watch around the clock. While one of the men was extinguishing his candle around 9.30 pm, his mosquito net caught alight. The flames quickly spread to the roof. The other men were awoken but were unable to control the fire, so they set to removing bales of wool. They were able to save nine belonging to Messrs John Headrick and Co, but all of William Fraser's bales were destroyed.

His wife, Annie, said, 'But you have insurance, William.'

'That money, when I finally get it, Annie love, still doesn't produce the wool. I have to wait for the shearing sheds to produce, and they are committed to others. And the rebuild will take time. I'll have to lay some of the men off.'

It was a double blow when William found that his insurance policy was for only £300, which was insufficient to cover the damage.

When he and Annie and their children, Jessie, 9, Donald, 8 and 2-year-old Millie visited Cremorne Gardens the following Sunday, they were invited into Edwin and Jane's home. The Fraser children, Jessie and Donald, together with the Macaree children, Ned, 16, Jim, 11, and Emma 7, were allowed free range in the gardens, but Ned was given the responsibility of keeping an eye on the tribe.

With mild temperatures and a cloudless sky, visitors had chosen, in large numbers, to walk across the bridge from the south side and along to the gardens where they strolled contentedly among the trees and flowering shrubs.

The children were playing on the swings, laughing and pushing each other when a 10-foot long carpet snake slithered by. Ned yelled, 'Snake!' and pushed the children towards the house.

'Go, get away!' he yelled again, grabbing a stick and chasing the snake.

Hearing the commotion, the adults hurried out to find Ned's cries had gathered quite an audience, although there was no sign of the reptile.

'Ah, just another carpet snake, my boy,' Edwin chuckled. 'They are more frightened of you than you of them. They'll never harm you even if they bite you.'

He turned to the startled onlookers. 'My dear guests, we organised this little excitement for you as a special treat. And now you may continue your walk as the wriggly fellow has made his way back down to the creek.'

Once everyone was settled back in the house, Edwin disappeared and returned with his human skull. 'Now William, what do you think of the study of phrenology?'

'Oh, Edwin, no,' Jane interrupted.

'Och, no, I'm interested,' William replied as Annie drew back with revulsion. 'Well, of course, I've heard of it, but I'm not too sure what I think.'

'The Society was formed in Edinburgh 50 years ago. I'm studying it at the moment from journals I get in the mail. The science involves the measurement of curves and bumps on the skull.' He cupped the back of the skull that now carried notations on marked sections. 'This,' he said, 'predicts intelligence. The more protruding the bump the more intelligence.'

Everyone's hand flew to the back of their head. Edwin chuckled. 'Self-diagnosis, is it?'

Jane brought back some normalcy when she called for a fresh pot of china tea.

'How is your auctioneering and land broking business going?' William asked.

'I recommend land up by the Boys' Grammar School.

Attractive for staff and parents of students. Are you interested?'

'I'm concentrating on rebuilding and on accessing sheepskins and fleeces at the moment,' William replied. 'And, Edwin, how are you finding the one o'clock gun for setting your watch?'

'Oh, did you know that carronade was found here in the Gardens about 16 years ago when the Penes donated it to the Council?' Edwin shook his head. 'No? It's a curse to the town. It's fired either too early or too late. Children are arriving late for school, and I even tried to send a communication this week from the Telegraph Office according to my watch, and the office was closed because the time gun was fired twenty minutes early, making them close twenty minutes early. What we need, William, is a reliable chiming town clock.'

'I hope you lobby for that.'

Edwin continued to be torn between Cremorne and Coorooman, and Ned travelled back and forth with his father. The usual rains didn't come, and with water from the creek they were able to water the cattle, but feed was scarce. Ned worked, somewhat slowly, either on the land or in the business premises in William Street.

'Mother, I'm to make my first appearance in court,' Ned proudly announced, arriving home from his father's shop.

'Oh, no. Whatever for?'

'Oh, the usual. Someone pawned stolen goods. I shall just have to give evidence.'

Jane was so concerned that she attended the criminal case.

Two men, Messrs Davidson and Brown were jointly charged with stealing a Bible, a coat and a jumper from the home of Mr Jones, the coachbuilder in East Street. They were accused of keeping the clothing and pawning the Bible at

Macaree's shop, where they received five shillings from young Ned Macaree. A constable found the Bible there, and Ned, giving evidence, said he passed it over to the authorities.

After Ned finished giving evidence he returned to work, but Jane stayed on to hear the outcome.

Davidson and Brown were unrepresented, and the jury found them guilty with the Judge subsequently ordering both prisoners to serve twelve months with hard labour in the Brisbane prison.

Jane left the courtroom puzzled by how desperate someone would have to be to steal such ordinary items and puzzled that the sentence was so severe.

Edwin came in that evening with the Capricornian newspaper tucked under his arm. 'They published my letter, Jane,' he said, sitting in his grandfather chair and unfolding the paper.

'And which letter would that be, Edwin?' Jane glanced up from her sewing. Not only was Edwin a prolific speaker, but also a writer.

'I refuse to be accused of misdeeds without a right of reply, so I said' – here he read directly from the newspaper:

'EMU PARK ROAD. TO THE EDITOR OF THE CAPRICORNIAN.
Sir, I hope you will give me space in your valuable journal to reply to some misstatements that appeared in your paper of Friday last re the meeting of the Gogango Divisional Board on Thursday last. Mr. W. Pattison says I have closed the road to Emu Park. Such is not the fact – the road is now open. Again Mr Jones says that the owner of the land wanted to make capital out of it. Such is not true. I do not wish to sell the land; and as there is a public surveyed road already running through my small selection of 240 acres, I cannot see

the justice of the hole and corner deputation's misstatements. To say the least, it is unmanly to attribute mercenary motives to an absent citizen, who cannot protect himself with a fair field and no favour. I stand by my colours. Edwin Macaree.'

'But Edwin, with those gates …'
'Yes, but they were able to be opened and closed again.'
'Always?'
Edwin avoided Jane's eyes and stuck his head back in the fold of the newspaper.

At the December meeting of the Gogango Divisional Board, after the favoured tender for the repair of the original Emu Park Road had been discussed, a board member maintained that the delay in commencing work was due to Edwin's not being able to make up his mind in allowing his property to be used while the original road was reinstated. It was agreed, after discussing their annoyance, to hold off letting the tender.

1883

The Salvage

For months into the new year of 1883, Edwin's lack of decisiveness was a bane for the Divisional Board to work around, till finally the new road was sorted, and tenders were also called for a telegraph line to Emu Park. Enthusiastic discussion then ensued on the potential construction of a railway line to Emu Park.

Edwin had managed to lease the Cremorne Gardens to Messrs Lachlan and Pratt, who were planning a zoo. They advertised for monkeys, snakes, lizards, alligators, cockatoos, and anything else people might suggest.

Bird breeding boxes were placed in an aviary filled with three exotic South American Soches and another bird called a double bar.

Hotel customers enjoyed the trilling of the birds. However, one day, when the chirping suddenly ceased, and an investigation took place, a six-foot carpet snake was discovered in the aviary. It was about to slither off after swallowing all of the birds whole. It just so happened that a Mr Easton was in residence in the hotel, and, having lived in India, was familiar with handling snakes. He was able to capture the snake and place it in another enclosure, where, he declared, it would not need another meal for a couple of months.

At least, at Cremorne, the customers and residents were

not disturbed by the one o'clock gun going off. Complaints were coming from the School of Arts on the south side as plaster fell from the walls when the powder money became over-enthusiastic. St Paul's Cathedral even sustained minor damage.

Jane decided it was time to move to Coorooman while Lachlan and Pratt added a veranda to the front of the Cremorne Hotel giving protection from the western sun to the bar and parlours, while still growing their zoological collection. They were able to muster considerable publicity for their venture, but not all of it was positive.

Jane was horrified when Edwin read to her from the paper about Mr Pratt cleaning out the monkey cage and being attacked. The largest monkey was called Captain Corcoran. He, with some of his primate friends, bit Mr Pratt on the hand so severely that he required medical attention.

The visitor population actually grew because of such reports. Not content with the zoo for entertainment, the lessees built a skating rink 70 feet long by 38 feet wide. At the end of the rink, they constructed a stage, 20 feet by 20 feet, to be used for concerts, especially during the winter months. They also issued season tickets.

The visitors were amused one Sunday to watch the antics of an escaped monkey with a chain attached who'd climbed into a high tree. He was unable to move when the chain became caught, so a visiting sailor climbed up after him. Whenever he got close, the monkey hurled branches onto him. Finally the sailor was able to untwist the chain and began to drag the monkey down, but the monkey escaped his grip and climbed again. No one was injured, and it provided a great spectacle.

When it was reported in the paper, even more guests attended the following week, hoping for more animal entertainment.

Wallabies, a black swan, an emu, and an ibis occupied a central enclosure where a tank was built to supplement the supply of water for them.

About four of the ten acres of Cremorne were planted with crops of seasonal nature, including pineapples and oranges. Water was being pumped from Moore's Creek during the dry season. The trouble was, this was the second year with drought conditions.

Edwin kept up to date with advancements at Cremorne, and Jane relied on his reports to stay in touch. The newspaper was highly complimentary of both the hotel and the gardens.

One of the earlier performances on the stage (now called the Bijou Theatre) was the drama, *Uncle Tom's Cabin*, by The Kate Douglas Company. It played to full houses on each of its three shows.

The White Ribbon Temperance Army concerts were patronised mainly by advocates of temperance.

Edwin received two cheques in his business from a man he knew; one for £4 8s and the other for £4. One he cashed, and silver jewellery was purchased with the other. The cheques were dishonoured by the bank on presentation. They were allegedly stolen from Richard Pettybridge, a miner.

Edwin was not the only person claiming to be defrauded. The criminal case was heard a week after the accused was remanded and subsequently found guilty by a jury. He was sentenced to two years' imprisonment with hard labour.

'I'm not sure if it's such a good thing, Jane, but I'm becoming even more acquainted with Mr Real now he's the prosecutor.'

Jane no longer concerned herself with the family members' appearances in court but she still worried when Edwin heard of a shipwreck.

Captain Cornelius Norris called into Edwin's office in July, in 1883, when he received word from the Harbour Master that a ship had run aground on Masthead Reef.

'We've just heard that she's the *Deutschland*, and it was her maiden voyage.'

'Tell me what you know about her Captain.'

'She's a wooden barque built in Germany, over 600 tons, Mac, and she's loaded with about 400 tons of cargo. Captain Braue, it seems, was following an old chart. He was many miles north of where he thought he was. When he ran up on the reef, the water flowed in and the pumps couldn't handle it.

'He's transferred the crew to Masthead Island and made camp by using the sails.' Looking at Edwin's raised eyebrows, he said, 'That's about five miles from the wreck.

'He went back to the wreck at low tide and saw her state. They revisited at high tide and collected all the fresh water and provisions, before taking the ship's largest boat with a few crew and reporting to our Harbour Master, Captain Sykes.'

'Ah, so the information's up to date.'

'Yes indeed and I plan to meet with Captain Braue to get more detail.'

And before long, Captain Norris, having all the inside information, told Edwin that the insurance underwriters, after promptly inspecting the wreck with Harbour Master, Captain

Sykes, concluded that both the ship and the cargo would be put up for public auction immediately.

Edwin's interest really piqued when Captain Norris shared with him the cargo manifest and belief in the *Deutschland's* salvageability. Much of the cargo's weight consisted of cast iron screw piles for the construction of the Port Alma wharf.

'Hmm. Excellent. What else?' Edwin asked.

'Well, there are also drums of oil, cases of hardware, barrels of ale, and quantities of cement in casks. And, on top of that, literally, are cases of wine, spirits and all kinds of merchandise, including the organ St Paul's Cathedral had on order.'

Edwin immediately sailed out to inspect the wreck. On his return, he and Norris quickly put together a small syndicate, including themselves, and Edwin went off to bid at auction on the syndicate's behalf. Mr G Curtis, usually a competitor of Edwin's, was the auctioneer. The ship, the *Deutschland* was put up first, and sold to Edwin's syndicate for £1,250 despite some fierce competitive bidding.

The Macaree-Norris Syndicate then bid on the cargo, valued at around £1,200, and won the bounty for £300.

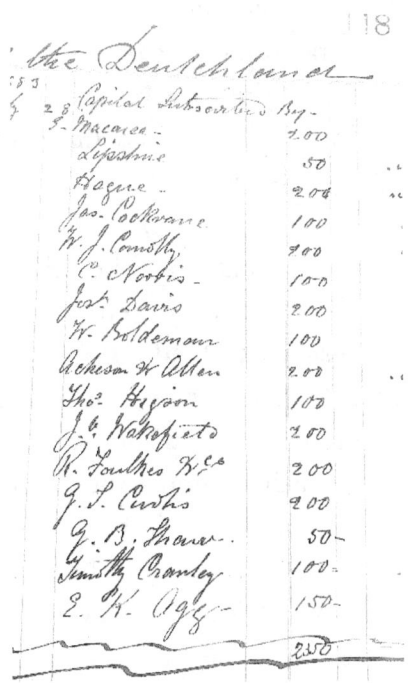

Deutschland *Syndicate from Edwin's Ledger*

1883 Capital subscribed by: E Macaree, Lipstine, Hague, Jas Cockrane, W J Connelly, C Norris, J Davis, W Bolderman, Acheson & Allen, Thos Higson, J Wakefield, R Foulkes & Co, G Curtis, G Shaw, Timothy Cranley, E Ogg.

Immediately following the auction, arrangements were made for Captain Sykes to take them out to the wreck, but they had to wait for favourable weather. Captain Norris took both his sons and a capable crew, including South Sea Islanders who were not only strong but also great workers and divers. Edwin accompanied them. When they were finally able to reach the *Deutschland* they settled in on board with some of the *Deutschland's* original crew. The remainder of the crew were taken to Rockhampton.

On removing the hatch, they discovered no water had penetrated the 20 cases containing the church organ.

Next, there were about five cases of gunpowder and explosives. These were immediately thrown into the ocean for safety reasons.

It was a dangerous operation, with the receiving boats at risk of broaching should the transferred cargo not be balanced item by item. The boats would come right up alongside and load only on the high tide. Speed was of the essence. They prayed the weather would hold, as bad weather might wreck the whole operation.

Regardless, under these circumstances, the operation took many weeks. Edwin travelled back and forth, auctioning off the bounty on shore, boat-load by boat-load, once it was unloaded. When the crew on board were not working, due to there being no workboat available, they were inclined to overindulge in consuming the supplies. They found a quantity of York hams and although these had been exposed to salt water, they were dried on the poop deck, packaged, and sent into town for Edwin to sell at auction.

When the majority of the cargo had been unloaded and access gained to the lower parts, Edwin returned. Norris's sons and crew were able to fix the pumps and make repairs in preparation for sailing the *Deutschland* off the reef.

The Morning Bulletin published a letter provided to Messrs R Foulkes and Co from Edwin on 4th October 1883, which he'd written on 28th September.

> *Captain Norris, Mr Nobleman, and myself are working with the men at the wreck. The Coomba, Ketch, in which we were passengers arrived with the timber and water here on Monday last. The weather was very fine, and we commenced at once discharging the timber, and sent one pile on board the Coomba. The next day the Coomba came alongside, the weather being still fine. She discharged the remainder of the timber, and shipped ten piles. On Wednesday nine more piles were put on board. Captain Norris is still of the opinion the Deutchland will come off if the weather continues fine in which I and Mr. Boldeman concur. The only visible damage to the ship at present is a short piece of planking which has gone clean out of the port bow, and the South Sea Islanders have already found the size of the hole. Captain Norris is preparing a very ingenious tapered plug to stop the leak. Of course, there are many seams in her sides and bilge, which will require caulking; other matters such as bending sails, etc., will have to be done before the final effort will be made to float her. We have been longer making these preparations than we would otherwise have been on account of getting the Coomba loaded. We are wholly guided by the weather, and unless you keep up our supply of fresh water we cannot possibly stop here.*

You might make arrangements for the Coomba to bring us out – say three casks of water. I have been on the island with Mr Boldeman, Mr. Brand, Custom House Officer, to get off the sails &c., to rebend, with a view to make sail on the ship. Captain Norris has been heavily taxed getting the piles out of the lower hold, a work of great difficulty, as every pile has to be dived for. The men are working very satisfactorily. While writing this the wind is getting up and the glass rising. The vessel is beginning to work, and now light winds will have great power over her so that we cannot tell whether we can complete the Coomba's loading tomorrow ... If the northwest winds prevail we shall be able to get the ship to a place of shelter with the sails. The vessel has now got a list to starboard, and the last four piles are being removed. At 12.30 p.m. weather cloudy. French Peter never came here as expected. The ship is beginning to move now (2 p.m. on 28th), which makes it difficult for me to write further.

They needed another few days to make her shipshape to transfer her to the Sea Hill anchorage where a buyer from the south was to take delivery.

However, the winds picked up to almost gale force and the crew were forced to abandon the *Deutschland* for Masthead Island. By morning, with the winds abating, anxiety was running high wondering about the state of the not-yet-prepared ship.

Their anxiety was well justified as they found her heeled over to her port side with water pouring into her. She had become a total wreck and was beyond repair. Cornelius Norris was devastated. 'To have been so close and yet ...'

'You could not have done more, Captain,' Edwin said,

shaking his head. 'You have been a genius and controlled everything perfectly, but you couldn't control the weather last night.'

The *Deutschland* still carried some cast iron screw piles which were needed by Burns and Twigg for the Port Alma wharf, so the remaining crew stayed on to salvage them on the low tide. The weather was again favourable. Captain Norris's two sons amused themselves when the tide was high and work was impossible, by playing with the white figurehead from the bowsprit of a long and shapely, but awkwardly curved female.

That figurehead found its way to Cremorne Gardens to join other figureheads from other wrecks.

After a lively discussion by syndicate members, where some wanted to donate the organ to Saint Paul's Anglican Cathedral, it was finally decided to charge them £50 as the organ was fully insured and much effort had gone into its retrieval and delivery to the Cathedral.

While the syndicate members experienced great financial success on the cargo, they lost heavily on the ship.

In September, Edwin donated a gold watch to the Fitzroy Pastoral Agricultural and Horticultural Society as a special prize at a show. The company intending to present it were disappointed in its quality and declared it was not worth the cost of engraving and recommended handing it back to Edwin. The Committee, however, decided to auction the watch and give the proceeds to the Benevolent Society.

'Well, I shall not be so generous if they ask again,' Edwin declared to Jane on hearing the insult.

William Fraser found the old method of wool-scouring at Frogmore unsatisfactory and purchased land at Balmoral on the Serpentine Lagoon where he erected a large building intending to upgrade to more modern methods. Besides, there was more water and wool scouring used copious amounts. Because he was an experienced tanner, he also treated the skins after the scouring.

At one of their many social gatherings at Cremorne, Edwin asked William to explain what he used for tanning.

'I'm currently experimenting with mangrove bark. I employ Islanders to collect it for me and make an extract. It ends up a reddish-brown colour. I'm also planning to install a bone mill and crush bones from the Lake's Creek Meatworks. Great fertiliser. For export too.

'Now, Edwin, you're not planning to enter the wool-scouring or tanning business, are you?' William added.

'I was a bit confused by what I read in the Bulletin.'

'Och, man, I know what you're referring to. I sold Frogmore, and they wanted to dissociate from my name. I'm moving to a different method where I will work with the fleece and wash it after it is separated from the skin. And Balmoral has a much better water supply too from the Serpentine Lagoon. I'm also advertising my business. And I'm off to England when I've got Balmoral sorted to check out the newest methods.'

'And how do you find living on Port Curtis Road so close to work?'

'Och, man, probably easier than you, with different places you have to work from. When are you next off to Coorooman?'

'Just as soon as I can, William. This isn't so much me,' Edwin said, waving his arms about to encompass all of Cremorne Gardens. 'At least with a lease in place it's someone else's headache.'

'Now, what is this about the new municipality being

created for North Rockhampton?'

Edwin leaned back and stretched. 'Yes, if I want things to get done around here, I'd better try to become involved. You know there are now 1700 people living over this side of the river? Mr Cribb, the Police Magistrate, will organise the first election of aldermen. The boundaries, though are an issue. It should have included the Lake's Creek Meatworks as well as the Lucas and Curtis properties, but they stay with the Gogango Divisional Board.'

Seeing William's eyes wander around the saloon and guessing at boredom, Edwin dropped the subject. 'Let's go and find the women,' he suggested, putting down his empty glass.

But Edwin was pleased nonetheless. The council would be formed late in the year and consist of nine members including aldermen, auditors, and a town clerk. The second election would be held just a few months later in February 1884. Edwin decided he'd nominate then.

When he heard about the first meeting late in 1883, where his friend, Cornelius Norris had been selected, he was pleased with his decision to wait. Captain Norris had his shipbuilding business interests as well as his home on the north side.

The papers reported that the meeting, minus Norris, was bogged down in who, what and where the declaration could and should be signed and other possible procedural violations. The evening concluded when meeting was adjourned till the following evening.

Topics covered in late 1883 by Messrs Face (Mayor) Nobbs, Wackford, Spencer, Patterson, Considine, Elliott, and Norris included: valuation of properties, collection of rates, appointment of a Town Clerk, conservation of gravel, disposing of rubbish and the like.

Jane listened to Edwin as he read sections from the

newspaper to her, and she heard his frustration.

'Get Cornelius to second your nomination in February, Edwin.' Anything, she thought, to get his frustration levels down.

1884

Another Foray into Politics

By January 1884 there was insufficient water in the Crescent Lagoon which supplied Rockhampton. The Rockhampton Council had the idea of pumping water from the Racecourse Lagoon into the Crescent Lagoon and, when they heard that William's wool scour had a centrifugal pump, they approached him and asked to borrow it, to which he agreed.

However, the newspaper reported that it had been borrowed from Frogmore. William was outraged with the credit being given to them, and the paper was quick to correct their error and report that it was William Fraser and his company's business at Balmoral that had come to the townspeople's rescue.

Not long after this, as was often the case in January, the monsoonal rains kicked in with torrential falls and the humidity escalated to a most uncomfortable level. The Fitzroy River broke its banks with flooding from Moore's Creek to Lake's Creek, and the bridge over Moore's creek was under water for a short time.

The athletic grounds at Cremorne Gardens were covered by water, forcing the cancellation of races organised by lessees, Messrs Lachlan and Pratt.

The following month, nominations for aldermen in the North Rockhampton Council were called. This time, Edwin was among them. Only four of those originally selected stood for re-election, such had been the early chaos, so there were six positions to fill.

Prior to the vote being taken, the Returning Officer, Mr Coker, asked if any of the candidates wished to say something to their voting public who were in attendance to listen to the nominations. Of course, Edwin came forward, and in his inimitable manner, soliloquised.

The Capricornian Newspaper of 2nd February, 1884, reported on his speech.

> Mr E Macaree said that as nobody else appeared to be willing he supposed they would not allow the maidenhood of that important borough to go without having a few words of the English language spoken in favour of its – it was to be hoped – bright future.
> As regards himself, they all knew he was an old resident of Rockhampton, and only on one occasion had he sought municipal honours. Then the ratepayers were shy in bidding for his wonderful – he might say – talents, and he was ousted in favour of Mr Caporn on the other side of the river. However, he should make another attempt, and would tell those present that if they returned him he would use his best abilities and energies to the advancement of North Rockhampton. They had plenty of scope and lots of raw material to work upon. The land on the ranges behind them was capable of being turned into mines of wealth. He had seen places both in Madeira and the Canary Islands which were now the lands of the fertile vine, and he did not see anything to prevent North Rockhampton becoming as productive if they put their shoulders to the wheel. With the assistance of irrigation it could be done. Enough water could be obtained to irrigate the whole of the valleys and mountains, and if returned he should endeavour not only to do that, but to make roads, and see that the money was spent judiciously

and fairly.

He should go in for a readjustment of the boundaries of the municipality. They had been deprived most unjustly by the Divisional Board of a very good paying thing. The Board had used their best judgement, and cut the grass from under their feet whilst they were in the straggling throes of child-birth, and before they had a chance to strike a blow for themselves, they had cut the boundaries to the detriment of the Council. If they returned him he should endeavour to show that they had been deprived of their just birthright, and get the municipality altered to its natural boundaries. Their demand could not be refused; if they were expected to give the Board compensation for the money expended they must get justice. (Hear, hear.) He did not wish to take up a great deal of their time to making a long speech, as some of his brother candidates might be desirous of addressing them as well. (Applause.)

Mr C Shannon responded, holding a map of the outlines of the borough, made in 1864. Mr Macaree and Mr Spike, (whose names appeared on that map), he claimed, were the two oldest residents of North Rockhampton and he praised their interest.

At noon on 6th February, the Returning Officer named the successful candidates: Messrs Macaree, Face, (who each received the highest number of votes) Hopkins, Spencer, Spike and Wackford.

Meanwhile, Edwin had written yet another letter to the Morning Bulletin editor, with the strange heading:

FROM AN ALDERMAN IN EMBRYO
TO THE EDITOR OF THE MORNING BULLETIN.
Sir, Would you kindly accord me space in your valuable journal for the following:- On several occasions I wrote the Municipal Council asking them, as a ratepayer (rates fully paid up), to form the road at the top of Archer Street to the Grammar School. My only reply up to the present time has been the wanton destruction of the proper road. On Thursday last I saw men with horses and drays (they said they had instructions from the Council) digging away the naturally formed surface of the road some three feet perpendicularly to suit their own purpose "carting it away" without any method, to the certain destruction of the public property and the decided disadvantage of the adjoining lands. Now, I ask, who is to blame? Have the Council any man to manage their affairs? "Have they a soul or sense?" It is certain when the present road to the Grammar School is closed another must be formed. I have paid rates for many years on the adjoining land, and up to the present time received nothing in return but quiet contempt. My letters remain unanswered. "There is something rotten in the state, &c" Trusting that this may meet with proper notice,
I am, &c EDWIN MACAREE

'For goodness sake, Edwin,' Jane said after dinner, when Edwin, drinking whisky, laughed at seeing his letter in print.

'Well, maybe now I'm an alderman on the other side of the river they'll take notice and do something.'

By now, Jane recognised that Edwin enjoyed stirring the pot almost for its own sake. Heaven help the aldermen working with him, she thought.

At their first Council meeting, Alderman Face was elected Mayor and Chairman. Edwin was elected to the Works

Committee.

Edwin proposed the health of the Mayor. He said that although he had aspired to the position himself, he bore no malice towards Alderman Face. He acknowledged that the man with experience had the job. Alderman Patterson said he had proposed Alderman Macaree and expected to see him in that position, but he would support Alderman Face. They drank to the health of their Mayor.

The telephone exchange opened with an initial 10 subscribers. While Edwin wrote letters, William Fraser, with offices in Quay Street, advertised his business, Wm Fraser & Co, of the *Rockhampton Fellmongering and Woolscouring Establishment* at Balmoral. He wanted to sign contracts with wool growers and was also willing to buy sheepskins, wool and hides. He even named his referees to lend support to his business as Messrs Aplin, Brown and Co, E. Livermore and William Pattison, all highly reputable and esteemed business people.

Annie, William's wife, gave birth to their third child, and their second son, William.

'Let's call him Will so there's no confusion,' Annie suggested.

There was never a dull moment with the North Rockhampton Municipal Council according to both Edwin and to newspaper reports. Captain Norris had returned as an Alderman to fill a vacancy.

One of the requests from Rockhampton Council was to ask the North Rockhampton Council to accommodate the one o'clock gun. Far too much damage was occurring from its present location on the south side. The North Rockhampton Council obliged, but soon they too were receiving letters of complaint.

One such letter came from Messrs Rees R Jones and Brown, solicitors. They said the gun 'produced such a concussion in their offices that the plaster fell and the walls shook.' They then suggested the use of a time ball, but instead, the carronade was moved to the paddock behind the Northern Star Hotel.

Finally, with planning, it was arranged that a ball would be hoisted at the fire station and a bell would be rung four times before the ball was dropped twenty feet at one o'clock and the bell would toll once.

The North Rockhampton Council hosted a visit from the Minister for Public Works, the Honourable W Miles. After formal introductions, Edwin, as head of the Works Committee addressed him:

'We wish to draw your attention to the Moore's Creek Bridge. First, its position is not in the line of road. Second, it was never designed for a bridge at all, as it is merely a few sticks laid across the piles that were put in for a dam that was unfortunately attempted to be made by the late lamented Engineer for Roads. We therefore pray that you will assist us in getting a new bridge across Moore's Creek, as it is the natural outlet for a large population on the river settlements, lime works, fruit growing, sawmills, farmers, and it is the main entrance to the Queen's Park Reserve and this road was the first surveyed road by the Government during the Peak Downs rush. And this being a new municipality it is quite out of our power to undertake a work of this nature as we have no funds for any works.'

On and on Edwin went, but at least the Minister was not exposed to Shakespeare. In response, the Minister suggested they write a letter which he would forward to the Colonial Treasurer. After a vote of thanks, they drove Mr Miles to the bridge to inspect it.

Very late the following Saturday night at the Cremorne Hotel, when all the guests had retired to their rooms, and the ground floor was in darkness, one of the occupants heard noises. The lodger arose and saw, in the darkness, four men passing items out of a bedroom window. He watched as one of them buried a looking glass at the foot of a tree about fifty yards from the hotel. The four thieves then ran off across Moore's Creek Bridge.

The lodger woke Mr Lachlan, the licensee, who rang the police.

Edwin and Jane were in residence in their house at the time but were not disturbed. Edwin's response was a shrug. He was off to Coorooman for a week, taking Ned with him. Jim and Emma were still attending school so Jane stayed at Cremorne.

Newspapers were delivered regularly to Cremorne, and one was always reserved for Edwin and Jane. A few days after Edwin had left and the children were off to school, Jane, settled in the sitting room, cup of tea in hand, read a letter in the Morning Bulletin from a traveller who'd visited Emu Park.

> *TO THE EDITOR*
> *Sir. Having heard a great talk of Emu Park I determined to take coach for the trip and accordingly booked myself in Pratt's coach from the Cremorne Hotel, North Rockhampton.*
> *We started in a four wheeler called the Invincible at 1 p.m. and with a good turn out let the leaders go for the road. The John seemed to be quite up to his business, and with a spanking team we soon made tracks. As one who*

has seen Rockhampton years ago, I could not help noticing the vast improvements that have been made on the road to Emu Park via Lake's Creek Works. When here ten years ago, not a solitary house with any pretention to that same could be seen. Now I find settlement has taken place, nearly all the way between the bridge and the Old Bush Inn. In days of yore the latter was a bark edifice.

It is now of more durable materials and ample dimensions. I was much struck by the majestic appearance of the Berserker Mountains in looking at them. I thought of other lands, where the slopes were clothed in verdure, and the fruitful vine, the yam, the cocoa, and Cassava root found a congenial home; and should your worthy citizens' views, especially Alderman Hopkins', be carried out re water conservation, you may yet hope to see a second Madeira for Fayal in that locality, and your exporters could enumerate wine, tapioca, coffee, tobacco, and many other tropical productions. "Now then, Jerry, time's up, all aboard," and off we go, none the worse for our reviver. The road, as it winds around the base of the mountains is not bad; but I am struck with the absence of settlement and cultivation. Here is the land; where are the people and the cultivation. Beyond a few head of fat cattle the land is deserted, until we come to the ten mile, where an attempt is being made to cultivate and apparently with good results. The soil appears to be first class. At Mr J Hayes' Stoney Creek, we have certain proof of profitable industry in the bright green waving corn just budding into maturity; and evidences of thrift and competence in ample dwellings and smiling happy faces. Prosperity is here at home. Passing Stony Creek we come to another range of mountains. I am told that there are vast mineral deposits in those New Zealand Gully Ranges, and that extensive gold reefs and veins of other minerals are hidden here to be unearthed by the enterprising speculator.

The country we are now passing over is certainly of a most peculiar formation. Here rises a bluff like an island in the Pacific Ocean and with every appearance of valuable mineral deposits. I am informed a copper selection is taken up here, but owing to want of capital cannot be started. The country between this and the half-way house I consider second to none, as regards its sugar-growing capabilities. "Here we are at Dan Hawk's." Who's Dan Hawk? A chinkee, and a most perverse one, but honest withal.

"Cup of tea – Yes, Sah. Me give him tea; you want him jam, you want him butter, you no take him tly (sic) flute, me no wants you, spose you no wants me. One shilling; me no talke too much – no goodee." Change horses. All aboard again; let them go, and they go. What place is this on the right? That is Cawarral head station, prettily situated on a delightful hill surrounded by a beautiful verdure and abundant cultivation. I hear this place has recently changed hands, and if the lucky buyers can only realise the true value of such a charming property they may rest assured it has few equals. Passing Cawarral station we come to Whitley's Orchard. Here also industry has its reward, and the orange, citron, guava, bananas, mango, custard apples, and every tropical fruit seem to bear abundantly and the smiling face of the owner speaks plainly of plenty and contentment.

We now come to Palm Tree Creek, running into Ross's Creek, where I am informed fish and oysters are abundant. The ground on the left is Macaree's land and not to know who is Macaree is lamentable ignorance. Here the road takes a turn to Coorooman Creek; but how

is this a charming site but no settlement? You mistake, if you look to the left you will see a garden filled with a large variety of trees in full bearing, and it is said the owner intends making extensive orangeries and other improvements. Coorooman Creek with permanent waters being passed, we have up-hill work for the next two miles, but our whip with his team well in hand is quite equal to the task. After a smart run we reach the locality of the turn off to Mr. Ross's and Tanby Hall Paddock. The latter, by the way, should be subdivided, and cut up into small farms and settled with a large population for the cultivation of sugar, &c., for which I conceive it to be well suited. Now we get through the timber and now extensive open undulating plains meet the eye on every side. Still no cultivation – a few hundred head of fat cattle seem to monopolise the land. These beautiful plains remind me of scenes far far away. We have reached the summit of the hills, and now the eight that meets the eye is beyond my poor powers of description. Emu Park! The Elysian fields of America sink into insignificance, but comparisons are – Emu Park is like a gem set in the bosom of the grand Pacific Ocean. The beautiful verdure, the delightful aroma, wafted from Neptune's curling looks by the trade winds, bearing sweet licence advance with the ever-present ozone, causes a fooling to pervade the whole system that at once dispels the lassitude of a city residence.
I find it is bathing time, and betake myself to the beautiful beach. A better or more enjoyable place to bathe I have never seen, "and I have journeyed over many lands." But I declare, I feel quite hungry – so resort to mine hotel, where I find fish and wambeen in abundance. After tea, I have a chat with the old Scotch shepherd, Mr Fulton, seventy years of age, with not an ache or pain but

hale and hearty, and as happy as can be, and likely to outlive many younger men. He declares he will never leave Emu Park. Where are all the sick people I ask?
There is nobody sick here – even children coming here sick, I am assured, at once recover good health. With such a watering place as this and a railway running to it, Rockhampton will have one of the finest seaside resorts on this side of the equator. But I fear my letter is already too long, so will conclude with success to your railway to Emu Park.
Yours, &c, TRAVELLER. J

Jane smiled gently when she finished reading, and a little bit of her wondered if Edwin was moonlighting as Traveller J since she rarely came across anyone who wrote so verbosely and poetically.

When Edwin returned, he was keen to attend a lecture by Professor Simon at the Hibernian Hall on physiology and phrenology. The hall was filled to capacity. The Professor was a trained surgeon and he stressed the importance of style of walking as an indicator of character before he went on to talk of features of the face such as a hanging under lip as an indicator of a lovable disposition. Edwin listened with great intent. He was disappointed that Jane showed no interest and had not accompanied him.

Jane suggested to Edwin that they employ a governess and musical instructor for Emma, now ten years old, and perhaps the governess could help Ned too. Jane was prompt in finding Miss S A Ryan, and Edwin drew up a contract to cover the initial four months at a salary of £40 per annum. Subjects to be covered included English, arithmetic, bookkeeping and also deportment for Emma.

Edwin's contract with new Governess

Rockhampton November 1884. Memorandum of Agreement Made and entered into at Rockhampton in the year of our Lord 1884 Between S A Ryan Governess on the one part and Edwin Macaree Auctioneer on the other part. The Conditions are that the said S A Ryan Hereby Agrees to engage with the said E Macaree as Governess and Musical Instructress And to teach English, Arithmetic, Bookkeeping and Deportment. And to give lessons ... as may be suitable for the Family at stated intervals. "And one young Lady Friend if required" as may be suggested by the Said E Macaree at reasonable times. And in Consideration for Such Services being well and truly performed the said E Macaree hereby agrees to pay the said S A Ryan at and after the rate of Forty Pounds per annum. And Board with the Family for the said term of three months connecting from the ... day of November 1884. Signed.

Edwin attended his regular Council meetings and enjoyed the cut and thrust of debate, although the newspapers were inclined to report the clashes of opinion somewhat differently.

The Aldermen agreed though, that tenders should be called for the construction of Council Chambers as the outgoings on rent were becoming prohibitive. Edwin was on that committee, but there was an objection by Alderman Shannon as he referred to hole and corner transactions.

This was a reference to Shannon's suspicion that Edwin might submit a tender to the Committee on which he sat, for the supply of timber or other materials he or his mates produced. But Edwin had the support of the Mayor and other aldermen. The Mayor voiced that he believed all could act honestly and maturely.

Edwin responded by saying, 'If an intelligent committee is not capable of carrying out a work of that magnitude, more shame for them.' After all, the proposed building was to be only thirty feet by twenty feet.

Edwin did recognise, though, that his position as a trustee of the Queen's Park and Recreational Ground Reserve might conflict with his Council decisions, so he resigned that post.

Late in the year, resentment was again building against the Chinese, especially those selling fresh produce in East Street on Sundays. All other premises were closed on Sundays, and the Mayor was opposed to the unfair advantage, so the police put a stop to it and forced the closures.

With Christmas coming, the Cremorne Gardens were offered as a retreat, with the 1885 New Year's Day celebrations looming large with its shaded walks, music, singing and dancing in the pavilion. Prizes were offered by a professor in phrenology for the best musical head, the best domestic head, and the best mechanical head. (Edwin couldn't help himself.) A one guinea prize was advertised for the winner of a two-mile bike ride and another for the best waltzers or Scottish dancers. All manner of animals from the zoo were mentioned. Edwin offered all this for just one shilling for adults and sixpence for children.

Following this promotion, he then advertised the following:

> *To let or for sale— Cremorne Hotel, Gardens, and Moores's Creek Island, in all about 12 acres; suitable for factories, shipbuilding, brewery, etc. Tidal creek surrounds the property. To an eligible tenant or buyer this is a certain fortune. Furniture, licence, goodwill, and stock at valuation. Apply early, principals only to Edwin Macaree.*

The ad was partially effective when Frank Isambert responded and became lessee of the Hotel.

1885–1886

Edwin Misbehaves

On 2nd January 1885, the Morning Bulletin reported:

> Mr E Macaree gave a lecture on phrenology, taking as subjects young men from the audience. He examined their heads with minuteness and created laughter by delineating their characters by that test and by their walk up and down the stage before a tittering crowd. He awarded a prize to Mr H Williams for the best mechanical head.

Jane tolerated Edwin's hobby, and the phrenological lectures and entertainment continued, but she was shocked that he would use an actual human skull as his example. She was relieved that the children showed little interest in the subject. Ned was a quiet young man who worked hard for his father, forever trying to please him. Jim was showing quite an aptitude for building and mechanics and was constantly pulling broken clocks and watches apart and putting them back together, usually with success. He had a good grasp of physics. Like his father, he was adept with his hands. Yet neither boy seemed to gain fully the approval of their father, which both craved.

'You're too tough on them, Edwin,' Jane said, smocking the bodice of a dress for Emma. 'You expect too much,' she added.

'Fiddle de dee,' Edwin retorted, looking over the top of his newspaper. 'I could do lots more at their age. With the bang Ned got on his head, I can accept he's a bit slower.'

'No-one can keep up with you.' She felt sorry for the boys.

The Cremorne Hotel and Gardens and all it entailed were a constant headache for Edwin. *The Invincible*, the coach service to Crocodile and Emu Park, was leased by Edwin to Mr Pratt. Edwin wrote to him in February, 1885.

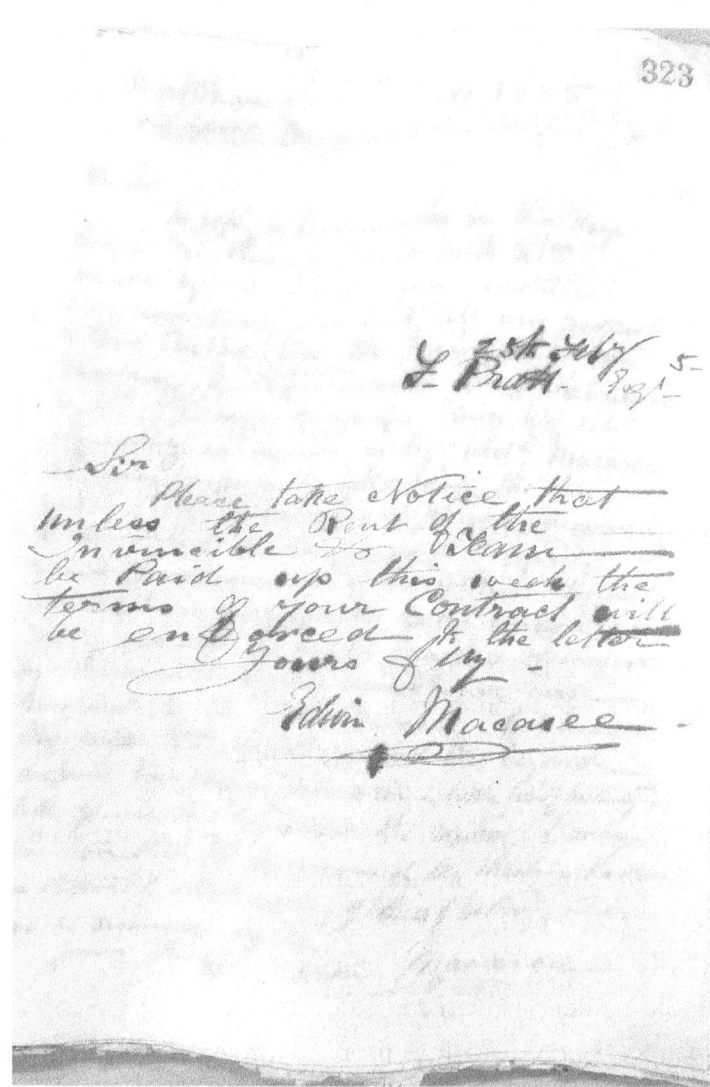

**Edwin's letter to Mr Pratt,
taken from Edwin's letterbook press copy**

25th February 1885
F. Pratt esq.
Sir,
Please take Notice that unless the Rent of the Invincible and team be Paid up this week the terms of your contract will be enforced to the letter.

Yours f'ly

Edwin Macaree

Captain Cornelius Norris again contacted Edwin, this time to tell him about the wreck of the schooner *Bannockburn* off the southeast of the Bunker group of islands. The *Bannockburn*, under the control of Captain Goss, had been sailing from Wanganui in New Zealand with a load of sawn timber for Normanton. She was found by *The Fitzroy* after she had unloaded a portion of the cargo onto an island. The crew were taken to Keppel Bay and then to Rockhampton.

'If only these captains would carry the latest charts and maps,' Captain Norris said. And yet again, Edwin put together a syndicate – this time just three of them – to buy the wreck and cargo, after Cornelius conducted his inspection. He felt sure all the cargo could be salvaged, and that he could re-float the *Bannockburn* on the next spring tide.

Norris, on the *Waterwitch*, a ship that he and Edwin had salvaged some years earlier, anchored five miles from the island. He sent a letter back to Edwin:

> *The spars are in good order and most of the gear, &c. The cargo is in very good order and there is only three feet of water in the vessel. ... A regular north-west gale has been blowing this last week, but the ship is well sheltered by the island and the breeze has no effect on her.*

The schooner *Fleetwing* discharged the cargo of timber on Norris Wharf on the north side of the river.

Once back from the salvage of the *Bannockburn*, Norris said to Edwin, 'We caulked and patched her up. Took down all the spars and sails. Then came a strong sou-easter. You should have seen her, Mac. We had cables stretched out, fully tense, and she rode there for three days while we watched from the island. She was pitching and crashing onto the coral. I've no idea how she rode it out, but she did.' He shook his head. 'And now she's safely here in the river.'

They toasted the success with whisky.

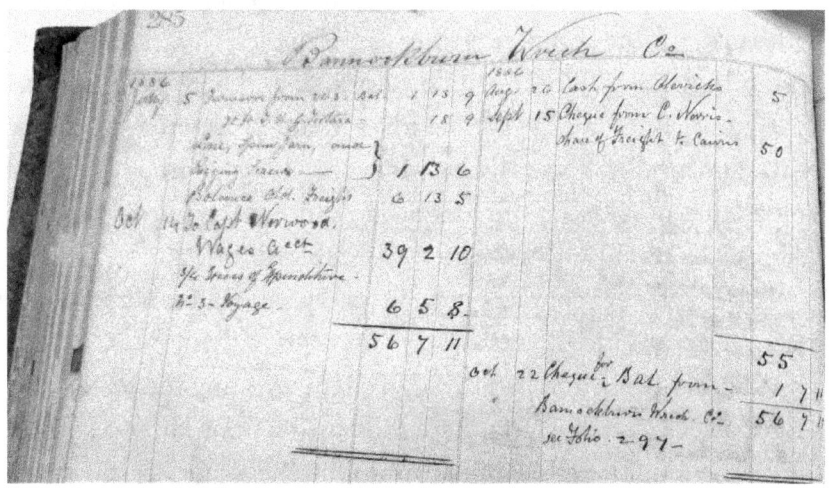

Edwin's record of "Bannockburn" from his ledger

Edwin hadn't seen William Fraser for some time because William had sailed to England to purchase the latest wool scouring machinery from Rochester. When William arrived back months later with the equipment, he immediately installed it at Balmoral.

Wm Fraser's Wool-scour at Balmoral

Annie wanted to see how it worked, how it was different from Frogmore, so William took her for a visit.

'First, we pump the water up from the lagoon. There's a plentiful supply here, unlike the first location at Frogmore,' he said, pointing at the water. 'It goes into these two 400-gallon tanks and soap is added. We've got the fire going underneath, holding the water at 100 degrees. That's the first wash. From there it runs into scouring troughs lower down for rinsing.' He moved Annie along. 'Then to the washing baskets.'

Annie noticed they had iron sides and were about four feet long and wide with perforated sides. 'Another wash?' she said.

'Yes, and then a second rinse in between pontoons in the lagoon. And the biggest addition is the drying machine.' He moved on again with Annie to show her the huge circular machines that spun the wool at 900 revolutions per minute. 'And lastly, we lay it out to dry on sheets in the sun. It's pressed into the bales from there and shipped off.'

'No wonder you need so much area and so much water, William.'

'We're already noticing how much more efficient this operation is, and the profits are already showing that efficiency.'

For William, the procurement of sheepskins and fleeces was still his biggest challenge. He was acquiring almost all the skins from local butchers and from Lake's Creek. Work opportunities increased for those who carted the wool and skins to and from the wool scour.

When William had been in London, he became entranced by the Whippet safety bicycle. Penny farthings had never made sense to him, but when he rode a short distance on the Whippet he knew it would be a success, and bought one for his son, Donald, who was eleven.

Earlier in the year, the Rockhampton Cycling Club had been formed.

For his daughter, Jessie, who was achieving outstanding results at reading and composition at school, William brought back a year's supply of Girls' Own Paper.

He also took the opportunity on his trip to purchase and import Gospel Oak galvanised iron, and it sold rapidly for roofing, especially in Emu Park. The Scotch whisky that came back with him proved just as popular.

William formed a partnership with Patrick Egan and they launched out as wholesale merchants in William Street.

The North Rockhampton Municipal Council meeting in October began with the Town Clerk reading the minutes when Edwin, still an alderman, burst into the room, bowed first to the other aldermen, and then to the reporters, and bellowed, 'Three sticks a penny.'

He apologised for being late and was chastised by the Mayor, Alderman Face, for interrupting the meeting.

Correspondence was first on the agenda, and Edwin, along with another alderman protested that too many issues were being handed to the Finance Committee and not to the General Purposes Committee. He moved, as an amendment, that the particular item be handed to the General Purposes Committee. Edwin added:

> 'May I do so, Alderman Hopkins? Your superior judgement must carry weight. It is no use, I know. The sheep are carrying everything. They should let the goats have a chance to nibble at any rate.'

Alderman Shannon seconded Edwin's motion. Edwin then added:

> 'We know it is no use. The ratepayers, however, most know of this little by-play of yours. No money shall be frittered away without my voice against it. No swindle shall be perpetrated unless I raise my voice against it ...'

The Mayor called for order.

Alderman Wackford suggested that if order were not maintained they should leave. He called Edwin a disgrace.

Edwin jumped to his feet in protest. 'I got up and said no swindle should be perpetrated. I did not say one had been.'

'Sit down, Alderman Macaree,' the Mayor demanded, but Edwin took no notice and continued his rave.

Again the Mayor ordered him to sit, and then for a third time. But Edwin became even more excited. 'No swindle shall be perpetrated while I sit here and have a common sense to prevent it.'

Alderman Wackford finally spoke. 'If I understand you properly you are drunk.'

'I say you are a liar,' Edwin retorted.

The meeting became a shambles. The Mayor threatened to

call for the police. Edwin challenged him to do so. The Mayor read from Clause 41 of the by-laws: 'Any alderman … who shall use any other language which, according to the common usage of gentlemen, would be held disorderly, or who shall say or do anything calculated to bring the Council into contempt shall be deemed out of order.'

There were two who supported Edwin's point of view, but not his expression of it, and six who did not.

And while the Mayor was reading the by-law, Edwin again jumped to his feet with more insulting remarks.

'I consider Alderman Macaree has been guilty of disorderly conduct and under clause 47 I inflict a fine.'

'I am well able to pay it if I like.'

Aldermans Hopkins and Wackford left the meeting as Alderman Shannon moved for an adjournment.

Edwin said, 'I will have justice or the ratepayers shall know it.'

The Mayor, still trying to bring some order said:

> *'I will soon have you arrested.'*
> *'… It is a public place, and before you arrest us you will find I will knock you and the constable down. You think you are going to rule the roost, and I will show you I will rule it.'*
> *'Mr Coker, take down Alderman Macaree's words.'*
> *'You have certain power, but when you refuse to receive an amendment you should leave the chair or be ousted.'*

Edwin's challenge went on and on. The issue really was that the Finance Committee was overspending, and Edwin wanted another committee to oversee the justification for the spending first.

'You say I am drunk. Anybody that says I am drunk is a liar. Do I look like a man that is drunk! I am capable of arguing a point and I am not drunk.'

'I inflict a fine as laid down in the by-laws for disorderly conduct to be recovered in the usual way.'

After some considerable time Edwin's rant ran out of steam and he became calmer. He seconded Alderman Shannon's motion to adjourn the meeting, but the motion was lost. The original motion was passed after the Mayor used his casting vote, although Aldermen Shannon and Wiley voted with Edwin meaning the original letter would go to the Finance Committee and not the General Purposes Committee as Edwin had fought for.

After the meeting, Edwin's friends loaded him onto his horse, patted its rump and the faithful steed walked the inebriated alderman down Bridge Street to the stables at Cremorne.

When Jane read the report in the Morning Bulletin the next day, the 8th October, she pressed her lips together. This was altogether too much. Edwin had gone off to work without saying a word to her.

A week later, he appeared in the North Rockhampton Police Court charged with disorderly conduct. He was fined £2 with £2 6s 2d costs.

'This is humiliating for all of us, Edwin,' Jane said, waving the paper at him. 'What did you say?'

'Ah, I did say "damn" I believe. I apologised publicly. I said I was sorry. I should never have sworn, but I do try to protect the ratepayers.'

Lips compressed, Jane sighed, knowing it was not the end of his outrageous behaviour.

His friends, Cornelius Norris, who had been an alderman for

North Rockhampton since its inception, and Albrecht Feez, a councillor on the Rockhampton Municipal Council and Edwin's mentor, spoke with him separately, both delivering the same message; cut down on the drinking and the language.

Edwin tried explaining to Jane that the money borrowed for the construction of the Council Chambers was not being protected, and there was no Council approval for the spending of £200 and he therefore refused to approve the expenditure after it occurred as it was beyond the limits of the loan budget.

'They don't understand how to do business, Jane. Only those who have their own business comprehend what is required.'

Edwin persisted in holding aldermen accountable on monetary decisions, but now he did that with more acumen.

On the 30th January, 1886 with Council elections only a week away, a few aldermen, including Edwin, presented their ideas to the ratepayers present. Prime issues included the rebuild or repair of Moore's Creek Bridge, and finding a reliable water supply for North Rockhampton. Edwin used humour, and one of those present called out 'How many sticks a penny?' which produced much laughter, and Edwin's gregarious nature won many over.

The following week, the outcome of the election was announced. Three successful aldermen gave a brief speech of acceptance, and Edwin, having lost, rose to address his loss. He actually turned his back on the ratepayers, striking his coat tails. This was met with a combination of laughter and groaning. He thanked those who voted for him, and added that a time would come when they would know what it meant to have a loyal person represent them. A devotee of Edwin's, who enthusiastically verbally continued to support him, had to be escorted from the room.

The following month, after the resignation of Alderman Hollingsworth, Edwin stood as a candidate. At a public meeting, the audience, including reporters, had the usual expectation of being entertained, and they were not disappointed.

Edwin and his opposition, Mr Smith each addressed those present.

As one reporter from the Morning Bulletin recorded:

> *Mr Smith was not in such good humour as his antagonist, and rather detracted from the value of his remarks by introducing offensive personal allusions. Perhaps, before Mr Macaree was done with his reply, no one more regretted his having done so than Mr Smith himself.*
>
> *'On public matters he (Edwin) expressed some sound views, and his remarks on the value of day work, and the way in which it is performed, ought not to escape the notice of Aldermen.*

With a three to one majority, Edwin was voted back on Council. He responded by admitting that he had been defeated in the past.

A voice then called, 'But you are not now, old man.'

He said it was no time to gloat over the losses of others, and that he'd shown his 'crusty side, smooth side and woolly side' to the voters, and he thanked them.

Afternoon tea on Sundays when Edwin was in residence at Cremorne, saw the Frasers continue to visit. Annie had given birth to Percy, her third son. Jane was well over childbearing age and Emma, her youngest was now twelve.

The men retired to the lounge. 'I'm getting into mining, Edwin. Have you ever been tempted?' William said.

Edwin smiled and shook his head.

'I'm acquiring one-tenth of the *Rise and Shine* claim at Crocodile, and one-twentieth of McLaughlin's *Mount Morgan* lease.'

'Highly speculative,' Edwin suggested.

'I heard talk in London. Some positive, some negative. It's a gamble.'

Nodding, Edwin said, 'Only way to get ahead – take a risk.' He liked William's steady and solid approach to investments, but now he was seeing the more daring side – something he admired even more. Why come out here to the colony of Queensland and play a conservative game, Edwin thought to himself.

Anyone who could travel for months halfway around the world with a family and start their life afresh had to have a certain amount of daring. He thought momentarily about his own initial trip up the Fitzroy and the hopes and dreams that travelled with him. He smiled smugly.

But he also realised that he and William were different people. William was a thorough gentleman, endorsed with a trade, whereas Edwin was an adventurer and a tearaway. Each, though, had respect for the other.

In April, Edwin was again elected to the Works Committee of the Council. Still the Council lurched from problem to problem, from heated discussion to heated discussion.

By May, the Mayor announced, towards the end of a meeting, that they were insolvent, with expenditure exceeding income. Each member, it was pointed out, was liable for a fine of £200.

Regardless, they continued discussing the employment of a works' overseer, and continuation of other projects.

The Mayor, in support of this, put several proposals on which much discussion ensued. But with no resolution and more disagreements, Aldermen Rutter, Norris, and Shannon, together with Edwin, abruptly left the room, so the meeting was forced to close.

Later, in May, under pressure from the taxpayers, a meeting was called at North Rockhampton Council Chambers on a less contentious issue – that of a rail link to Emu Park. Because Edwin's was the first name on the petition, he was asked to address the crowd. He was met with applause and pointed out that a promise had been made for tenders to be called in May, but May was almost over. Men from western towns were in need of work, but the expenditure of the colony's money was being lavished around down south with more and more railway lines. He pointed out that Brisbane was connected to ports by three railway lines, while Rockhampton had none. He finished by saying that tenders should be called for immediately and his suggestion was supported by Council who would demand action from Brisbane.

Edwin then headed for Coorooman where his family were in residence. The next day he received distressing news when a journalist arrived to interview him.

'Mr Macaree, have you heard what happened to the Cremorne Hotel early this morning?'

Edwin cocked his head. Jane had come into the sitting room accompanied by Ned to see who their visitor was.

'There was a shocking fire at the Cremorne Hotel. Poor Mr and Mrs Isambert lost everything.'

For a moment Edwin was silent, absorbing the news. 'Was anyone injured?'

'No. Apparently, a young lad by the name of Armstrong raised the alarm. He heard crackling and saw flames coming from an unoccupied bedroom, and alerted the Isamberts. They escaped their apartment with just a couple of personal items. They were able to save a few sticks of furniture and the cash tin. That's about it. The young servant girl managed to grab her few belongings.'

Ned broke in. 'What about the animals?'

'I was there. It was amazing to see them get the animals out of cages. Some didn't want to leave, even though they were terrified. The monkey in the cage nearest the kitchen had to be pushed out. He headed up the nearest tree. The crackling of the fire, and the screams of the animals … I can't tell you how awful it was. The Asiatic bear wouldn't leave, and when he did, he just ambled off through the gardens and people – there were lots of people there watching – they moved aside and let him through. Some boys caught him later and brought him back.'

'I'll bet they did. What time did the fire start? What do we know?'

'About 5 am. The Fire Brigade – there were fourteen of them arrived – about 5.30, but no-one could have done anything. The timber, and then the alcohol from the bar, fed the fire. They claim they could see it raging from up on the Range.'

Ned again broke in. 'What about the birds?'

'All the animals are safe, but those cockatoos and their hysterical screaming stirred the other animals right up. You have no idea how that heat radiated. The jackal was the smartest. First out he was.'

'So, Mr Macaree, would you, as owner of the premises like to make a comment?'

'I need to ask Isambert if he was fully covered by insurance.'

'He says with his two policies he was covered for £350, but he said he purchased the furniture and good-will from you for £700 and had made improvements.'

'What awful luck.'

'Are you insured?'

Edwin hesitated. 'I believe I had £500 of insurance on the premises themselves. That should more than rebuild it I would think.'

'And you will rebuild?'

More hesitation. Then, slowly nodding he said, 'Yes, I think I will.'

'May I publish that?'

'Since you've made the effort to bring me the news before anyone else, yes, young man, you may.'

After the reporter's departure, Jane said, 'I think we'll move out of the cottage at Cremorne for a while and stay here.'

'I'm happy to ride back and forth to work from here,' Edwin replied. He enjoyed galloping on his great grey steed, although rheumatism was beginning to affect his joints forcing him to use the carriage sometimes.

'No wonder you have aching joints. It's probably been caused by all that cavorting in the water,' Jane scolded. 'Fancy swimming over to Pelican Island just to plant a flag at your age.'

Edwin threw his head back, laughing. 'I'm glad I made it back.'

1887

Court Matters

Early 1887 saw the North Rockhampton Borough receive one resignation, that of Alderman Wackford. Three aldermen, including Edwin and Cornelius Norris, retired through rotation but were up for re-election in February. Even though the Council lurched from one drama to another, the Moore's Creek Bridge was finally undergoing significant repair, and, through government funding, the construction of the railway line to Emu Park, together with the associated stations, was finally underway.

In February, Edwin and Cornelius were re-elected.

Later that month, the Police Magistrate, Mr Lukin, began taking evidence in relation to the insolvency of Dr Charles Cripps, a medical practitioner and a friend of Edwin's. Dr Cripps also owned a chemist shop in East Street.

Mr Melbourne was the solicitor for the Trustee of Dr Cripps' estate.

The first witness to be called was Edwin, who initially failed to appear. He turned up when the National Bank of Queensland's accountant, Holyoake Woods, was giving evidence regarding amounts owed to the bank.

When Edwin, who held a mortgage over some of Dr Cripp's property, because of outstanding loans, took the stand, the sparring began.

Mr Melbourne (solicitor for trustee): You are a commission agent:
(Edwin) I am a financial agent.
Do you remember at any time getting a bill of sale from the insolvent?
Yes
Do you produce it?
Yes. Some time prior to this I received an absolute bill, but it afterwards resolved itself into a bill of sale. I made this statement because the insolvent got money from me before the bill of sale was given. I gave him £150 very soon after he returned from America.
(Mr Melbourne, solicitor for trustee) Allow me to say I am here to conduct the examination.
(Edwin) I have made the statement and I want a note taken of it.
(Mr Melbourne, solicitor for trustee) What is this?
(Edwin) I came here to speak the truth.
(Mr Melbourne, solicitor for trustee) What is the date of the transaction?
(Edwin) The 12th of February (1886), and the sale was registered on the 17th.

Mr Melbourne then read a document which stated that the original mortgage was for £150, with an additional £35 later added. Edwin confirmed that was correct.

Edwin was asked for proof of his payment to Dr Cripps of the initial £150, which he confirmed as the 15th June 1886. He was then asked to produce a document proving security over the mortgage. He confirmed several documents were involved at the same time as the payment was given. One was a rental agreement, another was furniture hire.

On 9th February 1887 a further £35 was advanced to keep the bailiff, who wanted to claim some of Dr Cripps' property,

at bay.
> Mr Melbourne (Solicitor for trustee). Did you pay any more money for him between the two dates?
> (Edwin) I might have paid the insurance on the furniture. I see from my books that I paid one fire insurance premium.

Edwin said he'd received £81 9s from the insurance company, and £24 3s 6d from renting Dr Cripps' furniture.

Dr Cripps' shop in East Street had been taken into possession.
> Mr Melbourne (solicitor for trustee): Do you know that somebody else carried on the business of a chemist at the shop the insolvent used to have?
> (Edwin) I told you I could not speak as to a fact. A man's life is so interwoven with mysteries that it is hard to get at the facts.
> Mr Lukin (Police Magistrate): Don't give us any of that, please.

Edwin stated that he had a clean Bill of Sale registered for £185. The £35 went to the bailiff, as he had previously mentioned, and Edwin repossessed the rental furniture, which had then gone into the bailiff's hands.
> Mr Melbourne (Solicitor for trustee): When did you take possession of these goods?
> (Edwin) Well, I have had possession once or twice. The time I paid the bailiff off was one occasion, for instance.
> Mr Melbourne: Answer me please. I am putting the question plainly enough.
> (Edwin) I took possession on the 9th of February again, under a fresh bill of sale. I did not take delivery of the goods, though I could have done so at any time.
> Mr Melbourne: How long did you remain in possession then?

> (Edwin) ...I cannot tell exactly.
> Mr Melbourne: Answer the question, please. What day of the month that you took the bailiff out in February?
> (Edwin) I will answer according to my memory.
> Mr Melbourne: That is all I want.
> (Edwin) If you get out of temper you will have to go outside and get cool.
> Mr Melbourne: I will ask your Worship to use the power you possess of committing the witness to prison. You can give him six months.
> Mr Lukin (Police Magistrate) Mr Melbourne asked you a question ... You must be courteous ...

Edwin asked for the question to be repeated. His reply then:

> Until today, I presume.

Mr Lukin suggested that Edwin admit if he did not remember.

Again there was unfriendly exchange back and forth until Mr Melbourne read out a letter written by Edwin and addressed to Mr Melbourne himself, in his role as solicitor to the trustee of the Cripps's estate dated January 21, 1887, whereby he stated that he held a registered bill of sale, which he intended to exercise and thereby be partially refunded.

Edwin then remarked that he never received a response to his letter.

Mr Lukin, the Police Magistrate, was becoming impatient.

Another letter was read from Edwin to Mr Dawbarn, the actual Trustee of the Cripps' Estate for whom Mr Melbourne worked.

With Edwin still unable to confirm specific dates, Mr Lukin, the Police Magistrate, rebuked him for not bringing all the evidence.

Edwin responded that he had no idea the examination would be so detailed. Edwin's evidence was adjourned so he could gather further papers, and Dr Cripps himself was then called.

He confirmed that he told Edwin he'd been served with a writ by Stewart and Co. He further confirmed that he was adjudicated insolvent on 3rd December 1886.

On January 28th 1887, Dr Cripps' goods were advertised for sale by Edwin and he thought they might have brought £150 to £180.

> *Mr Melbourne: You are like Mr Macaree; you give half a dozen answers. Say yes, or no.*
> *(Dr Cripps) I don't know.*
> *Mr Melbourne: did you get any money out of the proceeds of sale?*
> *(Dr Cripps) Not a sixpence.*
> *Mr Melbourne: Look at the bill of sale, and read the descriptions of the three horses – the chestnut, the dark brown, and the bay. Were they sold?*
> *(Dr Cripps) No. Only the bay. The brown horse was lost. It was a mistake including the chestnut in the bill of sale, because I had previously sold it.*

After a few more questions had been dealt with, Edwin returned to the Court Room, but the questions continued for Dr Cripps, many of them querying whether Edwin knew of Cripps' other debts, which were numerous. Cripps seemed unsure of the facts and hostilities were rising.

> *Mr Melbourne (to Mr Lukin): Under the Act, Your Worship has power to send a man to prison for six months if he does*

> *not answer a question satisfactorily.*
> *(Dr Cripps) I don't recollect whether I told Mr Macaree or not. I don't see why Mr Melbourne should talk about imprisonment, Your Worship.*

Mr Lukin concurred that Mr Melbourne's remarks were uncalled for and suggested that Dr Cripps respond with "I don't recollect."

Mr Melbourne asked Dr Cripps why he didn't put money into the Queensland National Bank.

> *Dr Cripps: Because I knew that if I paid in a £5 note the bank would keep it, and my family might have starved. I have a wife and nine children to support, and what money I spent during that time was on bare necessaries.*

Mr Melbourne persisted with expenditure information for which Dr Cripps did not have a record.

> *Mr Melbourne: Did you make – or cause to be made – that bill of sale with the intent to defraud your creditors:*
> *'No.'*
> *'Why did you make it?'*
> *'The real reason is that I was worried into it by Mr Macaree who thought the security he had was not good enough.'*

Mr Melbourne moved to questions regarding a debt to St Ignatius College. More verbal harangue ensued with Dr Cripps either not remembering or dodging the questions.

> *Mr Melbourne: I am loth to ask Your Worship to exercise the power you possess to send the witness to prison for six months. He will not answer and unless the Act is enforced*

it is a perfect farce.

Mr Lukin responded by asking the same simple question that Mr Melbourne had asked.

Mr Melbourne moved on to the sale of stock in Dr Cripps' chemist shop in East Street.

When Dr Cripps was finally released from giving evidence, Edwin re-entered the box with further records to support his testimony. He acknowledged that he put Dr Cripps' furniture in the possession of Ferguson McHaig, bailiff, where he paid him six shillings a day for eight days.

Edwin said he then appointed Dr Cripps as bailiff because of McHaig's excessive charges, and he said he advised the trustee.

Mr Melbourne brought up the question of the three horses. Edwin hesitated.

Now, even Mr Lukin, the Police Magistrate, was becoming impatient, and threated to lock Edwin up.

> *Mr Melbourne: What became of the horses?*
> *'One was advertised for sale on the 28th January, and one was lost.'*
> *Mr Melbourne: What became of the other? Did the doctor tell you he had sold it?*
> *'No.'*

Edwin received £113 18s 6d but all the items in the Bill of Sale were not sold.

> *Mr Melbourne: Hand in the account sales, please, and that will finish your examination.*
> *'Can I get a receipt?'*
> *Mr Lukin: We don't give receipts here.*

When Edwin returned home, he was not his ebullient self.

Jane immediately responded, 'What is it?'

'It appears that my good deeds may return to bite me and Charles is a goner.'

'And he has such a large family to support, too.'

'I am the eleventh of twelve children, Jane, and my father was not a doctor who owned a chemist shop. There is no excuse for Charles's mismanagement of his assets.'

Some time elapsed until the matter of Dr C Cripps and ex parte Macaree case was heard in the Supreme Court in Brisbane, although Edwin did not travel to hear the outcome.

It was alleged from the evidence already submitted in Rockhampton by the Cripps Trustee's lawyer, Mr Melbourne, that the proceeds of the sale of goods by Edwin should be paid to the Cripps trustee as it was a sham possession. It was intended, they claimed, that Edwin had tried to avoid being caught up in the insolvency. Edwin's representative in Brisbane contended that the transactions were legitimate.

A few days later, the Judge pronounced his verdict. Edwin was ordered to pay the trustee for Dr Cripps, Mr Dawbarn, the gross value of the goods, less the rent that had been paid. The trustee would be paid costs out of the estate.

Jane kept well out of Edwin's way when he heard the outcome of the case. Once he'd calmed she said, 'Well, remember when you finally received £350 from Samuel Rogers' estate earlier this year after that dreadful Mrs Birmingham tried to disrupt your rights in that old court case – maybe that can help?'

Edwin's face softened as he remembered his storekeeper friend and the fraudulent behaviour of the woman who tried to take possession of the home, but said dolefully, 'I spent that on property, Jane.' But Edwin was not prepared to let the case drop, and in protest, he wrote:

> TO THE EDITOR OF THE MORNING BULLETIN.
> Sir- An article appeared in your issue of the 21st instant that is calculated to injure me in my private business. I, therefore beg, for the love of fair play, that you will place the facts of the case before the public.
> Re Cripps's insolvency, before Justice Mein at Brisbane, in your paper it appears that I took a bill of sale from Dr. Cripps at the time of his insolvency. Such a statement is not true. The facts are that I advanced Dr Cripps one hundred and fifty pounds as far back as the year 1883, on a sale note of his furniture, and a further sum of thirty-five pounds to pay Dr Cripps's rent, at a later date, "long prior to his insolvency," at which time I took a bill of sale in good faith from Dr Cripps, not knowing anything of his indebtedness to others. I may mention, in justice to myself, that I should not have sold off Dr Cripps's furniture had I not been compelled to do so by the strain that was brought to bear on me by others. Those who run may read. I defy the breath of calumny, as my proofs will bear the closest scrutiny.
> Yours, EDWIN MACAREE, Rockhampton.

While Edwin spent much of his time in defence of his business, William's wool scouring business was thriving. At a major exhibition in Brisbane of the National Agricultural Association, the two bales he submitted won bronze. William, however was devastated, as his prize bales, which were much superior, had been left behind at the Balmoral scour.

He was surprised when Mr Young, the Land Commissioner in Rockhampton contacted him to report he had received complaints from residents in the area of the wool scour. They were not happy with the quality of the water in the lagoon, which they usually used for domestic purposes, but which were now too polluted for such purposes.

William explained to the Lands Commissioner that they were not actually washing the wool in the lagoon now they had new machinery, but the drainage was allowed to run back in. William then claimed the problem belonged to the Health Officer, and the Mayor reported back to William that their Health Officer had received no complaint.

William was expanding his land holdings. Emu Park was thriving as a holiday destination, and William bid for and purchased a prime residential block of half an acre atop the hill overlooking the Keppel Bay for £45 during a Government land sale, where the bidding was fierce. His intention was to build a holiday house for the family.

Along with Mr McLaughlin as partner, William applied for and acquired an extended quartz claim at Crocodile measuring 800 feet by 400 feet.

He next purchased a residential property in Mount Morgan, 66 feet by 166 feet through the office of the Gold Warden.

He paid £55 for a half-acre allotment on the Athelstane Range.

Having earlier acquired shares in the Mount Holly Gold Mine at Raglan, William was duly voted in as a director. He was already a director of the Rockhampton Permanent Building Society.

Edwin was yet again defending a claim in the courts – this time the Small Debts Court in front of the Police Magistrate.

When he arrived home grumpy, Jane said, 'I gather you lost? What was it about this time?'

'Staff at the Mount Etna Lime Works.'

'What is that to do with you?'

'Oh, I purchased the Lime Works some time ago. Did I

forget to tell you?'

Hands on hips, Jane said, 'Edwin, why did I not know that?'

'I put Peter Macdonald in as manager,' he said, ignoring Jane's question. 'I have Mr Black acting as the Rockhampton agent. He stores 200 bags of lime for 7s 8d a week, and gets a five percent commission on sales.'

'Yes, so what have they accused you of?'

By now, nothing surprised Jane with Edwin's quick business dealings.

'Well, Peter Macdonald drew on funds from the Rockhampton agent, Black. But Black maintained that I owed him the £20 14s that he gave to Peter Macdonald. Black reckoned I approved it, and had the paperwork to show for it. I didn't approve it, or, at least, I don't remember. I lost the case, and had to pay up.' Edwin, during delivering this brief outline of the case to Jane, had poured himself a whisky and was leaning back in his grandfather chair. He shrugged. 'What can one do? The Magistrate even charged me a fee of six guineas for the privilege of his arbitrating. Maybe I should become a Magistrate.'

Jane stared at Edwin, who was now in his early fifties. His hair had faded and his face, sporting a substantial bushy beard, was more weather-beaten. He was showing signs of physically slowing, but that was due to his rheumatics. Was he really mellowing? She doubted it. She shrugged back at him and picked up her knitting.

Ned walked in.

'How's it going out there?' Edwin asked, referring to the cattle at Coorooman.

'That timber is really hard to cut for fences, Father.'

'You're using the Citriodora?'

'Yes.'

'But you're getting the Islanders to chop them down, and cut into fence posts?'

'Oh, yes, of course. Peter's incredibly strong. Well, so are the other Islanders.'

Edwin knew Peter and the other workers, along with their wives, who lived in small houses on the property, kept a close eye on Ned, who was a slow and a gentle man.

Jim, Ned's younger brother, now seventeen, joined them. He was happiest with a tool in his hand, building or fixing or inventing. There was no end to the work needing to be done.

'Any fish caught for dinner tonight?'

'The women are preparing them now along with a couple of mud crabs.'

Coorooman Creek was a reliable source of food. Just a few kilometres downstream, mud crabs were plentiful. This abundance helped make Coorooman a favourite domicile for all the family.

Edwin said, since all the family excluding Emma were present, 'I'm thinking … since I am unable to sell the Cremorne property, that we actually supply the hotel with beer. We can produce it here. The water from Coorooman Creek is pure and therefore ideal. I'm just starting investigations.'

Jane's hands flew to her ears. She didn't want to hear any more. She thought she'd heard everything, but this seemed a swim too far into deep water.

'We have the railway line to Emu Park being built to go right by with a Coorooman Station stop. All we need is to build a small siding to transport the product,' Edwin added.

Jim smiled knowingly. The North Rockhampton Station was just down the road from Cremorne Hotel. He understood why his father was involved on the ground floor of so many developments. It was quite often, he'd realised some time ago, to his father's financial advantage.

'You just found a new licensee for the hotel, Father?'

'I can't get away from Lukin. If he's not playing Police Magistrate, he's playing Chairman of the Licensing Committee. He approved the transfer to William Bergmann, and then had the audacity to complain about the refreshments on Saturday night at the hotel along with his glass not being clean. He did admit, though, that it was an enjoyable affair regardless.'

The boys laughed. They had little to do with the hotel since most of their commitments were to the Coorooman selection or to helping their father in the business in the township.

Late in December, in 1887, Cornelius Norris came into Edwin's office frowning. 'Have you heard the rumour about John Rutter?'

'What's going on?' Edwin rose from his desk, sensing the seriousness of what Captain Norris was about to say. John Rutter had started working for Rees R Jones, the solicitor, but had branched out into his own accounting business. He was also the current Mayor of North Rockhampton, so he was well known to Edwin and everyone else in the town.

'They say he's been arrested for forgery.'

'*Is whispering nothing?* Let us be fair till we know. I would be stunned.'

'There is substance to it, Mac.'

It was just a short while later the rumours proved to have validity. The entire town was in shock.

At 6 pm the previous evening, after being unable to find John Rutter in his office, the police appeared at his home on the Range where he was arrested.

'Poor sod,' Edwin said to Jane when he was relating the outcome the next day. 'First, he asked them to delay the arrest till he had time to right the wrong. They refused. Next he asked to stay home till after dark so the rumours wouldn't be confirmed and his family would not be humiliated, but they insisted on taking him to a cell immediately. At least they had the decency to escort him in his own private buggy.'

'What has he done, Edwin?'

'They claim he forged documents to the amount of £12,000.'

'What! That's an enormous amount. I wonder why? Where is he now?' Jane could see that Edwin was still in a state of disbelief.

'Lukin, the Police Magistrate, allowed him to be released from jail on £800 bail. The sureties were Caporn and Curtis. Anyone decent would have done that for him. He was released fairly promptly. Rutter himself must be somewhat deranged. I am at a complete loss to understand how he thought he'd ever get away with defrauding the bank. He's accused of forging a bank official's name on several promissory notes with the Union Bank of Australasia. The first one matured on 22nd December, and was instantly identified as a forgery.'

'What happens next?'

'He'll appear in court next Tuesday. I'd imagine most of the town will be there.'

'And you?'

'Yes, of course.'

Edwin duly turned up on Tuesday at the new Police Court for the 10 o'clock hearing. There was no sign of John Rutter, but the witnesses, including bank staff were ready.

Rumours began flying around the gallery until Police Inspector Stuart applied for a remand. He said:

> '...I have received an intimation that the defendant is very ill. I have therefore sent the Government Medical Officer to examine him, and report upon his condition. At 12 o'clock I shall be able to state the result.'

Mr Melbourne (representing Mr Rutter) responded that Dr

Stuart was attending him, and that he was dangerously ill. He questioned the pointlessness of a two-hour remand. In response Mr Lukin the Police Magistrate said:

> 'Simply to get the evidence that he is ill. Yours is only second-hand evidence, Mr Melbourne.'

Inspector Stuart said he would ask for a remand for a week, depending on the seriousness of the illness.

There was a general agreement, with Mr Melbourne asking about the bail if Mr Rutter was unable to appear. The question was to sit unanswered until after midday.

At that time the constable of the Court formally called John Wallis Rutter, who did not appear.

Inspector Stuart suggested that Dr Stuart be called to explain Mr Rutter's inability to attend.

Mr Lukin said that if there was no valid reason for his absence, then bail should be forfeited.

The Inspector called Dr Stuart, who was sworn in.

Dr Stuart said he was called to Mr Rutter's home at 9.45 am. He saw him in a bedroom, lying down fully clothed. He found him in a state of collapse, with almost no pulse, and barely breathing. He telephoned for another doctor from the hospital and applied remedies till Dr Brannigan arrived. At the point Dr Stuart said he examined Mr Rutter and found something sticking out of his left side. When he pulled his shirt and singlet up, he found a crochet needle buried in his skin.

Dr Stuart produced a small ivory-handled barbed needle, about four inches long. When he was asked how far it had penetrated, he responded it was to a depth of the whole steel section and halfway up the ivory handle. Dr Brannigan had watched him withdraw it.

He said that Mr Rutter was in a serious condition right now

and was completely unfit to appear in court. Dr Stuart went on to say that he was not fit to be left alone, and was too ill to be transferred to the hospital.

On responding to further questioning, Dr Stuart said he and Dr Voss intended examining him further and hoped to move him to hospital in the evening. Mr Rutter had been only partially conscious and was incoherent.

Dr Vivian Voss, who was Acting Government Medical Officer in Rockhampton, was called to the stand. He confirmed that he had also attended Mr Rutter and concurred with all that Dr Stuart had told the court. Mr Rutter was being attended by a constable who had been ordered not to leave his side.

Mr Melbourne, after hearing all this evidence, asked that the case be adjourned for a week, and the sureties be discharged.

Mr Lukin (Police Magistrate): When there is any doubt as to the defendant being unable to appear we generally make it eight days.

> *Inspector Stuart: It will put me in a very peculiar position, Your Worship, and after the evidence which has just been given by the doctors I shall be compelled to arrest him for attempted suicide. I cannot get out of it.*
>
> *Mr Lukin: Have you got him under arrest at the present time?*
>
> *Inspector Stuart: There is a constable in the house.*
>
> *Mr Lukin: Is he under arrest? If you say you have him in custody I will discharge the recognizances.*
>
> *Inspector Stuart: He was in such a condition that he was not fit to be at large. Yes, he is under arrest.*
>
> *Mr Lukin: Very well. Then I discharge the recognizances, and the case is adjourned for eight days. Of course, if he is in a fit state to be brought up in the meantime, the ordinary remand warrant will be made out.*

Those in the gallery had been shocked into silence during the proceedings, but with the case adjourned, they clattered and chattered their way out of the courtroom. In a sombre mood, Edwin stood with the North Rockhampton aldermen outside.

A few of them were closer to John Rutter and his family than Edwin and offered to follow through on what they might do to help.

'As if he wasn't in enough strife,' Edwin posited, 'without being charged with attempted suicide. He, *the noblest Roman of us all.* The shame must have gripped him in such a vice.'

Edwin's friend, Cornelius, contacted him in the afternoon, to say that John had regained consciousness, and had been transferred to the hospital at the jail. The bleeding had stopped and he was under the care of Dr Voss.

1888

Edwin takes the reins

In early January 1888, the Aldermen of the North Rockhampton Council met, after receiving the resignation in writing from their former Mayor, Alderman John Rutter. The Town Clerk chaired the meeting. Alderman Shannon nominated, and Alderman Norris seconded Edwin to fill the office of Mayor till the elections in February.

But as was usual with these Council meetings, it degenerated into chaos over procedural rules when Alderman Face tried to suggest someone from the Finance Committee, rather than the Chairman of the Works Committee (which was Edwin's position) would be better suited for the position. Everyone noisily joined in the discussion.

The Town Clerk found it impossible to control the aldermen, and the argy-bargy continued until Alderman Shannon said, 'When a motion is made it is the motion, and it is put unless there is an amendment, and then the amendment becomes the motion, and all the aldermen are debarred from speaking until the amendment is accepted.'

When the vote was finally put, it was seven to two in favour of Edwin.

Edwin took the chair and read and signed the declaration before embarking on a brief speech.

> 'It is customary when a mayor or alderman is returned, or honoured as I feel honoured, by your returning me, although

it is for such a brief period – to express thanks. There are several remarks which have been made which I do not agree with, but I do not intend to combat them. I never asked any man for his vote, because If chance will have me king, change will have me. I have well considered the matter in all its bearings, and I have come to the conclusion that it is better to have a man unacquainted with the finance of your Council. Perhaps fresh blood will do good, even at this late hour. ... During the next three weeks I shall take such a method in my madness ... I have no desire to be personal at all. ... It is not a matter of rejoicing that I sit here. I rather look upon it as a kind of mourning for the unhappy events of the past weeks. I feel very proud of the honour you have done me. ... Give every man fair play as I have done. Many thanks, gentlemen.'

In February, after Edwin had demonstrated his ability to act as Mayor, the Aldermen voted him in to serve again for the ensuing twelve months. Meetings went no more smoothly under his control than they had prior to his taking the Chair. A shortage of funds hindered much of what they wanted to achieve.

In March a deputation from Council, led by Edwin, met the visiting Premier of Queensland, The Honourable Sir Samuel Griffith MLA, accompanied by the Minister for Works. Water Supply headed the list on the agenda, as the people of North Rockhampton were dependent on three wells. Edwin wanted to use the Government's diamond drill, lying idle, to drill deeper for water.

Other infrastructure requests, including a wharf for the North Side, went to the Premier, but his standard response was that the Council could apply to borrow funds. The outcome was a zero commitment.

Edwin and the Premier debated the advantages of a deep water jetty at Emu Park, as Edwin held that the Port Alma Wharf was too far from the town. Edwin said that, with all the materials present at Emu Park, it could be done for £20,000. The Premier was adamant it would be around £500,000. Edwin went home quite dejected, with not one win under his belt.

A short time later, Edwin chaired a meeting in the Council Chambers in support of solicitor, Mr Rees Jones representing North Rockhampton in the Queensland Parliament.

During the introduction, there was some friendly heckling, after which Edwin apologised for the poor lighting. 'There has been some misunderstanding or else we certainly should have been better lighted. You see the beastly state the lights are in. Even the glasses are not cleaned, and somebody will have to come in for their share of it.'

It was after this meeting that Edwin was handed a petition signed by many North Rockhampton residents requesting that he consider standing for parliament himself. He declined gracefully without giving it much consideration. He was up to his armpits in brewery construction and development, as well as searching for a good brewer to manage it. He was also managing his other businesses and he enjoyed the challenges of his role as Mayor.

This didn't stop his continuing support for Rees Jones. The Morning Bulletin reported, with humour, the lobbying and electioneering of both Mr Macdonald and Mr Jones.

> I hear Macaree is prepared with an extract from Shakespeare upon slavery to launch his member's devoted head at the next meeting. Macaree, not knowing Macdonald's preference for the cheap heathen Chinee, had at a previous meeting, enveloped him with all the influence and dignity which it is in the power of a Mayor to bestow,

> *and described him in a proprietary fatherly sort of way as "Our" candidate. Some of Macdonald's attempts to hold country meetings have been magnificently ridiculous. He was going to Emu Park, but the reply to his telegram said the four electors at that place were pledged to his opponent, that they had all gone to town, but that if he wishes to hold a meeting, the ladies would attend and bring the children if he would promise to say something amusing. ... His meeting at Yeppoon was very funny also. He advertised to speak at the same time as Jones, at the school house. Jones, however, got there first and took the ear of the electors, so when Macdonald arrived, he had no choice but to sit down and wait until Jones had done. But when Jones was done, Pattison took the floor and wired into Macdonald in a most alarming fashion. The meeting carried a vote of confidence in Jones.*

Mr Macdonald also had the opportunity of addressing electors at the North Rockhampton Council Chambers. Edwin didn't chair this meeting. Macdonald said that it was known that Mr Jones was part of a syndicate who were antagonistic towards the working class. He claimed that Jones didn't think the Fitzroy River was essential as a port, and was supportive of the Port Alma Port and railway, but had now turned his interest to Broadmount. The Bulletin reported:

> *If Mr Jones had been in favour of deepening the river (I) never would have opposed him. They said they wanted an honest lawyer, but if this were really the case with Mr Jones, he was the only one in this part of the country; and the best thing they could do was to keep him in Rockhampton.*

After a long speech, Mr Macdonald asked for questions from the floor.

Since Edwin was present, he couldn't help himself. There was no question, just a statement. The Morning Bulletin summarised:

> Mr Macaree made a long speech in his characteristic style, which caused both considerable amusement and applause. He alluded to the Opposition candidates on the other side of the river as "thundering political mountebanks," and "thundering big bellied fellows strutting about the town;" and incidentally advocated Emu Park as a port – although he said he had no interest in it. He also warned the voters against imbibing "Tom McLaughlin's beer," and then informed the meeting he was going to start an opposition brewery on the north side. Mr Macaree further warned the electors not to allow their independence to "be sold for a mess of porridge."
>
> In concluding he referred to the actions the Griffith Government had recently performed for North Rockhampton. ... Mr Macaree's speech caused the greatest amusement and one gentlemen shouted out: "Why, Macaree, you are worth a thousand pounds an hour."

An audience member, trying to shock the listeners, claimed that Mr Jones employed a black fellow as a coachman and a black woman as nurse.

After a vote of confidence was seconded and passed, the meeting concluded.

Polling places for voting the next day included Edwin's Emu Park Cottage.

The following week, after votes were counted for the new seat of Rockhampton North, the Returning Officer appeared on the platform, together with Mr Jones and Edwin. Mr Macdonald was not present. The total number of votes counted was 551, with Edwin's Mr Jones winning by a majority of 155 votes.

Edwin's rheumatics were bothering him more and more. He had difficulty mounting and dismounting his horse. He was looking for relief and a friend put him on to *Warner's Safe Rheumatic Cure*. It genuinely helped for a while. Discovering his position and standing in the community, the manufacturers asked him to endorse the product in return for a free supply. The advertisement ran for some time in several east coast newspapers.

The current licensee of the Cremorne Hotel was Mr William Bergmann. He applied to the Licensing Authority to have the licence transferred to Edwin, who, of course, was planning to have his own beer available there later in the year and to have control over who would market it there.

Mr Jones represented Edwin because Mr Pattison had filed an objection on behalf of merchants Messrs W G Capora and Co and Messrs W P Walton and Co. The objections were on the grounds of the welfare of merchants in the town.

Mr Jones, on Edwin's behalf, said that he 'had never seen more impertinent objections filed by anyone.'

Mr Pattison claimed that Edwin resided at Coorooman, not North Rockhampton, but it was responded to by Mr Jones saying that Edwin was Mayor of North Rockhampton, and therefore did reside there. Another objection raised was regarding funds owed to Messrs Walton and Co. The response was that Edwin had paid them over £177 from his own pocket, which was actually owed by one of his tenants and not Edwin himself.

From the Bench, Mr Lukin interrupted, saying that it didn't matter where one resided because the applicant seldom resided in the hotel until the licence was granted. The only objection to be considered when granting a licence was if the person applying was found to be improper, and since that was not shown, the licence was granted.

It was only a few months later that Edwin found the licensee he wanted to run the hotel and sell his new beer, and subsequently the licence was transferred yet again, this time to the Irishman, Daniel O'Brien. The brewery construction was progressing rapidly.

Edwin was attempting to divest himself of his low-profit investments, so he put the Mount Etna Lime Works on the market along with its 800 acres of land.

Edwin had heard that the ship *Geelong* had run up on rocks a considerable distance north of Rockhampton. This time, though, it was William Fraser, and not Edwin, who showed an interest. William contacted Edwin, having heard of the auctioning of the wreck and her cargo.

'I think I'm stretched too far for now, William, but talk to Captain Norris. He understands salvage.'

'The cargo is food stuffs mainly.'

'Ah, then it will fit with your store merchandise.'

A few nights later, Edwin lifted his eyes from the newspaper and told Jane that Messrs Fraser and Craig were successful in their bid for the wreck.

Jane heard a few weeks later that Annie had given birth to her fourth son.

'Oh, Edwin, they've called him Prince Albert,' she said. 'What do you think?'

Edwin shrugged, lifting his eyes from the newspaper. 'Well, if they were English it would be more likely, but even the Scots like our Queen and her deceased husband. He was creative, and that would appeal to William.'

He became quietly absorbed by an article. After a while he said, 'I see William and his partner Craig have held their first meeting of their new gold mine.'

Jane turned to listen. 'And talking of names, they've called it *Who'd-Have-Thought-It Gold.*' He chuckled. 'Who'd-have-thought-William had a sense of humour? William's the Chairman and Craig is the Secretary. They expect to pay a dividend to shareholders earlier rather than later. Good luck, I say to them.'

Both Edwin and William joined the newly opened Rockhampton Club. Both were also members of the Chamber of Commerce and joined with other members to present a list of considerations to the Parliamentary member for Rockhampton, the Honourable W Pattison MLA, who'd recently been promoted to the Ministry.

The first consideration was a railway to Longreach. Now the Central Queensland Meat Export Company could freeze beef to export to England, the same could apply to sheep from the central west, making the railway line imperative. Wool for treatment and export was another reason. The Hon W Pattison was in favour and agreed to lobby for it.

The second consideration was the Port Alma railway so that Port Alma itself would become the major port. Mr Pattison admitted he was not in favour of deepening the Fitzroy River as the time taken to have large vessels reach the wharves in Rockhampton was disadvantageous. Mr Pattison said he was gathering more information.

Just before the completion of the deputation, Edwin spoke. 'I see a strong necessity of erecting a fort and an electric battery for firing torpedoes at Broadmount (Thompson's Point) and elsewhere, for the defense of the town.'

Mr Pattison responded by saying, 'I'm not an alarmist who thinks Rockhampton is worth robbing, and I can't see any necessity for a fort. The magnificent mudflats you have in the river are sufficient protection.'

His comments were met with laughter before the deputation withdrew.

Edwin's brewery was close to completion when he organised a visit from a reporter from the Morning Bulletin newspaper to meet with his brewer/manager, Mr Coomber.

On the evening of the 18th October 1888, Edwin smiled smugly into the newspaper as he read aloud the more-than-favourable report to Jane.

> *It has been mentioned in our columns, that Mr Edwin Macaree, Mayor of North Rockhampton, was building a brewery on his Inglewood Park Estate, at Coorooman Creek. It is not generally known, however, that the brewery in question has been completed, or so nearly completed that already two "brews" have taken place. The new premises are in charge of, and under the management of, Mr Herbert Coomber, a skilled brewer of reputation in this district, and who was formerly with Messrs. Younger and Company, of Edinburgh. On applying to Mr Coomber for permission to inspect the new premises, he cordially took us over the building, shortly explaining the mode of manufacturing;*
>
> *"Beer, beer, beautiful beer,*
> *Cheering, frothing, bright and clear"*
> *at the Coorooman Creek Brewery.*
>
> *Some of the new brew was sampled, and proved a most palatable beverage. It is so well-known that Pressmen are*

not connoisseurs of any kind of intoxicants, that it is scarcely necessary to say the opinion expressed is merely that of an amateur. The beer leaves no unpleasant taste in the mouth, has more "body" than is often the case, and is apparently slightly darker in colour than that manufactured at other places. It is clear to the eye, but at present it has a rather sweet taste, which, we are informed, arose from its newness, and which we were assured would entirely disappear in the course of a week. The good quality of the beer is ascribed to the suitability of the water – which Mr Staiger, after analysis, stated was similar to that used by Bass, of Burton-on-Trent – and to using nothing but the best English malt and Kent and Bavarian hops.

Inglewood Park is distant twenty miles from Rockhampton by road or rail, and eight miles from the township of Emu Park. The railway to the Park crosses Coorooman Creek within fifty yards of the brewery, going right through the land comprising the estate. The brewery is not more than two or three hundred yards from the main road, and of course is plainly visible from it. The land is quite level, and has been securely fenced off. At present it is rather heavily timbered, but clearing has already been started, and all but heavy foliage trees will be removed, and the ground improved by ornamental trees, flowers, etc. The site of the brewery is close to Coorooman Creek, the devious course of which is thickly planted with Alexandra palms, Leichhardt trees, she-oaks, ti-trees, and many other varieties of Australian timber. There is at present a splendid reach of deep, fresh water close to the bank, on which stands the brewery, and, except in times of prolonged drought, the water in the creek runs in some volume. When the ground has been cleared and improved as intended, the Coorooman Creek brewery will occupy one of the most attractive and picturesque nooks to be found in the district. Being so close to the Emu Park Railway, Mr Macaree intends to lay down a tramway to connect with the railway. This will be a great convenience, and will materially facilitate the receipt of stores, etc, and the despatch of the product of the establishment. The capacity of the brewing plant is 100 hogsheads per week. When the brewery is going in full swing, it will give employment to about ten or twelve men. The buildings have been erected with sawn hardwood, and covered with galvanised iron. They were designed by Mr Coomber himself, and erected under the supervision of Mr McGurrin. The main building is 80 feet long by 27 feet wide, of which 60 feet are to be used as cellars. The cellars have at present merely an earthen floor, but it is intended to lay down a concrete floor at an early opportunity. The brewery is worked on what is known as the semi-gravitation principle. The tower is 46 feet high, 27 feet long, and 20 feet wide, On the top of the tower is an open tank capable of holding 8000 gallons of water. The water is pumped from a creek below by a pulsometer pump, made by Messrs Burns and Twigg. Mr Coomber is in raptures with this pump, which he says is one of the best he has ever seen. It works splendidly, without the slightest vibration, raising 8000 gallons to the height named in one hour. The water at present is pumped directly from the big waterhole in the creek, but as this water, in time of flood, will be slightly discoloured, it is intended to sink a well twenty or thirty feet in from the bank, when the soakage through the drift will clarify and purify the water. Descending from the top of the tower, the first space reached is the boiling-room, where the beer is boiled by steam. The room contains a hot water tank, a beer boiler, and ground-malt hopper. The beer is boiled by naked steam by a patent revolving T piece, which, as it revolves, emits dense clouds of hot steam. Underneath the boiling-room is the mash-room, where the malt is mashed by a patent cascade mashing machine, filtered through an iron bottom, fitted with copper studs. From here the "wort" is conducted to an underback on the ground floor, to which is fitted a copper steam coil. The beer is then pumped back to the beer boiler, already referred to, on the top storey, where it is boiled with hops, etc, and in its heated state passes over a peculiarly arranged and powerful refrigerator, and from thence, through a hose to the fermenting casks in the cellar. Hot and cold water is laid on to every floor from top to bottom.

Some little time hence another storey, 60 feet by 27 feet, will be erected over the cellars, to be used as a store room for hops, malt, etc. The business offices are to be on the ground floor, and the manager's office and experimenting-room on the second floor. Verandahs, 16 feet wide, are to be erected all round the main building. The whole structure is strong and commodious, and there is ample room for any necessary extensions and developments. The motive power is supplied by a 14 horse-power Tangye engine, one of Messrs. Burns and Twigg's 18 horse-power Cornish boilers furnishing the needed steam. The boiler is fitted with a patent Vauxhall feed pump. The engine, pumps, etc., work splendidly, and Mr Coomber is not sparing in his praise of the proprietors of the Vulcan Foundry for the manner in which they have performed their portion of the contract. Arrangements are about to be adopted for cleansing empty casks by steam, which will not only save labour, but do the work more effectively.

As already stated the Coorooman Creek Brewery is not yet quite completed, but it is sufficiently advanced to enable the manager to continue the manufacture of beer, which will shortly be placed before the public. It is gratifying to notice the increase of local manufactories of any kind, and it may be hoped the manufacture of beer will soon be followed in this district by industries which will more widely tend to the welfare and benefit of mankind. Mr. Macaree is to be congratulated on having a manager who so well understands his business, and it is probable that ere long Coorooman Creek beer will be in brisk demand throughout Central Queensland.

'Well, Jane,' Edwin gloated, folding the paper, 'I could not have praised the brewery more if I'd written the piece myself. And the timing is impeccable with the railway to Emu Park to be finished by the end of year.'

Once Edwin began marketing his brew, he joined the Victuallers' Association. His first meeting was an eye-opener. He had expected a different kind of response. One of the major tasks was to elect a new President of the Association.

An extensive discussion of three-penny drinks, though, dominated general business. Mr Trickett was selling a glass of beer at half price, and that, to those present, was very disturbing.

The Morning Bulletin reported some of the discussion in the publication of November 30th, 1888.

Mr Wilson: I want to ask a question of Mr Macaree, who I see is present. Are you supplying beer to the publican who is selling threepenny drinks …?

Mr Macaree: When you got your last discharge from the service, how was it signed?

Mr Wilson: Answer the question.

Mr Macaree: I decline to answer it.

Mr Wilson: Are you serving Trickett with beer to sell at 3d a glass?

Mr Macaree: I decline to answer.

The Chairman: And I rule you out of order, Mr Wilson.

Mr Wilson: I am asking a straight-forward question.

The Chairman: When I first landed in Rockhampton most things were a very good price, and I am sorry we reduced them …

Mr Wilson: If you go to work and reduce the price of beer, as a matter of course, you will ultimately expect other things to be reduced.

Mr Macaree: As you have mentioned my name I may state – (interruption)

Mr Wilson: Now, only the other day I saw five of your casks coming out of Trickett's cellar.

Mr Macaree: It is not true.

Mr Wilson: No. I think it is.

Mr Macaree: I never saw anything come out of your cellar.

Mr Wilson: No. You never will; not that we shall be the worse friends for that. Mr Pershouse said yesterday he was informed by a leading wine merchant that a certain local brewer offered to sell beer to a publican at £3 per hogshead, on the condition that he dealt exclusively with him. He could give the name if necessary.

Mr Macaree: Name … (interruption)

Mr Pershouse: It can be obtained if it is necessary. I think Trickett made a move in the wrong direction … I consider that such a man ought to be boycotted. … I hope every other publican in the town will do like-wise. …

Edwin said that since his name would be mentioned in the paper he wanted to put the record straight. He'd never offered to sell his beer lower than what his friend Tom McLaughlin charged. Mr Wilson said he'd vouch for what Edwin had said.

On and on the discussion stretched, and they even talked about price-fixing. There were only three brewers in town.

Eventually, the Chairman drew them back to the agenda and

the matter of electing a new President. Once complete, the Acting Secretary pointed out that most present were not yet members, and therefore the vote was invalid. The meeting was adjourned to a future date.

When Jane read the article, she was bewildered. When she asked Edwin what it meant, he laughed. 'You had to be there, Jane.'

Later, on considering Jane's comments, Edwin had his agent write a letter to the paper. Unsatisfied with the outcome, he decided to write his own response.

> TO THE EDITOR OF THE DAILY NORTHERN ARGUS
> *Sir* — *In your issue of the 2nd. inst. you were good enough to insert a letter from my agent, Mr Withers, giving a contradiction to my having any participation in, or knowledge of an untradesmanlike and unworthy incident, on Monday last, severely and unjustly commented on by your contemporary, and as his letter has by some few of our licensed victuallers been deemed an insufficient denial, I shall esteem it a favour, will you kindly publish this, my most emphatic denial, of any complicity in the affair. I should not add lustre to the name of the party to the incident did I ask you to publish it, although I have to thank him for his unwittingly giving prominence to my product and thus gaining for it a further proof of its goodness, a result the reverse of that intended, and without doubt, contemplated, or desired. Apologising for trespassing on your valuable space*
> *Yours, &c., EDWIN MACAREE*

Jane could see that Edwin's beer was an extension of Edwin's personality, and it had been wounded. Hopefully, she thought, after reading this letter, Edwin would let the issue rest.

In early December, the newly appointed Queensland Treasurer, their very own, The Hon William Pattison, was guest of honour at a celebratory function of about 100 guests. The Mayor of Rockhampton, Mr Sidney Williams, occupied the chair, and Edwin was vice-chairman.

When it was Edwin's turn to speak, he acknowledged he'd known Mr Pattison for many years and even though they might not share the same politics, he reckoned he was the best man to represent Rockhampton and was the best fit for the position of Colonial Treasurer.

'Prior to the elections,' Edwin said, 'we had some misunderstanding with Mr Pattison's party, but when we were wiped out, I was with him and his party all the way. They have been attentive to our needs. North Rockhampton Council almost became insolvent, and water has always been a major problem for us. Others,' he said, 'promised everything and did nothing. But this Government has sunk a bore for us.'

Edwin mentioned the Member for North Rockhampton, Mr Rees Jones, and his support too, before proposing a toast to the Hon William Pattison.

The much-awaited Emu Park railway line was completed and opened in December 1888. The line ran from close by the North Rockhampton Council Chambers for a tad more than 29 miles. The line had been built close to the road, making access during the construction much easier and quicker.

The first train was filled with 120 politicians as well as those involved in the rail development, which, naturally, included Edwin.

After the line crossed 114 feet of bridge across Twenty-Mile Creek, Edwin entertained the carriage pointing out that Coorooman Creek was next.

'This bridge' he said, 'is the longest on the route with a length of 504 feet and a height of 32 feet above the bed of the creek.' As they passed by, he pointed to his brewery on the left-hand side. 'The siding will be built right there,' he indicated.

After a smooth trip, stopping only for water for the steam engine and for picking up passengers at designated stations, the special train duly arrived at Emu Park, where the party refreshed themselves at Comley's Hotel before they proceeded to Tanby Paddock, just beyond Tanby Station where the event was hosted by Mr Johnson of the Belmont Arms.

The relevant Government Minister was unavailable for the official ceremony, and so as not to delay the opening, Mr A Archer, MLA, had volunteered to perform the act amid much celebrating where food and drinks and humorous speeches were in abundance.

Edwin took his turn in responding. He was done up to the nines, and having received comments on his attire, said that there were many present who'd seen him working dressed in shirt and moleskins and covered in sweat.

Calls of 'That's Shakespeare,' were shouted at him for others to recognise who he was. It was followed by laughter.

In response, Edwin said, '*Ye old men, and members of the fourth estate, it gives me wonderful pleasure, and great is my content to see you were before me, and to see the line to Emu Park an accomplished fact.* That,' he declared, 'was Shakespeare.' By now everyone was laughing madly, and another call of 'Coorooman Creek beer' kept Edwin entertaining the crowd.

He said he'd heard from a clairvoyant, Miss Clara Baldwin, three years ago, that the railway line would be completed within three years.

'So we knew it would happen,' he said. Again, the audience, recalling that specific entertainer in Rockhampton a few years prior, laughed and cheered.

Edwin's speech was followed by more humorous speakers, and he was then called upon to propose a toast to the Parliament of Queensland for their support.

Another major December event was the meeting called to discuss Separation, where Edwin, naturally, was in attendance. The issue of creating two more colonies within Queensland, with their own centre of parliament, had been mooted for decades. The interests of Brisbane, they claimed, were not the interests of Central Queensland, nor of Northern Queensland. The Separation League was a serious body. Mr A Archer, MLA was a proponent. Both an offensive and a defensive alliance with northern members was proposed.

1889

Brewing

On the 8th January 1889, The Morning Bulletin published a list of Queensland magistrates extracted from the Government Gazette.

Edwin left the newspaper open on the dining table for Jane to find, with a pencil circling the list. Jane glanced at list, and nearly dropped the paper in shock. The new Justices of the Peace were listed in alphabetical order. Half way through was the name Edwin Macaree. Good heavens, she thought, they've actually made him a magistrate.

The following month, to add to his profile, in case this was needed, Edwin was again elected Mayor of the North Rockhampton Borough. Shortly after, another minor conflict occurred at the meeting. For a while Edwin held tightly and mysteriously to some inward correspondence. The Aldermen were curious as to what game Edwin was playing. When he finally shared the contents, it proved to be regarding the administration of liquor licences, which fell to a magistrate. Edwin knew, since he was a brewer of beer, that he could not take on the role. Nonetheless, he toyed with the idea. Alderman Nobbs, also a magistrate, expected the position to be given to him, and was most annoyed when it went, unjustly, he believed, to Alderman Thompson. Edwin constantly enjoyed the kerfuffle he caused.

Water – the perennial problem of North Rockhampton – was permanently on the Council's agenda. With local man, Mr

William Pattison MLA now the Colony of Queensland's Treasurer, Edwin saw the opportunity to make something happen with one of his orations. The Brisbane newspaper headlined Edwin's effort:

> *'Bores and the Dearly Beloved Pattison':*
> *I wish myself, gentlemen of the Press, to take this impression, that for seven consecutive years I have tried to impress on the people, impress upon every member that ever presented himself as a candidate for our suffrages, both north, south, east, and west, that they would go in for bores; that is, drills, diamond bores. Now, I see, gentlemen of the Press, that there is a tender accepted for 10,000ft of bores. Well, gentlemen, you know that we have received the assurance of our dearly beloved William Pattison that he ... (interrupted by laughter.)*
> *Take it down verbatim, gentlemen. We have received the assurance that he will look out that we get bored down to our very bottom. (Loud laughter.) Put it down just as I give it, or otherwise do not put it down at all. I give it, not as orthodox, but extempore – just as it occurs to me. Now is the very time and hour of our discontent, and we salute them as the five points of the promises (Edwin turned to the reporters) Got it?*
> *(Alderman Nobbs here rose from his seat, remarking, "I'll come back when it's all over.") We salute them in the five points of the regulations that they would give us a bore, that furthermore, that the honourable the Treasurer, William Pattison, has assured us that our bore should be one of the first bores put down in the colony of Queensland. Mind, this is all truth. We have got it in writing. Therefore we promise – suggest that our bore should be attended to forthwith.*
> *(Seriously:) Now, mind you, who is going to make a motion on this? A motion – make a motion – make it if you can. In*

the minutes, as read, you can make a motion, or otherwise the Press will take notice of it.
(More seriously :) Considering this question in a public light, and considering several bores have already been attended to.
(To the reporters:) Got it – that more bores of subsequent arrangement, that our bore should come on now as speedily as possible, as the requirements of the case are most urgent. Now, I think, that this is the last of it.
(Aldermen simultaneously: "Hear hear.")
Now you see we have not neglected our bore.
(To the rate-payers:) Mind, the rates will come very heavy, and when the water rates come in they will be heavy. But we want to get the bore. Mind, there is no motion. It is for the edification of our reporters – not for the edification exactly, but for the public to show that we are trying to do what we can – for the North Rockhampton Times in particular, because they say – the Press – the mayor and aldermen are neglectful of the interests of the borough. That will suffice. What do you call it? Quandam stuff the cat. (After a pause.) Make a motion – make a resolution. I remind you it will strengthen them. This is merely of a conversational character. I advise you to do it for your counsel; otherwise it has no effect.

Sometime later, the Morning Bulletin responded thus:

A party by the name of Macaree is mayor of North Rockhampton. North Rockhampton is a funny place, and contains (besides Kanakas) some funny people. But Macaree is the funniest. Some time ago he delivered a speech on 'bores and dearly beloved Pattison' which made him famous throughout the length and breadth of the land. So famous that the Mayor of Rockhampton feared less the

> *oratory should be attributed to him. Consequently Archie Archer M.L.A. wrote to the Courier that to North Rockhampton fell the honour of having elected as their Mayor one who could deliver himself in that eloquent manner. One specimen of the eloquence — e pluribus unum. ((Translation: out of many, one.))*

The article went on to quote sections of Edwin's speech, including 'Quandam stuff-the-cat.' ((Translation: Quandam: somebody.))

Well, the delightful outcome of all this talk of bores arrived at noon on a December day, on the corner of High and Berserker Streets when a drill sank into the soft earth after Edwin had said a few formal words. Mr Rees R Jones had christened the undertaking and Alderman Nobbs had expressed his hopes that the water would be measured not in the thousands of gallons, but by at least a million gallons.

None of the audience realised that the drill had already reached a depth of twenty-five feet three days earlier.

Whilst both Edwin and William still met each other at various club meetings at which they were both members, their business paths rarely crossed. William, with another partner, Mr McLaughlin senior, purchased a wool-scouring plant at Barcaldine, closer to the source of the quality wool. For water, they successfully sank an artesian bore. Bales of scoured wool were sent to Sydney and their superiority was acknowledged.

Once this business was up and thriving, William sold his share and partnered with Mr Dan Craig. They acquired 30,000 acres of the Coreena resumption near Barcaldine which they called Balmoral. They invested in improvements, including a bore, and they subdivided it into paddocks and stocked it with sheep. Once again, when it became profitable, they sold it.

Edwin received word while at his Rockhampton office that there were staff issues at Coorooman. On arrival, Jane filled him in.

Edwin's diary note on Mr Coomber's bad temper

Started for the Creek. Had trouble with Coomber (the brewer). He has been traducing the governess and the boys. It puts me at my wits end. The Governess was sad – sore distress. Whatever can we do with such a bad tempered man, I do not know.

Back at Coorooman, Edwin approached the problem.

Edwin's diary ask Mr Coomber to apologise to Governess

At Coorooman Creek. I wrote a letter (press copy) to H Coomber asking him to make a written apology to Miss Moore the Governess, but he denies everything and will not sign the apology. I went over to the brewery and he asked me if he should put in a brew. I told him he could if he liked but I did not care for Sunday work! He asked me to send his things over to Lamberts.

Edwin had solved the problem but lost a brewer.

Always thinking of ways to make money, he discovered yet another opportunity at Coorooman. He was surrounded by thousands of trees – mostly quality hardwood – and he now had a railway line passing by. A sawmill, somewhat compact in size, with the ability to saw between 10,000 and 20,000 feet per week was to be built, along with the siding to connect it to the rail line.

'Jim will manage it under my supervision,' he told Jane. There's plenty of construction going on at Emu Park, and all along the rail line to guarantee sales.'

Jane was pleased that Jim could have some degree of autonomy – well, at least she hoped he would. She was optimistic that Edwin's interference would be minimal.

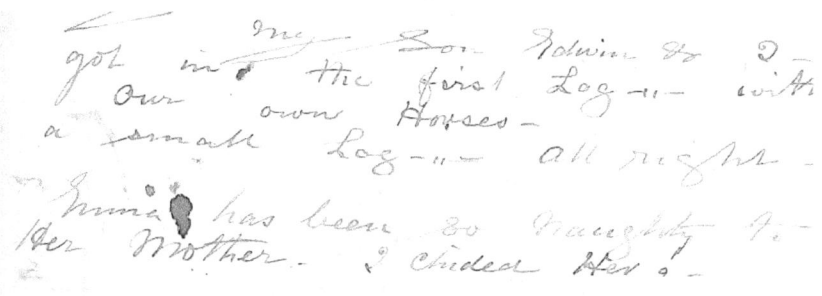

Edwin's diary, first log to the Sawmill

My son Edwin and I got in the first log with our own horses – a small log – all right. Emma has been so naughty to her Mother. I chided Her!

It was early one evening, not long after this disclosure that Edwin hurriedly left his buggy with the groomsman at the stables at Cremorne, and theatrically threw the door of their home open. 'At last, Jane, at last,' he panted.

'What's happened now?' Jane felt like a receptacle for all Edwin's moods and dramas, but at least this one sounded promising.

'The Separation League is holding a public meeting, and there's huge support. I'm on the provisional committee.'

'It's been going on for decades, Edwin. Why should this meeting make a difference?' Jane had become accustomed, over the past twenty-eight years, to her husband's spending more time in his public life than in his family's life.

'Wait till you hear of the support.'

Edwin was correct. On the platform at that meeting were three Members of Parliament, Messrs Archer, Murray, and Callan. The Rockhampton Mayor, Mr John Murray was chairman, and Edwin, as Mayor of North Rockhampton, sat alongside this distinguished group. His friend, Rees R Jones MLA had sent his apologies along with his written support.

In the opening address, the Mayor stated that this was a serious fight for Central Queensland's rights. There were sound business reasons for the whole area to separate, which included the coastal regions and the western regions.

A telegram of support had come from Emerald from Mr Gay, a delegate of the Labourers' Union.

North Queensland's Separation League had begun their battle, so there was power in allegiance and in timing.

In giving examples of the need for self-rule, the speakers claimed that business was constantly disadvantaged. One example given was the Registry of Titles Office located only in Brisbane. When locals complained, The Southern Government sent a representative to open a branch in Rockhampton. Next was a request for a tea sampling representative, as samples had to be forwarded to Brisbane. There were many more needs, and

Central Queenslanders, they claimed, should not have to go to Brisbane, cap in hand, and ask each time, just because the government was not proactive.

The public support of the meeting ensured that a permanent committee was formed to pursue the necessity for separation. George Curtis, the auctioneer, became the first president. Edwin, however, was not on the permanent committee. While his passion had not waned, he had other plans.

1890

More Fraud

With the North Rockhampton Council annual elections only a month away, one ratepayer wrote a scathing letter to the editor of the Morning Bulletin, accusing the Council of 'cliqueism' because, initially, Edwin appeared in advertisements as the Returning Officer. Next, he appeared as a candidate, and the writer was disappointed there were not more candidates to choose from.

When Edwin next attended a meeting, the 30th January Northern Argus reported:

> *When Mayor Macaree strode into the meeting-room of the Council Chamber yesterday, he saluted the reporters with the remark, "Ah, members of the press, don't oppress us." He then hurled at the head of our unfortunate reporter a huge quotation from Shakespeare, but the romantic Mayor's articulation was so "throaty" that the concluding words only of the quotation could be distinctly heard, from which, and the succeeding words, it appeared that Mayor Macaree considered himself "invulnerable" to the remarks of the press. He felt specially aggrieved at some comments in our issue of yesterday, but instead of cursing our representative in good round Saxon, Mayor Macaree elected to abuse him with unintelligible Shakespearian quotations. Someone next remarked that the Returning Officer Face was going to attend, and Mayor Macaree rubbed his hands*

with glee in anticipation of the shindy that was sure to open up, when, however, Returning Officer Face, prompted by his usual cuteness, went away before the meeting. Mayor Macaree expressed his disgust in no mincing tones with "people who are afraid to see it out, and turn their back on the fight." During the council's proceedings Mayor Macaree called Alderman Schwarten to order promptly for saying a certain action was foolish, and when aldermen were putting their heads together as how best to secure votes by appearing to desire certain work to be done, Mayor Macaree reminded them that the seeming levity of the proceedings was not fitting to the occasion of his last sitting. After the meeting a certain alderman, in wishing to impress reported how unnecessary it was for him who had been in the borough for 25 years to address the ratepayers, concluded with the startling revelation that "The proof of the pudding is in the heating of it." This is merely putting a new dress on an old friend.

Ned, 25, Jim, 20, and Emma, 16, confronted their mother now they had a greater understanding of their father and his behaviours.

'How does he get away with it, Mother?' Jim asked, having read the newspaper.

'Better not to bother yourselves with it,' she said to them lightly.

'He spends a lot of time sampling his own beer,' Ned said bravely.

Jane compressed her lips. She saw her children now, not as children, but as adults. Yet she could not – would not side with them against Edwin. 'Have some respect,' she said sharply and turned away.

Edwin, with property at Emu Park, and being a well-known member of the church, accepted an invitation to the committee under the direction of the Rural Dean, to pursue funds for the purpose of erecting a church for the Church of England on land already secured by them.

Hearing this, and taking heed of her children's words, Jane said, 'Edwin, you have obligations now at Emu Park, Coorooman, North Rockhampton, and Cremorne, not to mention your business in town. And you're – what? – more than 55 years old. You've got your rheumatics to contend with when you travel. Goodness knows you can barely ride your horse anymore. Is it time to give something up?' She was thinking mainly of the consumption of alcohol. 'Go back to the theatre perhaps?'

'Can you see me dancing the hornpipe now?' He chuckled, ignoring Jane's comments, and picked up his newspaper.

After the written request to Edwin, as Mayor, from the ratepayers and Aldermen, he called a public meeting in early February, prior to the election, to discuss to desirability of forming a Separation League branch for North Rockhampton.

On 5th February 1890, Edwin was elected on to Council yet again, with the second-highest number of votes. In his speech he admitted he was glad someone else would be mayor, as he couldn't give the time and attention to the duties required. He promised, though, as an alderman, to work for the fairness of the ratepayers.

Ten days later, at the meeting to consider a North Rockhampton branch of the Separation League, Edwin's absence was noticeable. His rheumatics were playing up severely. The new Mayor, Alderman G Thompson, read Edwin's apology saying he would happily have given Edwin the chair had he been there.

In late February, with Edwin spending more time at Coorooman, he told a local reporter that he was keen to hold a meeting at Cawarral to form a local branch of the Separation League and to 'see the thing through.' It would happen as soon as he was up and doing better.

At that meeting, which Edwin did not chair, Mr George Curtis, President of the movement was reported to have said:

> 'We have tangible proof that for many years past upwards of £100,000 per annum has been received in the Brisbane Custom House, on dutiable goods shipped to Rockhampton and consumed in the Central District, making a total estimated owing to this district of more than two and one half million pounds sterling, all of which has been spent on Brisbane and its environs. The exports by sea from the port of Rockhampton in the past year have been £2,500,000 sterling in value, which does not include wool despatched from the Western country ...'

And the explanation of the massive perpetration of defrauding Central Queensland of its due continued to be read out.

Edwin moved a simple motion: That the Member for Rockhampton North be requested to use his influence to promote the interests of the Separation movement. The motion was supported. He went on to explain that a territory far larger than Queensland, in fact, more than twice as large, was revolutionised overnight. He named that country as Brazil, and explained that the people united with the army and deposed the Emperor, saying that they would govern themselves.

While he was not advocating such action, he said they should show the Government that they could unite and manage their own affairs. Emotions continued to run hot long after the meeting ended.

A few months later the Governor of the Colony of Queensland, General The Honourable Sir Henry Wylie Norman GCB GCMG CIE, visited Central Queensland.

Edwin saw an opportunity to garner support for the Separation Movement when he discovered that a visit to Emu Park was on the Governor's agenda. In full dress adorned with medals testifying his distinguished service in the Crimean War, and to Her Majesty via his service in the Navy decorating his chest, he waited patiently at Tanby Station. But the trip by the Governor was abandoned, and Edwin remained uninformed of the cancellation.

When he finally heard, he responded sharply, 'If we can't get a Governor to stay with us for one day in the year, it is time to have a governor of our own.'

Jane was knitting a layette for Annie Fraser's baby, expected in a few months, when Edwin stormed into the home and slammed the door. Who's upset him now, she wondered. He was scrunching the paper as though he were about to strangle it.

'What is it, Edwin?' she said calmly. Not that her calmness ever rubbed off on him, but she refused to adopt his mood unless it was warranted.

He hurled the newspaper onto the table. 'Read that!'

She picked up the crumpled Bulletin, smoothed out the pages and read:

> It will be news to many North Rockhamptonites to know that the extent of the borough is 19,840 acres, or 81 square miles, and most people will admit that a very much smaller area would suit the capacity of our local parliament. Alderman Macaree objected to letting the Council Chamber

for dancing purposes, and pointed out that the Cremorne Gardens could be used.

Of course he did; so would I if I owned the gardens, but then, my dear Alderman, there might be a few stiff-necked ones who would enjoy a select dance without the assistance of Coorooman beer.

Jane turned away to hide her grin. 'Oh goodness.'

'I swear they're out to get me, Jane. Ridiculous to think the Council Chambers would be large enough for that sort of activity, and the rest was unnecessary.'

Edwin's grumpiness grew when the flood rains swelled the Fitzroy River to such proportions that it damaged the bridge. He became stranded on the north side and was unable to attend his business.

His hotel manager, who heard all the gossip from the customers, told him that at about a quarter to eight that morning on the bridge there was a loud cracking sound, and then another two. Those who were on the bridge ran for their lives. The Lake's Creek bus was on the bridge at the time. The passengers thought they had a better chance on foot and leapt out. The driver, though, whipped his horses into action, and they all made it across.

The bridge was quickly closed.

Engineers found a large crack in the girder that connected the pillars near the south side. The current had dragged the planks sideways. The Harbour Master, Captain Sykes, together with the Mayors from both sides of the river arranged with private boat owners to ferry people across till repairs could be carried out.

Edwin was called to a special council meeting to hear that their Town Clerk since inception, Mr James Coker, had been arrested for embezzlement of Council funds. The auditor had picked up the discrepancies.

'How much?' Having been head of the Works Committee before he became Mayor, Edwin wondered if some incidents had gotten past him. But it was the responsibility of the Finance Committee to follow through on such matters.

'Well, the police are still investigating. The amount is about £5 at the moment, but they expect more will be revealed.'

Within days, James Coker appeared in the Police Court, but the case was held over pending further investigation.

The aldermen at the Council met informally to discuss it.

Edwin said, 'I'm not surprised to hear, after what happened to John Rutter, that they have refused bail and are holding him in custody for his own protection.'

When the court reconvened the following week, the embezzlement charge had risen to £10 10s 7d. The funds had disappeared over a period of four years.

Having pleaded guilty to the charges, James Coker awaited sentence in the Court. The Aldermen of North Rockhampton Council were all in attendance.

> *His Honour*: Well, prisoner, you seem to have been contrite, but it is a very serious offence – a breach of confidence extending over four years, and not disclosed until it had been discovered by the auditor. I am quite unable, upon reflection, to give you the benefit of the First Offenders' Probation Act.
>
> You have apparently occupied a position of comparative respectability for twenty-one years, in the enjoyment of the character which you fairly won; but instead of continuing in it you have gone in for a series of frauds, extending over four years, towards your employers. The greater their confidence in you the

more should you have been bound in honour not to have abused it. I do not wish to say anything that will give you pain, but when a man stands in your position it is necessary that he must, to some extent, be made an example, which will deter others from the commission of similar offences.

Therefore I cannot give you the benefit of the First Offenders' Probation Act. There is one source of regret which is ever-present in the mind of a Judge in cases such as yours; that is the fact that your family must to a considerable extent be affected by the position in which you have brought yourself. It is always very sad to a Judge, and no doubt it is very saddening to you. I have taken into consideration your conduct since, and I hope your readiness to acknowledge your guilt is a sign of penitence. I shall therefore limit your punishment to the extent of making it an example to others, not with a desire to give expression to that natural resentment which society feels at such an abuse of confidence as in your case. I therefore give you the lightest possible sentence I can reconcile with my views of the matter, and that is that you be kept to penal servitude for four years.

Edwin and his Council friends gathered outside the Courthouse in a sombre mood after watching their former Town Clerk taken away by police.

When Edwin arrived home and told Jane, she was somewhat nonchalant. She'd given up on trying to keep up with Edwin's associates, Edwin's businesses, and his public life.

Ignoring his announcement, she burst out with, 'Annie Fraser has just given birth. It's another boy. They're calling him Harold. I must go and see her tomorrow and give her the layette.'

Arriving, Jane noticed another family portrait of the two older children with their parents had been framed and hung in the hallway.

*The Frasers: Donald and Jessie standing,
Parents, Annie and William seated*

1891–1892

Difficult times

The summer rains had not eventuated. Although Coorooman Creek ran all year, it couldn't make the pastures grow. Central Queensland was suffering the beginnings of another drought, and Edwin was feeling the pinch.

He appealed to the Rockhampton Council to have his rates remitted on a property he owned in Bolsover Street. The cottage had actually been demolished five years prior. His request was declined.

Emma's seventeenth birthday was approaching.

'I'm going to give her land,' Edwin said to Jane. 'Those allotments on the Range are not selling well, and I'd rather they stayed in the family.'

Jane nodded her approval. Her husband was generous. He'd already taken care of Ned, and Jim was going to inherit the family businesses, as they were beyond the abilities of Ned.

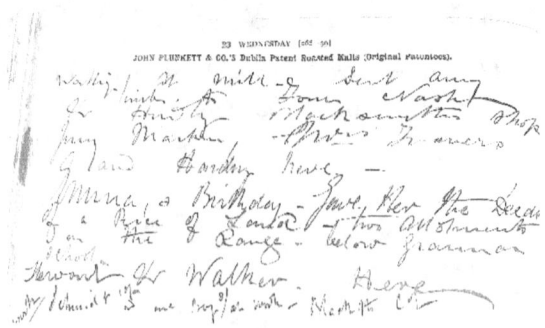

Edwin's diary, Emma gifted land for her seventeenth birthday

Working at the mill. ... Emma's Birthday – Gave Her the Deeds of a piece of land - two allotments on the Range below Grammar School ...

The Annual February North Rockhampton Council elections saw the resignation of Cornelius Norris, but Edwin was as keen as ever to renominate and was duly re-elected. It helped him keep his eyes on business opportunities, although he recognised that current times were now more a time for consolidation rather than expansion.

There was a bit of a fuss about the sale of gravel. Council took as much as they wanted from Moore's Creek for roads. Edwin said there was also plenty in Kalka and Frenchman's Creeks. But other aldermen were worried that selling it for 3d per yard would soon deplete supplies.

'We only sell it for that price to ratepayers,' Edwin said. 'Others pay more. It's an income for Council.'

Edwin and Jane's time spent socially with William and Annie and their family continued. They'd sometimes stay over at Coorooman in the guest house and also get together when Edwin was at Cremorne on weekends. Late one afternoon at Cremorne, Jane received a hand-delivered note from Annie to come immediately. The groomsman quickly arranged her carriage and when she arrived, she was ushered into a darkened front parlour, where a tearful Annie sat. William stood silently behind her.

Uninvited, but reading the seriousness, Jane moved and sat beside Annie. She threw herself into Jane's arms. 'Our little Prince Albert is dead,' she sobbed. Prince Albert was not yet two and a half.

Jane stroked Annie's hair. She knew this pain. The accumulation of the loss of her Emma, Peter, and Mary gripped her. She too sobbed. Neither noticed William leave the room.

Neither spoke to the other as their individual grief took hold and spread through their welded bodies.

Edwin returned to Coorooman after the funeral. He often left Ned in charge, as he'd done in this instance.

'Father, we have a problem. It seems that white heifer you admired so much has been slaughtered by Samuel Andrewartha.'

'I beg your pardon?'

'Yep Tin looks after the slaughter yards. He alerted me,' Ned said.

'Let's go.' Edwin took the buggy over and spoke with his bullock driver, Mr Bean, as well. Mr Bean escorted Edwin to the hide-house where a white hide was hanging under other hides. Edwin pulled it out and checked the branding which was ME 9. It was his hide also because of its rarity.

Yep Tin told Edwin that he saw Mr Austin was having a problem yarding the cattle. He was finally able to yard the white one which he slaughtered and skinned. He then cured the hide.

'What in the tarnation do these Cawarral butchers think they're doing?' he said to Ned. 'I share paddocks with them, allow them to use my yards, and they, in return, allow me to use their timbers for fencing. We do deals, but we talk about it first.' Edwin was furious and decided to press charges against both Mr Austin and his boss, Mr Andrewartha.

At the trial, Andrewartha said in his own defence: 'I took the cow without the intention of stealing it; I was led to understand that Mr Macaree would see Mr Hill (another employee) about it and Mr Macaree said if it was so he would get me to sign a document.'

Austin declared he was an employee just doing as he was told.

Andrewartha responded by saying that Edwin owed him a

cow, and he had meant to come and tell Mr Macaree about the cow being slaughtered, but he forgot. He said that the white heifer was the easiest to yard, even though it wasn't the one that was arranged to be slaughtered.

'I had no intention of stealing it. I buy cattle from Mr Macaree to slaughter for my butcher shop,' Andrewartha said. 'And he buys timber from me. I offered Mr Macaree £2 5s for it. I don't want to be considered a rogue. I am an honest man. All that happened was that the wrong cow was killed, and I forgot to tell Mr Macaree.'

Austin was dismissed, but Andrewartha was held on remand till the next day. When the case resumed, the judge subsequently dismissed the case against Samuel Andrewartha, much to Edwin's chagrin.

At the next Council meeting, a letter from Mr E S Lucas and others criticised Edwin for having neglected Queen's Park's fencing. He'd withdrawn from its committee when he became an alderman, but they still saw it as irresponsible on his part.

Also among the inward correspondence was a letter from Mr James Macaree offering to supply Council blue gum or ironbark timber 12 inches by 2 inches, or 8 inches by 12 inches for £1 per 100 superficial feet.

After the following Council meeting, Jane was reading the Morning Bulletin, when she came across another article singling out Edwin. She sighed as she read:

> The North Rockhampton Council meeting ... was chiefly remarkable for a passage-at-arms between his Worship, Mayor Nobbs and the "one-and-only Macaree." The latter wished to table a motion that all appeals made within seven days of the meeting of the Appeal Court be heard. This Mayor Nobbs refused to receive on the ground that it was

against the Act. And then the band commenced to play. Macaree accused Nobbs of attempting to block his motion, and of not giving him fair play, while Nobbs, preserving his temper with admirable self-control, smiled sweetly upon the irate Macaree like a seraph upon a damaged arch angel. The storm raged for some time but as it was all one sided it soon subsided.

It was time, Jane thought. Time for Edwin to desist. Time for them to have a serious talk. Time for Edwin to cut back. Time for Edwin to wrap a cloak of calmness about him.

She tried.

His response was to hop in the buggy and head for Coorooman. She acknowledged that he was happier and calmer there. His calling card gave Coorooman as his address, not Cremorne. Both the South Sea Islander men and women there looked after Edwin and treated him as though he were royalty.

Edwin's calling card

The report from the next Council meeting showed Edwin again dissenting. Not only was he supportive of North Rockhampton's ratepayers, but also those who lived north of the Council Chambers.

The Council's Lighting Committee read their report from the Rockhampton Gas and Coke Company which offered to supply and erect ten public lamps for £95, with terms of payments laid out. Supply of gas was £6 5s per quarter per lamp. The Committee recommended the offer be accepted and the work carried out promptly. The motion was accepted by all but Edwin who asked why there would be no lights up to Moore's Creek Bridge where murders and robberies had been committed. The sketch showed gas mains to Lake's Creek only.

The response was that they should be content with whatever they were offered.

When Jane heard the decision, even she felt annoyed. It really was time for Edwin to withdraw.

However, by the end of the year, a huge advance had been made when the gas lighting was extended to the Cremorne Hotel as well.

William, unlike Edwin never sought a public image, but quietly expanded his businesses. He purchased the Lake's Creek Sawmills and began converting them into a tannery by sinking 38 pits, bricked and cemented to allow for tanning on a large scale. He was awaiting the latest machinery from England in order to turn out first-class leather for use in harnesses, shoes and bags. He continued to use the steam power of the old sawmills, and he expected to be in full production with 30 men producing 300 hides per week by February the following year.

William also purchased half an acre of land with improvements on the corner of Stanley and Alma Streets for £1800. The family took up residence in the upper story above Martin's butcher's shop which sat on the land.

Yet again the North Rockhampton ratepayers wanted Edwin as an alderman on Council in 1892. At their first meeting, he was asked to represent Council on the Fitzroy River Bridge Board and on the Lighting Committee as well. Once all positions had been filled, the new mayor, Alderman Linnett moved that they adjourn to the Railway Hotel to celebrate.

'Gentlemen, charge your crystals with the elements you most love,' Edwin said, raising his glass. He followed with a few kind words about Mayor Linnett, for which he was thanked.

The meeting degenerated from there onwards, with comments about earlier mayors being extravagant and frivolous. Edwin took exception.

'By the time I left the Chair, the overdraft had been reduced by fifty percent,' he pointed out. 'This Council is in as good a financial position as any in the country.'

Alderman Nobbs, the previous Mayor said he hadn't accused Edwin of anything.

'I'm just defending my mayorality,' Edwin quipped, before he proposed a toast to the press, which brought proceedings to a close.

William was pouring funds into the Morning Bulletin by advertising for staff for his tannery as it came into production.

He also advertised the private sale of twenty one-acre lots, which were part of the Coonpoora Estate on the Lake's Creek Road, opposite his business, and close to the Williamstown Station.

When he and Edwin met at the Rockhampton Club, William said he was trying to sell off any assets that were not profitable, especially land. 'You're the politically astute one, Edwin,' he said. 'But I'm hearing that England's feeling a financial squeeze, and there's less capital coming into Australia.'

'You're right, William. I also hear the banks are pulling back on lending. They overextended themselves on loans in the eighties for land, for private development too, as well as for urban development. It was great for my business back then. But it's coming unravelled now – there's not much property being sold, and what is selling is worth half what it was a few years ago.'

'That's probably why we've seen some of the smaller banks go under?'

'And the others raise interest rates, and adopt stricter conditions on lending,' Edwin replied. 'I don't think we've seen the end of it yet. We can't even get a Government loan for the Council now for infrastructure.'

Edwin felt more concern than he was showing. He'd been forced to negotiate with his bank and allow them to hold the titles of six properties for added security.

His brewery was not doing well. He couldn't afford to keep producing at a loss, and lack of finances meant he was forced to let it run down. Never one to show any weakness or failing, and always one to turn a negative into a positive, he said to William, 'I've got a new development in the pipeline. I'm going to form a limited liability brewing company to expand the beer production. One can never go wrong with supplying alcohol.'

William was supportive, and Edwin wasted no time. The Rockhampton Brewery Limited was subsequently formed and registered. Two hundred shares were available at £25 each and were quickly taken up, many by publicans in the district. The brewery and plant were leased to the company for fourteen years. Mr W Humphreys, a well-known brewer, moved in, and there was action again at Coorooman.

Jane continued to spend most of her time at Cremorne, but welcomed Edwin back each time. He was continually full of news of the area and of further afield.

'It was poor timing for Archie Archer and John Ferguson to travel to England to appeal to Lord Knutsford to discuss Separation. I can't see anything happening with this economic climate.'

'That's not stopping the women from acting, though,' Jane responded. 'Madame Thozet is heading up the Women's Separation League Committee, and she is very persuasive at the meetings I attend. We have thousands of signatures ready to send to Queen Victoria.'

'Well, the mother country is not doing well, Jane, so I don't like our chances.'

'We are women appealing to another woman. A woman with power. Perhaps she will listen to us.'

While rumours were rife that the country was in the throes of a depression, the newspapers were careful to talk the economy up.

Writing about a simple land sale by Edwin, they reported:

> Land sale completed by Mr Macaree this week indicated the progress made in the material prosperity of the town. He disposed of the allotment of land at the corner of Bolsover and Derby Streets, with a frontage to the former of 33 and to the latter of 160 feet, for £1000 cash to Mr T T Faunce, agent for the Commercial Bank. Not long ago Mr Macaree was tempted to take £750 for the block, but he refused the offer, and has now substantial reason to congratulate himself.

Edwin, as a North Rockhampton Council representative, dutifully attended the monthly meetings of the Fitzroy Bridge Board, which were considerably tamer than the Council meetings.

Outstanding debts to the Bridge Board included monies owed by owners of cattle herded across the bridge on their way to the Lake's Creek Meatworks. More than £25 was owed to the Gas and Coke Company for just three months' supply, so it was decided to investigate the cost of electricity.

An engineering report from Mr W Burns was mostly favourable, but one of the anchorage chains, nine feet in length, was corroded.

Edwin, with his experience in boating, shipping, and salt water, recommended that, instead of procuring new chains, the corroded links be replaced and massive savings of around £200 obviated.

Back at the Council, Edwin was in his element. To advance the Separation movement, he recommended that both Mayors should confer and invite the Governor of Queensland as the subordinate of the Crown to visit, laying before him the rights of the Central District to have autonomy. The motion was seconded, but Alderman Stewart objected to any ratepayer's money being spent, as he claimed the Governor received a large salary and did nothing.

Edwin spoke, and the paper recorded his speech. 'We are prepared to fight for separation. Not at the point of the bayonet, but by constitutional means by laying our grievances at the foot of the throne. The voice of the people will be heard, and sound as through a trumpet, both far and near. Inviting the Governor to Hades (Rockhampton) where the voice of the angels will hover round him, is agitating in the right direction.'

The motion was carried, and the meeting closed. Discussion among the aldermen post-meeting then turned to the outcome of the petition by the townspeople for the early release of John Rutter, their ex-mayor, who'd been sentenced to eight years' jail at St Helena for fraud.

After an initial denial by the system in Brisbane, word had just come back that, because of good behaviour, the denial had been overturned and John Rutter was due to be released on 3rd October.

1893

Romance

Once again February brought about the Council elections, and once again Edwin nominated. Six candidates came forward for the three vacant positions, none of which was filled by Edwin. The Morning Bulletin reported:

> *Alas! The gay and festive Macaree has been thrown out. What could the ratepayers of North Rockhampton have been thinking of to have shown so little regard for Shakespeare as represented in the person of his devoted admirer, Edwin Macaree? Could it possibly be that they preferred to enjoy Shakespeare in season and at their own homes, in place of all at times and seasons, whenever the spirit moved Mr E Macaree? Very probably!*

'There's a message, there for you, Edwin,' Jane said. 'Off to Cooroooman with you.'

Edwin didn't take much convincing. With his two boys there, the brewery active, and sawmill wanting attention, not to mention the cattle, the call was heeded.

Every time Edwin travelled back to Cremorne, Jim travelled with him. Jane was the first to notice Jim's regular visits to the Frasers.

'Oh, Edwin – I think something is going on between Jim and Jessie Fraser,' Jane said with a lilt in her voice.

'Mother, you're so naïve,' Emma said. 'That's been going on

for years.'

Edwin looked from one woman to the other. 'Why am I the last to know?'

When Jim arrived home, Edwin and Jane captured his attention.

He looked a little sheepish, but said firmly, 'I'm going to ask Mr Fraser for Jessie's hand in marriage.'

'Good for you, son. They're a fine and decent family. She's a smart girl. And how old is she now?'

She's twenty. I'm nearly twenty-two. Yes, she is clever. And she plays the pianoforte and sings. And she's good with the little ones.'

Both parents nodded. 'I think her father may ask for a longer engagement. She is rather young,' Edwin said.

When Jim was alone with his mother, he said, 'How do I do this, Mother? Should I make an appointment?'

'Oh, goodness, Jim, next time you're there, just ask Mr Fraser if you can have a word with him. I presume you've already asked Jessie?'

'Not yet. But we play chess and backgammon together, and …' He looked down, leaving the sentence unfinished.

Jane smiled gently. 'I'm sure it will all progress smoothly. Just tell us when so that we may organise a dinner here at Cremorne for both families.' Jane was excited at the prospect of a wedding.

As was predicted, the engagement went ahead. It was to be a lengthy one as Annie and William thought Jessie was still too young.

The time had arrived to officially open the 'new' brewery. Although Edwin was now only a shareholder in Rockhampton Brewery Limited, albeit a major one, he acted as host, sitting astride his huge white steed, much to the guests' amazement as they arrived on the train.

Climbing 50 feet to the top of the tower where the 20,000-gallon water tank was housed was beyond Edwin's rheumatic knees so he left the tour to Mr Humphreys, the brewer. The pure Coorooman Creek water was pumped from a 70 feet deep well near the creek.

The visitors were then taken to the 30 by 20-foot boiler room below. Pipes pumped the fluid to a tub for mashing malt. The beer was boiled and the hot liquid then passed over a refrigerator to the fermenting room below. The group was then taken to the 60 by 60-foot cellar on the ground floor where there was storage for 100 hogsheads, although only 60 were currently stored.

Edwin was waiting on the ground floor and took over providing the information. 'The beer stores well here,' he said. 'And the plant is serviced by an 18 horse-power engine driven by an 18 horse-power boiler made by our friends, Burns and Twigg.'

Although many of those present were publicans, or people in the industry, one guest asked, 'What ingredients do you use?'

'Ah, the best,' Edwin replied. 'Mr Humphreys makes sure of that. He acquires English malt, Tasmanian and Bohemian hops and Millaquin sugar.'

'And the water from the creek is first class,' Mr Humphreys added. 'You'll note that the rail siding runs right to the cellar door, and the siding is only 100 yards from the main rail. We have a staff of five.'

At this point, the tour finished, and they gathered in front of the building for a group photo, and began testing the produce. Edwin moved to the piano where he and Mr McKean became the life of the party as they entertained the guests with lively songs.

The Brewery celebrations

Over lunch, Mr Fend proposed a toast to local industries especially singling out businesses whose owners were present, including William Fraser's tannery, Mr Ingham's eucalyptus works, Edwin's sawmill, as well as his own refrigerating plant.

Edwin responded, and so the toasts went on and on, with any excuse to re-charge the glasses.

Celebrations were short-lived for Edwin. His sales and loans and commission businesses, as well as his timber mill, struggled because banks were not only not lending money, but were closing their doors at a great rate. He continued to advertise his produce and properties for sale or lease.

> *Coorooman Creek Sawmill, Emu Park Railway. Cheap timber piles, girders, headstocks etc.*
> *To let or For Sale – THE AMERICAN COACH WORKS, Fitzroy Street. Fortune to suitable party.*
> *Also Farm of Land alongside Emu Park Railway Line. No floods but permanent water. Low price, easy terms. Sale or*

Lease; horses or bullocks lent, with ploughs, harrows &c to good enterprising farming men; railway to the door.
Town Properties, farms other localities.
"There is a tide in the affairs of men if taken at the flood, leads on to fortune."
Apply EDWIN MACAREE

William contacted Edwin after he read his ad. 'I'm building a house at Emu Park for the family, right on top of the hill on that land I purchased. Let's do our own private deal on the timber and any other supplies. I'm not going near the banks, Edwin. Too risky. I've removed some of my funds already.'

'What else have you heard, William?'

'Och, man, there's only nine of the twenty-eight banks left standing, as you know. And some are now suspending payments on deposits. God help us all if that gets any worse.'

Edwin didn't really need the warning. Everyone in business was concerned. Edwin was using all and any means he could. He'd even written to the Rockhampton Council to offer to sell them timber. Their response was that they contracted it out.

The tough times didn't stop Edwin from continuing to contribute to public life. He'd worked hard for the Church of England, where, finally, the Diocese of Rockhampton was established, with Bishop Nathaniel Dawes becoming its first bishop.

'Surely this acknowledgement from the Church contributes to showing our need for autonomy from the south,' he said to Jane. 'Talk about that at your next Separation meeting.'

Young Jim was being sued. Mr Smith had originally claimed that Jim Macaree had stolen his fishing net at Emu Park, but he had not filed the case so the net in question was then returned to Jim. Smith now claimed the net was his and wanted it returned along with £10 for its detention.

Rees Rutland Jones appeared for Jim and it was shown in evidence that Jim and some of his friends had made the net. When the net was brought into the court, it was revealed that a piece of the original net had been cut off, and a new section added by Smith.

The case was dismissed. Jim, though, on request, agreed to give Smith the new piece that he had added to Jim's net.

Jim was spending much of his spare time at the Fraser's new home in Emu Park, a short horse ride from Coorooman. Jessie was the main attraction for him, although he found he held interests in common with her father. William was more approachable than his own father.

Jim helped plant a row of young Norfolk Pines across the back of the house, which William and Annie decided to call The Pines. They had a brass plaque made and Jim attached it to the timber wall on the front of the house for them. Cane furniture and a few squatters' chairs became the favourite relaxation spot on the long veranda across the front of the home where there was always a breeze. Sometimes though, that breeze reached almost gale force.

Jim and Jessie never tired of the views of the islands, including North and South Keppel on the horizon, but Jim was not good at sitting and relaxing and was forever building or fixing or making things.

For his twenty-first birthday, his parents had presented him with a three-volume set on engineering, carpentry and miscellaneous construction and repair. He would absorb himself in them while Jessie read. Her preferences included Jane Austin's works, but she was working her way through Charles Dickens' books from the bookcase at The Pines.

'Dickens always features some poor creature who's suffering,' she said to Jim. I do prefer Austin's work.'

'And I've had enough of Shakespeare to last me a lifetime,' Jim commented. They both understood the nuances of that comment and chuckled.

James Macaree's 3 Volume set of books

Jim and Jessie sometimes took Jessie's youngest brother, Harold, who was only three years old, to the beach. Jim, with steady hands and great imagination, built the most elaborate sandcastles for him, with turrets, moats and bridges. He and Jessie laughed as Harold's bumbly little fingers tried to decorate the castle with shells, managing only to knock it apart.

The two mothers, Jane and Annie, met regularly to work on wedding plans, with the mother of the bride-to-be leading the way. The date set was still a year away, well after Jessie would turn 21. It was to be held at The Pines, which, although just built, was a favourite with everyone.

In September, Mr Stewart resigned from the North

Rockhampton Council. A major issue to be resolved, once the vacancy was filled, was the renewing of the slaughter yard licence for the Co-operative Butchering Company. Edwin was pro-business, but there was a resistance within the electorate to renewing the licence. Edwin was re-elected by just two votes over Mr Woods.

A short time later, the all-important meeting, with just one item on the agenda, took place. When Edwin arrived home late, somewhat inebriated, he laughed and said, 'Chaotic again, Jane. But it's good to be back.'

Jane didn't want to hear details. Edwin was content. That was enough.

The next day, she and Annie were again meeting to advance wedding plans, when the newspaper was brought in. 'Let's have a little peep at the Council meeting report, Annie.'

They stood together and read under the heading: Slaughter Yard at Kalka.

> *The Mayor: The business is the consideration of this letter from the Co-operative Butchering Company*
> *Alderman Macaree: Alderman Lewis is going to pour oil on the troubled waters.*
> *Alderman Hogan: I move that Alderman Macaree take the chair.*
> *Alderman Kearney: I second it.*
> *Alderman Canovan (To the Mayor): You ought to leave the chair before we appoint another chairman.*
> *Alderman Lewis: I move that Alderman Reaney takes the chair.*
> *Alderman Canovan: I second the amendment.*
> *Alderman Reaney: I won't take the position now.*
> *The Mayor and Alderman Thompson left the room and Alderman Macaree left his seat and walked towards the*

chair, and while doing so he was repeating passages of Shakespeare.

Jane stood back from the newspaper and grinned at Annie. 'They are worse than schoolchildren.'

Nudging Jane's shoulder, she said, 'Let's read on. It's better than any stage comedy.'

Alderman Canovan (as soon as Alderman Macaree had taken his seat at the head of the table): I would remind you that this is not a Theatre Royal, Alderman Macaree; This is a Council Chambers, and we want to do the business of the Council here. Confine yourself to the business of the Council. Might I ask if you are in order in sitting in that chair?
The Chairman: Am I in order? Yes.
Alderman Canovan: You are not in order, and I call upon you to retire.
Alderman Lewis: I move that Alderman Macaree leave the chair.
Alderman Canovan: I second it.
The Chairman: The Town Clerk will tell you whether I am legally in the chair or not.
Alderman Lewis: You are not in the chair until this Board puts you in.
The Chairman: Oh, yes I am. Even if you carried your motion, I would decline to leave the chair.

Jane was giggling softly as she lifted her eyes from the paper and looked at Annie again. 'Oh, those poor souls. They have no idea the games Edwin plays. It's a wonder the meeting ever finished. Let's just read on a little more.'

> *Alderman Lewis: But the motion was never put to the meeting.*
> *Alderman Macaree here resumed his ordinary seat, leaving the chair vacant.*
> *Some inaudible chatter went on.*
> *The Mayor and Alderman Thompson returned, the Mayor taking the chair again. Presently there was a lull and Alderman Lewis exclaimed before sitting down, 'We are to go by our rules, and we are not going to be put down by any tragedian or any quoter of Shakespeare. I for one, at any rate am not going to be bounced.'*
> *On seeing the Mayor in the chair again, Alderman Lewis jumped up and exclaimed: 'You are out of order. You have no right in the chair.'*
> *The Mayor: I ask you to sit down Alderman Lewis. (Alderman Lewis resumed his seat.*
> *Alderman Macaree: We had better send for the police.*

'Enough, Jane, enough,' Annie said, laughing so much she had tears in her eyes. 'Just tell me, did they approve the licence?'

Jane, equally amused, glanced at the bottom of the article. 'It looks that way.'

'So is Edwin like that at home?'

'From the day we were married it's been like living with a whirlwind comedian. Picked up, turned around, off the ground, never sure of what's next or where we'll land. What's it like to live with William?'

'About the opposite, I'd say. Steady, methodical. But he does take risks, calculated ones, I think. He doesn't share much with me though, like Edwin does with you.'

Annie took to reading the newspaper that followed the fortnightly North Rockhampton Council meetings. The reports were never dull. When William arrived home, she'd read them out to him. William's eyesight was poor.

'Do listen, William. It's interesting and it's partly relevant to us.'

General Business.
Alderman Schiekowsky said that some time ago it was decided to call for tenders for the supply of 2000 yards of muck to put in Kalka Street, which was in a dangerous state, in trafficable order, and now that the finances were in a pretty good state the work should be gone on with. He therefore begged to move that tenders be called for at once.
The Mayor: Specify the probable cost.
Alderman Lewis: I beg to second the motion. It will cost about £150.
The Mayor: The motion is, then, that the work be done at a cost not exceeding £150.
Alderman Macaree asked if the work was the first on the list of the works authorised to be carried out, and called on the Town Clerk to produce the documents he was asked to produce at the last meeting.
The Mayor: Kalka Street is second on the list.
Alderman Macaree: Which is the first.
The Mayor: Elphinstone Street.
Alderman Thompson: The first that was passed should be carried out first, then the second.
Alderman Macaree: I move as an amendment that the work be carried out as passed.
Alderman Thompson seconded the amendment.
Alderman Reaney: I believe Ford Street is second on the list.
Alderman Macaree: Let the works be carried out in the order in which they are passed. If what has been said is a lie, let it be contradicted. Why should we come here and lose our time for the sake of fifty town clerks. I do not believe in being humbugged.

> The Mayor: I call you to order.
> Alderman Macaree: I want the truth, the whole truth, and nothing but the truth.
> The amendment was then put and lost by the casting vote of the Mayor.

'Oh,' Annie said, glancing further down the newspaper. She looked up at William who had a crooked smile on his face. 'They just list who voted what. But listen to this.' She began reading again:

> Alderman Reaney: I wish to move an amendment.
> The Mayor: Oh no, you can't. I must put the motion first.
> Alderman Reaney: Can't I move an amendment?
> The Mayor: No. Not after a show of hands.
> Alderman Reaney: I can.
> The motion was then put and carried.
> Alderman Lewis: I move that £50 be granted for Elphinstone Street which is the first on the list now.
> The Mayor seconded the motion and it was carried.

'I'm just skipping another bit, William, where another lot of repairs is discussed and approved but the good bit is coming up now.' Annie read:

> Alderman Macaree: Everybody appears to be having his own little game, so I move that Your Worship lay aside, say £10 for the purpose of purchasing a grindstone to be placed outside the Council Chambers so that each of us can grind our axes there. And if any ratepayer wishes to grind his axe there he can do so. It will be much better than spending money on things that we do not require.
> Alderman Lewis: I move as an amendment –
> Alderman Macaree (interrupting): The motion has not been

seconded.

Alderman Lewis: I move as an amendment that the grindstone be placed at the Botanic Gardens.

Alderman Thompson: I am surprised to hear such opinions enunciated by an old member of this Council. I thought he had more respect for the dignity of the Council than to do such a thing.

Alderman Macaree: A little nonsense now and then is relished by the wisest men. But you are too wise to live.

'Can you believe the shenanigans they go on with, William?'

'It would drive me to madness, Annie. I guess that's why Edwin creates a little light relief at the meetings. Now that the children are in bed, what is for my dinner?'

William did not spend time reading the newspapers because of his eyesight, and the thick lenses of his glasses were not a great help.

While he ate a lamb stew, prepared by their maid, Annie said, 'At the end of that article I was reading the Council seemed to be about to repossess some properties because rates haven't been paid. Can they do that?'

'These are very difficult times. Banks are repossessing, as well as Councils.' William was surprised that Annie was showing an interest in such matters.

'Are we alright?'

'Of course.'

'But you dissolved a partnership.'

William cocked his head on one side. 'Och, aye. So you are reading everything in the paper. Yes, Robert Cheesman and I are going our own ways. Wiser in this climate for me to be responsible for me alone.'

William did not want to unduly alarm Annie, but he himself was alarmed by hearing of the United States of America in the midst of a severe downturn. Like Australia, many of its banks had closed too. He changed the subject.

'Did you see the call for old residents to attend a dinner? You had to be living here more than thirty years to be eligible. I'll wager Edwin will lead the way.'

And so it was. Around sixty men attended the Belmore Arms Hotel, with Edwin playing Master of Ceremonies. Each guest was encouraged to write on their menu the year of their arrival and the name of the ship from which they disembarked. Edwin wrote 1861 and *The Light Brigade*.

Speeches were interspersed with music and songs, where Edwin also contributed. Those present included Messrs T S Bird, Robert Barry, H J Boreham, B L Dibdin, and almost all present were friends and acquaintances of Edwin.

'Rockhampton is known as the City of the three S's,' he said. 'But I like to call it the ABC of Australia, that is, A Beautiful City.' He went on. 'This is a lesson to the bachelors that so many married men could come together after living so many years in one place.

'I have sons who could carry me a mile, and drink a long sleeve of Coorooman beer at the end of it.' This drew considerable laughter. He then recounted his arrival in Rockhampton with 7s and 6d in his pocket, where there was a tiny wharf, and clearing of mangroves along the river was being undertaken.

'The town was a mere collection of humpies, tents, and a few brick houses, and the population was small, the streets were unformed, and Rockhampton was then a mere hotbed of fever and ague. Everyone in this room had something to do with bringing Rockhampton to its present state.'

Edwin then spoke of some of those unable to attend, including Colonel Feez, whom he called Rockhampton's king with the generous heart and ready helping-hand. He next mentioned William Pattison, who, he said, should be presiding over the meeting.

When Mr Harden was called upon to speak, he said he arrived in 1859 and sailed up the river with a black-fellow. While landing he heard a voice speak in French, saying, 'Beware of the blacks as they are dangerous about here.' He initially thought it was the black-fellow talking in French, but discovered it was Mr Thozet, who later became his friend.

Feeling a need to record some family history after this dinner, Edwin demanded a family photo be taken.

The Macaree family: Standing, Ned, Jim and Emma
Seated, Jane and Edwin

1894

Tough Times

1894 did not begin well for Edwin. He was just one in a list of creditors in the Insolvency Court making a claim on the distribution of assets in the estate of the Ellis Brothers, graziers, of Malvern Downs to whom he had loaned money which they were unable to repay.

'Jane, I'm going to put our Emu Park cottage up for rent.'

'Must you?' Jane loved summers at the beach.

'I don't think you understand this financial crisis. It's world wide, Jane. Not just here. Britain, The United States – everywhere – banks are collapsing. We must be careful.'

Jane had never heard Edwin in this mode. She acquiesced in silence.

The ad ran:

> *To Let at Emu Park, Mrs MACAREE'S COTTAGE (2 storied), Furnished. Easy Terms; made lighter for long residence, Apply by letter. Address Mrs MACAREE Coorooman Creek, Emu Park Line.*

The wedding date for Jim and Jessie was set for the 18th December at The Pines at Emu Park, so Jane was hopeful she'd have her cottage back by then.

The Sawmill at Coorooman under Jim's control was doing reasonably well by keeping its head above water financially. But

Edwin was the one who wrote the letter to the Gogango Divisional Board when he heard he was to be fined for snigging timber along the public road. Not that he actually did it, but one of his, or rather, Jim's, employees was guilty, as he explained in his letter.

He stated he always ordered his timber-getters to keep off the public roads unless compelled to use them, which was the case this time.

The public road was so bad, he explained, that the driver had to keep unloading and loading because the wheels kept getting bogged. The bullocks pulled so hard that the coupling and pole-rings broke, so the driver had no recourse but to snig for a short distance, that is, he had to unload the logs and un-bog the dray, fix the coupling then reload the dray by dragging the logs along by chain, which chopped up the roadway even more. He then had to re-load the logs. The workman went through this process several times over.

He asked for the pardon of the Board, saying he would not snig any more logs on the roads.

Edwin explained that the driver's wife was in town under the care of the doctor and consequently the driver had to hurry home to his young children to care for them.

The Chairman, when he was reading Edwin's letter responded:

'I suppose, gentlemen, in the present instance we had better take this explanation and the promise made not to offend again. I move that Mr Macaree be informed that in future under no consideration whatever will we allow timber to be snigged on the road. At the present time he will be excused on account of the circumstances, but under no circumstances hereafter will we allow such a thing to occur.'

Edwin needed something to go his way and was relieved with not having to pay a fine.

Jane was in residence at Coorooman when her friend Annie gave birth yet again; this time prematurely, to a boy, George. Jane rushed up to Rockhampton to support her, but little George died before she arrived.

'Oh, Annie, I am so sorry,' Jane said, with tears in her eyes. The same thing had happened to Jane when she gave birth to Mary at age forty-two. 'I think our worn-out bodies just can't bear little ones when we are this old,' she added, knowing that Annie, who was now forty-two, had given birth eight times. She still had the four boys and Jessie and Millie and they spanned seventeen years of Annie's adult life.

Jane contemplated her own situation while she and Annie clung to each other like marooned sailors to driftwood, fearful of letting go. She'd given birth to seven babies and had lost four of them. She thought only about her losses when she was in situations like this.

She wanted to share her favourite quote from the popular German philosopher, Friedrich Nietzsche: *That which does not kill us makes us stronger.* Her better judgement took over and she thought she'd save that discussion for another day since she didn't feel very strong either.

After Edwin's failure to be re-elected to the North Rockhampton Borough, he decided to nominate for a position on the Gogango Divisional Board, due to a resignation. He was surprised to see that William had done likewise as had another sixteen gentlemen. Neither he nor William was elected.

The Directors of the newly formed Rockhampton Brewery Company Limited, taking over the Coorooman Brewery, together with their staff and a few journalists, enjoyed a celebratory lunch at the Belmore Arms which was owned by Harry Johnson, the Chairman of the Board. They then boarded the train for the visit to Coorooman.

Edwin entertained the carriage-full all the way, pointing to the landscape and telling both the history and the anecdotes relating to the pre-railway days when there was just a handful of residents.

Edwin told the tale of His Royal Highness, the Prince of Wales' visit to the Burton Brewery on the Trent. He flourishingly related how Prince Albert had labelled stout as "excellent", the ale as "delicious" and "very fine". Edwin encouraged his audience to find their own descriptions of the Coorooman brew.

The general verdict of the tastings, therefore, contained similes including 'immense' and 'nice bitter twang'. One of the journalists wondered if the enthusiasm shown was derived from spending too much time in a smoke-filled carriage that built up a thirst.

The trip was followed by a tour, again led by Mr Humphreys, their brewer, and although they had all, including William, done the tour prior, the positive publicity it drew from reporters from other Queensland papers seemed worth it.

While Edwin was pinning his hopes on producing an income from the sawmill and the brewery to see him through the tough times, William was relying on his investments in mining, as well as wool. His latest foray into gold was with the *Gold Fleece Gold Mining Company* producing gold at Mount Larcombe. William was a director of the company. His initial Mount Morgan investment had already rewarded him.

There were now only a few banks in Queensland operational, and even they closed their doors for a few days, not allowing withdrawal of funds. Alarm bells rang loudly for everyone.

As the end of the year drew close, financial stresses or not, for two families, the excitement of the imminent wedding grew.

Nothing was to be spared for Annie and William's first-born child, Jessie Stuart Fraser when she married Jane and Edwin's second son, James. The Pines hosted a fabulous affair on the 18th December with much aplomb.

James Macaree and Jessie Fraser's wedding

1895

Tougher times

With December festivities behind him, Edwin confronted his shocking financial predicament. No-one was purchasing property, or, for that matter, timber or hogsheads of beer. He could not meet his loan repayments with the bank.

'Well, Jane, the time has come to let go. We'll make a comeback when the good times return.' His voice though, Jane noticed, did not hold his usual enthusiasm. His Midas Touch had abandoned him.

She felt a deep sadness when he placed the following advertisement in the Morning Bulletin:

> FOR SALE. READ THIS.
> WANTED, SEPARATE TENDERS for the undermentioned PROPERTIES.
> MUST BE SOLD
> Lot I.-The Cremorne Hotel and Gardens, about seven acres.
> Lot 2.-The "North Rockhampton Times" Printing Office, Dwelling House, and land on which they stand.
> Lot 3.-The Mount Etna Lime Works with 275 acres of Freehold Land ; a bargain.
> Lot 4.-Three acres with House, &c., securely fenced, Musgrave and Painswick Streets, opposite Town Pump.
> Lot 5.-One thousand acres of Land (more or less), with Dwelling House, &c. Dairy, Stockyards (all sawn timber, and securely fenced), with or without the Milking Herd; a

comfortable desirable home, near the Emu Park Railway; permanent water; free from all flood.
Lot 6.-Two acres of Land in East-street, at the corner of East end O'Connell Streets; the only original large block left in East Street.
Lot 7.-The Dwelling House and 1/4 -acre of Land, next to the Presbyterian Manse (Dr Hay's), Bolsover-street.
Lot 8. -The Blacksmith's Shop with Cottage at the back, and two-storey Iron Building, &c, Fitzroy-street, next to the Scariff Hotel and near Fire Brigade Office; and sundry other lands, of which particulars can be had of
EDWIN MACAREE, Sawmills, Coorooman, Emu Park Railway.

Edwin ran this ad a few times a week for weeks on end. But no-one was courageous enough to borrow money in the financial downturn that was smothering not just Australia, but other countries as well. No one was game to predict when it would all end either.

The brewery was still not thriving. Edwin, on behalf of the current shareholders, placed an ad looking for more shareholders in order to raise more capital.

SOCIAL REFORM WANTED TO BE KNOWN by the people of Rockhampton and District that it is the intention of EDWIN MACAREE of the Coorooman Brewery, Emu Park Railway, to PLACE THE BREWERY AT THE DISPOSAL OF THE PEOPLE.
Not having sufficient capital to carry it on himself, he means to make a "virtue of necessity" and let the people make their own beer, as that those who like a glass of good beer and like big Dividends – as they pass by may step in and try the flavour of the Coorooman cheers, and drink their own beer. The Brewery is now replete with all modern

appliances, and right here the people are invited to inspect the Brewery, the water, and the picturesque surroundings. So roll up for old Mac – a thirty-four years' resident and for the People's Brewery, and show me the man that can tread on the tail of his coat.
Hip! Hip! Hurrah! From east and west.
Local Industries and Social Reform.
A Prospectus with an influential Directorate will shortly appear. Cheer, Boy – Cheer.
"Bless my eyes if ever I tries to rob a poor man of his beer."
E. MACAREE, Hon. Sec.

Shortly after, Edwin named the provisional Directors. They included William Fraser and other highly respected and influential townsfolk. The Prospectus stated that they hoped to raise £5000. No shareholder should hold more than twenty shares. Payment for the £1 shares should be made thus: two shillings and sixpence on application, and two shillings and sixpence on allotment. This would ensure the commencement of operations, and no other call should be needed. There was to be equal division of the profits.

Edwin would remain Honorary Secretary and would be a shareholder.

'We need to overcome this adverse publicity,' Edwin told his directors. 'I'm going to have someone experienced test the water to show, once and for all time, that it is quality water along with the ingredients.'

Once subscriptions began, his next step was to advertise that the beer and stout were selling again. He also published a glowing report on the water quality used in the brewing.

Late in November Annie and Jane became grandmothers for the first time, with Jim and Jessie having a baby girl, Violet Muriel. She quickly and affectionately became known as Moo.

1896

Ned, Ned, you should have stayed in bed.

In his own inimitable way, Edwin sued George Bunce, the licensee of the Cremorne Hotel, and tenant, for £18, the value of six hogsheads of beer he claimed were not paid for. He accused George of using insulting language, by saying he would pay 'When he damn well liked.' Edwin produced his books and said he allowed a 10 pence rebate on hogsheads when the money was paid within a reasonable time. The rent, Edwin acknowledged, was paid up.

Delivery dockets were produced, and Bunce's signature was verified by the deliverers of the beer.

George Bunce said he was buying West End and Fitzroy beer and paying £7 10s for 3 hogsheads. When he bought some of Edwin's beer in September, he claimed it was no good, and complained to Edwin, and said he would take no more, as he was losing money on it. At that time he paid Edwin £2 for a week's rent and threatened to close the place if Edwin did not reduce the rent. He said Edwin told him that he wouldn't reduce the rent, but he would give a hogshead or two of beer occasionally if he would buy half of his beer from him.

When the carrier arrived with each of the hogshead deliveries, George claimed Edwin asked him to sign the receipt for the protection of carrier.

'He only sent it to me when he couldn't sell it to anyone else,' George claimed.

He said that this dispute only arose when he had an argument with Edwin over fixing sanitary arrangements at the hotel. When Edwin refused, Bunce said he'd complain and get the licence cancelled.

It was then shown by the Police Magistrate that George Bunce paid £3 for each hogshead from West End and Fitzroy beer and not the amount he'd earlier asserted.

George Bunce's wife also gave evidence, saying they didn't sell much of Macaree's beer as it spoiled their trade. She couldn't recall dates of deliveries, although she agreed with her husband that they'd entered into an agreement for free hogsheads with Edwin instead of lowering the rent.

In judgement, the Magistrate found in favour of Edwin for the amount of £15, with £2 2s professional costs, 10s witnesses' expenses, and 5s 6d court costs.

A short time later, George Bunce appealed, but when the case arose in the Court, George decided to drop it. He was, however, still charged a second set of court costs.

A short time after that, with the now untenable position of having Bunce in charge of the Cremorne Hotel, Edwin knew he had to act. Before a Magistrate in the Licensing Court, a transfer of licence was granted from George Bunce to Edwin Macaree Junior. At least, Edwin thought, his own beer would be sold. But Ned, now thirty-five, would need some support managing staff.

'I can't leave the sawmill, father,' Jim said, pre-empting any request.

'Jane, are you happy to stay at Cremorne again?'

Jane was enjoying life at Coorooman with all the help from the Islander women, and she hosted many visits from friends. She saw the Frasers regularly. The train line and the fast service made all the difference. She could easily travel back and forth, so she acquiesced with grace.

Jim travelled to The Pines for the weekend with his wife, Jessie. Her parents were in residence. Late on the Friday afternoon, they went looking for Hoppy Billy, a well-regarded South Sea Islander with his own sailing boat who regularly brought in fresh fish and oysters. But Hoppy Billy didn't arrive back into Emu Park.

Word spread about 8 pm that two aborigines had come bursting into the hotel with words of urgency about a boat capsizing.

Jim went back into the township while they set up a search party, but there was nothing he could do, so he returned to The Pines. Early Saturday morning when he returned to the township, Jim found the place abuzz with excitement. When he heard what had occurred, he went home and related it to Jessie and her parents.

'Hoppy Billy went out to South Keppel for oysters. He was on his way back with three lads and two Aborigines on board. A big squall came in and tipped them over.'

'How big is his boat?' Jessie asked.

'A twenty-four-footer.' He continued, 'Apparently one of the lads couldn't swim, so Looa, the old black-fellow from North Keppel, grabbed him and put him where he could hold onto the keel. Looa and his son volunteered to swim to shore for help. Hoppy Billy stayed with the three young ones.'

'Risky thing to do,' William said.

'So brave. They reckon old Looa will be awarded a brass breastplate for his bravery. They estimate they were swimming for an hour and a half. They landed somewhere between Tanby Point and Emu Park.

'After Looa and Paddy swam off, the squall eased, and Hoppy Billy encouraged the boys to help him right the boat. They couldn't get the water out because she was sitting too low in the water, but, with constant bailing, they stayed safe. It must have been a miserable night drifting, soaking wet. I heard they got excited when they drifted towards Emu Park. They were so close they could see the lights of the hotel, and even into the ballroom where there was a dance going on. Then they drifted north, and out to sea, poor sods.'

'How frightening,' Jessie said.

'A big crowd stayed up all night watching and waiting. Just after daylight, they saw the rescue boat. It was skippered by Mr Long, the headmaster, and it was towing another boat. Then everyone got despondent. They couldn't see any sign of life in Hoppy Billy's boat. But when they realised that all four were safe, well, it's a wonder we didn't hear the cheering from here.'

William said, 'I'm so glad he's fine. And his boat?'

'I think it's lost all its rigging.'

'He's such a decent chap. Always happy to do a deal. I think we should set up an appeal and help him recover,' William suggested. Others had the same thought.

An article appeared in the paper a few days later.

> APPEAL FUND FOR REPAIRING RECENTLY DAMAGED BOAT OF MR 'BILLY' SMITH OF EMU PARK.
> TO CENTRAL QUEENSLANDERS and Rockhamptonites: There is no better known identity and seaman than "Billy" Smith of Emu Park.
> Life has its "ups and downs" and Bill has his share 'tis true. It is only a few days ago that Billy launched his boat for summer pleasuring, oystering and fishing on the Bay, after having spent weeks of toil and care on making his craft (his only means of subsistence) sweet and pleasurable to those who love the briny; and sad to relate the recent rough windy weather has dismantled his craft of sails, masts, jib and decking to such an extent as to require some thirty-odd

> *pounds to make her seaworthy again.*
> *Towards this purpose a local committee has formed, namely, Mr William Bell, Chairman, Mr P F Goodwin, Hon Secretary and Treasurer, and members, Messrs P Allan, T W Biddulph and T Myers.*
> *All sympathisers kindly forward subscription to the secretary who will have same acknowledged in the columns of the "Morning Bulletin."*
> P. F. GOODWIN

Queensland's new Governor, Lord Lamington, went on tour. He planned not only to visit Rockhampton, but also Emu Park. In preparation, Edwin organised a wild Coorooman welcome, even though he knew the Governor was not making a stop there. The guests on the train included MLAs Curtis and Callan, as well as Colonel Feez, Mr Littler, the Mayor, and around forty other gentlemen.

The Morning Bulletin reported:

> *The only special incident on the trip down was the appearance at Coorooman of the old warrior, Edwin Macaree and a number of would-be warriors with flags waving and a mock battery of sawdust on which were planted several imitation pieces of naval warfare, in the shape of cannons, manned by two gunners.*
> *The party were much entertained by this unexpected demonstration as the train moved past.*

When Jane read this, she was relieved that she was still at Cremorne, otherwise she had no doubt Edwin would have roped her into playing a role. But at Cremorne, she could plainly see that the running of the hotel was too much for Ned. He was too gentle to command the respect needed, both by staff and by customers.

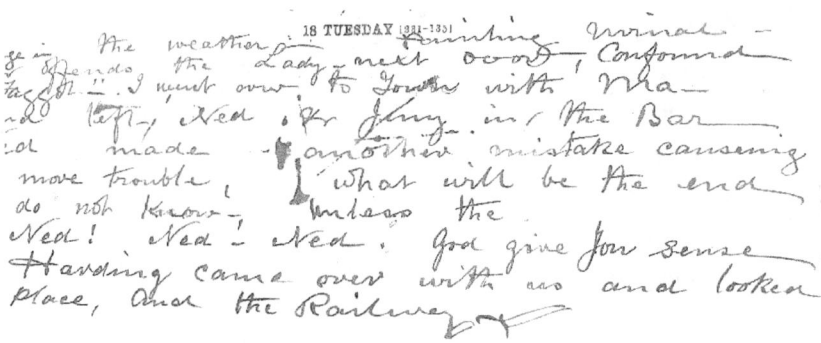

Edwin's diary. Ned makes a mistake at the hotel

... I went over to Town with Ma – and left Ned ... in the Bar. Ned made another mistake causing more trouble. What will be the end I do not know. Unless the ... Ned! Ned – Ned. God give you sense.

Edwin could see that profits were non-existent. He sought out and found someone willing to take on the role of licensee so Ned could return to his job with the other men tending the cattle. In November, the Licencing Court approved the transfer to Ellen Dwyer.

This was not a good year for Ned. He was drinking far too much and testing Jane and Edwin's patience. He'd branded the wrong cattle and he'd moved the wrong herd, and was becoming accident-prone.

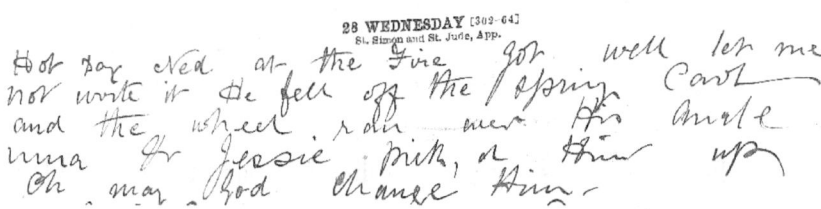

Edwin's diary. Ned falls from spring cart

Hot day. Ned at the Fire. Not well. Let me not write it. He fell off the spring cart and the wheel rolled over his ankle. Emma and Jessie pick'd Him up. Oh may God change Him.

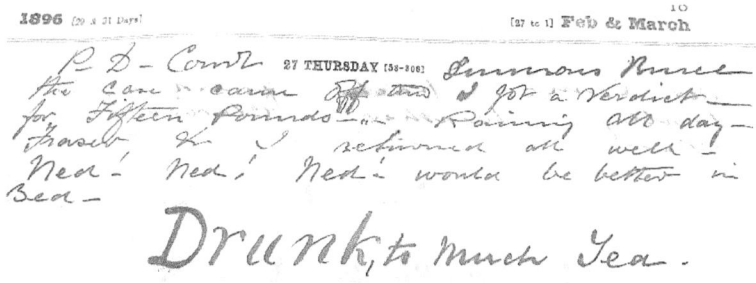

Edwin's Diary. Ned had drunk too much.

...Raining all day – Fraser and I returned. All well. Ned! Ned! Ned! Would be better in Bed.

William often saw Jim at The Pines on weekends.

'I'm experimenting with mangrove bark for tanning by extracting the tannin bark. I'm paying Islanders to collect it for me. It's a bit reddish, but it's readily and cheaply available,' he told Jim. 'And I'm installing a bone mill at the tannery too. I get the bones from next door at the Lake's Creek works at no cost. There's a ship sails from Nerimbera every month for New Zealand. The crushed bones sell well as fertiliser.'

Jim could see that where his father was going backward with what were once assets, but now anchors around his neck, William was forging ahead.

'I'm off to England,' William told Jim, 'to see if I can interest them in the mangrove bark for tanning there. I can show them samples and hopefully develop an export business.'

During that trip, William met with no luck because the English tanners preferred the wattle bark.

1897–1898

Jessie's brother, Donald

Edwin continued to appear in court, occasionally on the Bench as the actual magistrate, but more often on the floor as the defendant. They were still tough times for him, and he succeeded again in court by collecting partial funds for rent owing on one of his business properties.

Edwin had other financial issues. He wrote and complained to the Gogango Divisional Board. Their employees, he claimed, were driving his cattle to the pound when the Board's employees found them beyond the Coorooman property boundaries and it was happening too frequently.

'Jane, they've taken five head with the calves this time. And someone has been taking down or breaking my fences. How dare they.'

'How dare who, Edwin?'

'I don't care … lazy travellers who can't be bothered putting fences back up when they pass through by road. The Board is ultimately responsible. They've held all these cattle for three days without bothering to notify me. They expect me to pay. They are using my rate money to employ men to drive my cattle far from where they found them. Ridiculous.'

Discussion by the members of the Board when they received Edwin letter was varied, but Mr Jones thought the ranger might use discretion in such cases.

'The ranger found some of Mr Macaree's cattle on the road.

He went and told Mrs Macaree who got a boy to run all the cows the lad could find back into the paddock,' Mr Beak, an alderman said.

The Chairman said the ranger had a job to do and should do it.

Mr Boyer pointed out that the owners had roads running through their selections, and people passing through just tossed the rails down on the ground. These are the cases where the ranger should be lenient. Edwin was let off lightly.

To worsen conditions for Edwin, there was a tick plague. It began in Gracemere but soon spread in the hot steamy conditions. All cattle owners were forced to put their herds through a dip, a new innovation, to try to control the pest. It was both costly and time-consuming.

The brewery was not selling enough beer, so Edwin again advertised it for sale, but there were no takers.

Donald Fraser, Jessie's brother, now almost twenty-two, had taken up bicycle racing the previous year. The Union Cycling Club had been formed, with six founding members, not in any antagonism towards the existing Gymnasium and Cycling Club, but to foster more competition, they claimed. The club grew to some eighty members and partnered with Rugby Union to lay down a new track. In return, the cycling members supported the Rugby club to carry out their weekly sports meets during their season.

A year after formation, the first cycling club annual general meeting was held, and the club showed a profit from the sports days it held. At this meeting, Donald was elected Captain.

A request was made for women to join. Donald seconded the motion, and, while they were not full members, women could now ride with the club.

During the previous twelve months, when Donald was a

novice, he was initially leniently handicapped, and succeeded in the races he entered with ease, winning three heats, three finals, and gaining one third out of seven starts. The favourites, the reports said, never looked dangerous.

Once handicapped appropriately, he continued to win convincingly.

Don went off to Sydney with a young cyclist, Ben Goodson, who was hailed as a possible international star. Donald, who'd been racing at that time for less than a year, won two handicaps against intercolonial competitors. Both he and Ben rode Imperial Rovers.

After the first AGM, Donald said, 'I'm going to set a record for the ride from the Post Office to the Hector Hotel and back.'

'How far is that?' a club member asked?

'Fifteen miles.'

And the following Saturday afternoon at 3.30 pm, with the road in fair condition, Donald set out on his Red Bird weighing 25 lbs, geared to 76 inches. Ben Goodson acted as timekeeper and other officials watched along the way. He arrived at the Hector Hotel at 3.51 pm and turned back for the Post Office against a strong headwind. It took him 23 minutes and 54 seconds for the return trip, taking a total of 44 minutes and 53 seconds, axing 3 minutes from the previous record.

Time and time again, Donald won his races, over several different distances, and on different cycles, with varying handicaps imposed.

As captain, Donald often chaired committee meetings where his leadership skills were being honed. He'd learnt from his father, whom he helped in business, that there was winning, and there was nothing else.

Don and his cycling competitor, Ben Goodson, attended another international sports carnival in Sydney. Bill Martin, an American and a world champion was present, and he had a bundle of Seattle newspapers which he shared. They were full of glowing accounts of the Klondyke gold rush.

Don arrived back in Rockhampton fired up. He had hoped to travel to Klondyke with another cyclist, but when he dropped out, Don decided to go it alone. He approached his father.

'Would you invest in a prospective gold mine? I'm going to Klondyke and staking a claim. We could share the profits if you'll back me.'

But William rejected the idea. Undaunted, Don paired up with another mate, Hugh Walker, a young engineer, who had been investigating the Cawarral gold for a Scottish syndicate.

The Union Cycling Club Chairman said, 'If you could ride a bike after reaching Juneau City, you'd make short work of it. We wish you every success in bringing riches from the Canadian Eldorado to Rockhampton.'

The following month, William escorted Don to Melbourne and farewelled him off on the *Leura* sailing to Vancouver.

In Vancouver, Don and Hugh set about collecting the equipment they'd need for the trek to Klondyke. This included parts for a boat that they'd have to build when they arrived in Yukon.

From Vancouver they sailed for Skagway. The ship was overloaded. It was carrying 150 horses, mules and cattle, as well as many passengers. It pitched and rolled in the rough seas and the poor livestock were tossed from one side of the deck to the other. Night was filled with the cries of terrified animals, not to mention terrified passengers. Amazingly only one cow lost its life.

Once at Skagway, the ship's captain said to them, 'You have just arrived at the worst town on earth, past, present or future, and I advise you to stay on board if you don't want to be doped, robbed or murdered.'

On the ship with Don and Hugh was Frank Slavin, a

champion Australian boxer. He defied the warning and went ashore with a mate to find the gambling tables. Don somehow found himself the witness to a row between Soapy Smith and Slavin. Soapy Smith was the leader of a gang who robbed miners returning from the goldfields. He was as infamous there as Ned Kelly was in Australia. Fortunately, Slavin found his way safely back to the ship with Soapy, and Don had the extraordinary experience of shaking the hand of Soapy Smith, the same hand that usually held a menacing gun. Shortly after that, though, some other ruffian shot Soapy dead.

Having replenished supplies, the ship sailed for Dyea, located a little north of Skagway, where everyone disembarked and began the trek for the dreaded Chilkoot Pass. The climb was so daunting that even those with limited funds soon paid for porterage.

At Lake Lindeman Don and Hugh assembled their boat and loaded up, waiting for the ice to melt. The boat leaked a little, but the two landed in Dawson City twelve days later, having managed to get through the White Horse rapids, which many others didn't. Dawson City had a population of 50,000 men who had come from all parts of the globe.

The major leases were on Bonanza Creek which joined the Klondyke River about twenty miles north of Dawson City. Don and Hugh met up with a Scotsman, Alexander McDonald, who was willing to allow his claim to be leased for 50 percent of the gold mined during the winter months. They took up the offer and did reasonably well out of it. When they were ready to move on, they still had to wait for the ice to thaw before they could travel. When they did, they were forced to carry their own equipment since no pack animals were available.

Hugh Walker, Don's mate, wrote a letter to his family.

I was wakened at three o'clock this morning to receive your letter. Day and night are all the same here, you know. There will be an immense amount of gold come out of here next year. I have just been on one claim where I picked up little nuggets scattered around like a wheat field. We are cleaning-up tonight and will get about $3000 from this wash. I am working very hard, and will leave with a full survey and accurate information of every claim on the best creeks. It is very hard work continually climbing mountains as high as Ben Nevis, and all the time sinking to the ankles in moss. My health is perfect and I am as hard as nails with a great appetite. The trouble here is getting about. We must foot it all the way and carry everything. It costs a dollar per pound to get food over to my last camp, and we had to hump back 30 lb. apiece for twenty miles over a hill about 4000 feet high. After a day with me Donald Fraser just drops down anywhere and is asleep in a moment. He is well. I was up a good deal of the night watching the sluicing and cleaning up.

The gold in this claim is not large — generally the size of a grain of wheat. It looks very pretty lying in the sluice boxes with the water rushing over it. We cleaned up about 300 oz. last night for a two days' run. We will have close on 600 oz planted under the stove by the end of the week. Robbery is almost unknown and a drunken man is seldom seen. For a long time there was nothing to drink, and when it did arrive a dollar a drink is rather an impossible price. Corruption and bribery are rampant. Men stand for hours in a long row outside the post office or the Gold Warden's office waiting to get in.

Of course five dollars to a policeman or a clerk gets you served at once. Unless some change is made miners must leave the country or have a big upheaval. The Government officials must all be getting very wealthy. Donald Fraser was in fine feather yesterday.

He shot a bear while we were at the head of Eldorado Creek and felt quite proud of his achievement. At dinner his pride was shared by us all when we luxuriated in bear steak. I had a piece of roast beef yesterday — the first fresh meat since leaving the coast. One slice for Donald and myself costs just 20s. (A friend) who is not *very well got a bottle of whisky and water for which he paid $3 10s. Teetotallers have the best of it. The weather is very hot during the day and the season is exceptionally dry, so bush fires are common. The moss covering the country takes fire like tinder and the numerous travellers are careless about camp fires. It is a strange sensation standing on ice with the perspiration pouring down one's face. We have not an hour's dark in the twenty-four, which is quite refreshing. Everything here is paid by gold dust and nuggets. I intend to come home the way I came – namely, via Victoria – instead of via St Michael's, and, all going well, you should receive a cable from me from Victoria on the 1st September, and I should be in England about the middle of October.*

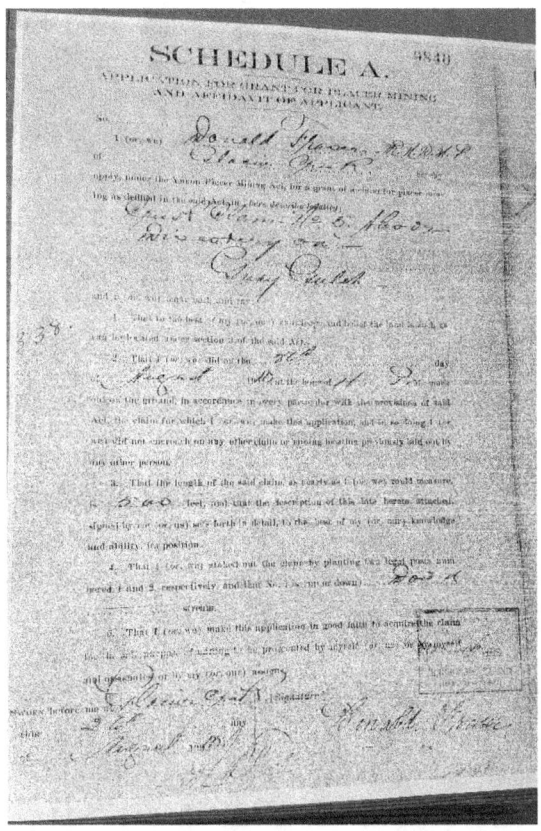

*Donald Fraser's first claim at Klondyke
(photo, courtesy R & C Jensen)*

with a new partner, Frank Martin. They found gold on the claim, but costs were high. Don left Frank at the lease while he travelled back to Dawson City to arrange credit, which took some time. While waiting, Don wrote home and explained the trip to get there.

> '... I saw a clean up of gold after two days washing of poor wash, and they got 282 oz; this was considered a small return, as they have got as much as $28,000 worth in the same quantity of wash. Everything is paid with gold dust here, and when a man goes in and has a drink he hands his sack of dust to the bar-tender, who weighs out the quantity and returns him his sack. Of course a man does not know how much is taken, and a great deal of swindling is carried on. A drink of beer or whisky costs a dollar and a lemon squash 50 cents. A meal costs from two and a half to five dollars, according to whether you want steak and eggs or not. Board by the week costs on thirty-six dollars, and a bed (no blankets) two and a half dollars, with blankets five dollars. So you can guess that one cannot live in this country for nothing. Many men who came in a couple of years ago are now worth from $300,000 to $500,000. The richest man in the district is Alex Macdonald who owns a great number of claims and he is estimated to be worth $15,000,000. This man came here a couple of years ago, and was worth about $1000; now he is a millionaire in pounds five times over.
> All the country round the Klondyke district that is worth anything is pegged off, and I expect I will have to go up to the Stewart River before I can peg anything of any value. A most peculiar feature of this country is that alluvial gold is found right up on the top of the hills on what is called bench claims; and on the French Gulch and Skookum bench claims the miners are rocking out with an ordinary cradle 1000 dollars worth daily. I pegged a bench claim off last week, but as the locality is not yet prospected I cannot tell whether it is worth anything.

The trails here are very bad, being wet and boggy with the moisture thawing out of the ground and we have to walk everywhere we go. We find it very tiring. We usually start out on our journey about six o'clock at night, so as to travel in the cool, and as we have perfect daylight all night we have no difficulty in finding the trail. The temperature runs up to over 80 degrees in the shade, so it is no joke travelling in the day time. I have decided to stay here this winter, so you must not be anxious if you do not receive any letters from me for a couple of months at a time, as the mail runs very irregularly in the winter from Dawson. I have got plenty of tucker, and I intend joining another fellow and going up to the Stewart River to take up a claim as there are good reports from that place. I think I will be able to make a good lot of money here in the next twelve months as there is sure to be a boom next year.

A great number of the claims cannot wash up as there is a shortage of water in most of the creeks, and consequently the output of gold will not be as great as estimated but will reach $12,000,000 or $15,000,000 and probably next spring this quantity will be doubled.

The Government charge royalty of ten percent on all gold taken out besides many other charges, which reduce the real value of claims, but notwithstanding this sales have been made at $600,000 for claim 500 feet long at Eldorado. On account of the royalty of twenty percent which is charged, a great quantity of gold is smuggled out of the country so as to escape paying it.

All the shafts I have been down have been in frozen ground, and it looks awfully pretty to see the walls encased in a sheet of clear ice, and icicles hanging from the roof of the drives. A fire of wood is lit on this frozen ground or washdirt, and when thawed it is taken out in the usual way and dumped in a heap, where it becomes frozen again. This is thawed again by the sun in summer, and washed in a sluice drain with ripples which catch the gold.

I like the climate very well and do not notice the cold in the slightest although we often have the water frozen half an inch thick in the morning. I was travelling the other night carrying my

> *coat on my arm, and when passing a creek noticed that there was coating of ice on it half an inch thick, yet I did not feel the cold in the slightest.*

Don asked to be remembered to all his friends. He enclosed a wild rose with the words: There are thousands growing everywhere.

On Don's return trip to the lease, after securing finance and posting his letter, he felt ill, but when he arrived back Frank Martin restored his wellbeing by telling him they'd found decent gold, worth £500 to £600 per day. This was the rate of measurement.

The ground they mined was still somewhat frozen so they thawed it by lighting fires and heating boulders. The dirt could then be taken out and cradled.

Once the financial returns dropped they sold the claim, purchased another, and again made a good find, which they kept secret till they could secure the adjoining claims. They bought in, though, too heavily, paying 10 percent interest. Someone else therefore made the greater profits, while Don and Frank Martin did all the work.

Don again wrote home, praising his earlier experiences with Hugh, who'd been representing an English syndicate. He spoke of the mining, the methods, and especially the graft and corruption.

> *... the laws of the Dominion are rotten and cannot be relied on, as they are being continually altered. ... Another cause of complaint is the way some officials treat the miners. In one case a man found out that a claim on El Dorado Creek had been pegged off but not registered, as the man who first staked it had left before the creek had been proved so rich. The miner restaked it and went to register, but was told that he had made a mistake, as it was*

> *already recorded. He therefore went away, and immediately he did so the official went up the creek and staked it off for himself, and kept the claim. This kind of thing is quite common here and presumably the officials are allowed to do it. It is certain that they have all the best claims.*

Don actually enjoyed the climate and said:

> *...the winter is not half so bad ... although one wants to be properly clothed to stand it and look after oneself. The glass runs down to 60 or 70 degrees below zero in a cold snap.*

He wore heavy woollen underwear, three pairs of socks covered by a pair of German stockings, along with buckskin moccasins, and a thick woollen suit in these conditions.

He explained how and when to travel and what to expect. He said, though, that if you have constant work in Queensland you might be just as well off staying there. He listed the costs:

> *Rockhampton to Dawson, steamer fare £40, outfit consisting of eight months' provisions and clothing for winter £60, and about £30 for packing over Chilkoot Pass from Linderman to Dawson and freight, with about £50 to £60 for hotel expenses. A meal in Dawson costs from $2.50 to $10, eggs 4 dollars a dozen, ... and everything equally high. A man wants 15 dollars a day to stand that class of thing. I am now in splendid health and over 12 stone in weight.*

The Frasers delighted in hearing from their son and sharing with friends. They affectionately kept each and every letter.

They let out The Pines to their friends, the Paterson family, in the early Queensland summer. Emu Park was hit full on by the gale-force winds of a cyclone. The chimney gave way and crashed through the roof into the kitchen. Everything in it was wrecked, but, fortunately, no one was in the room at the time. Other homes and buildings sustained even more severe damage than did the Fraser's home.

1899

William and Annie Fraser were relieved that the wool-scouring business was thriving, as were William's other investments, which he was able to off-load when he judged it was the correct time. They were spending more and more time at their home in Phillip Street, Emu Park.

Their spirits were lifted when they heard Donald, after twenty months away, was arriving home.

Donald, naturally, was ebullient with stories. After the initial town greetings from friends, his parents whipped him away to The Pines at Emu Park for a rest, where he caught up with his brothers and his sisters, Jessie and Millie.

'Yes, I've left my partner in charge back there,' he said. There was a barrage of questions. 'We have nine claims, and they've got to be worked or you lose them. One hundred hours per week on each claim is necessary, and that isn't asking too much.'

He explained to his father, 'I've got a hydraulic concession, which means we can move large quantities of earth. Most of the claims are alluvial. But we've also got a quartz claim.'

Annie, concerned that her son looked lean, although toughened, asked what he'd been living on.

As Donald wolfed down a large steak from Coorooman, he said, between mouthfuls, 'Well, mainly bacon and beans. Let me give you some idea why. Beef and moose and caribou in United States dollars costs one to one and a quarter dollars per pound. Flour is about $16 per 100 lbs, butter about $2 per lb. I saw a watermelon sell for $35. We made our own bread. And drank lots of tea and coffee.'

Annie's eyes were wide with disbelief.

Seeing her expression, Donald added, 'A shave, haircut, and bath cost $7.50. That's about £1.10s.'

William took over the interrogation. 'Tell us about living standards then.'

'Oh, we built ourselves a log cabin. That will be excellent when I return. I wish I could describe to you the sight of the colours and movement of the Aurora Borealis on a winter's night. Magnificent is the only word I can think of.'

'And your nearest town is Dawson City?'

'Ah, the customs there. You actually pay $1 to dance with a girl and have a drink, and the girl takes 25 cents of this amount.'

Don's younger brothers, Willie 15, Percy 13, and Harold, only 9, were wide-eyed, hearing this.

'How will you manage the trek back in when you return?'

'They've built a railway from Skagway to Bennett over the White Pass. That means I don't have to tackle the Chilkoot Pass again.'

'And what are your plans for the return?'

'I'll head off early next year. I should arrive by June at the latest. That will allow Frank Newton, my partner, to travel back to England while I take charge.

Jessie boldly asked, 'Did you make lots and lots of money, Don?'

He laughed. He was very fond of his sister. 'Some of the claims were rich and returned $77 to the lb.,' he said, giving little away. 'And it's close to the surface.'

When Don returned to Rockhampton from Emu Park, reporters were keen to interview him. He was considered quite an adventurer and hero. He rattled off more of the facts and figures. After that he was asked:

Q: And did you meet with any incidents worth quoting?
Don: There was one poor fellow who lost his arms and hands through being frostbitten. He got wet and was unable to crawl to his camp. He had only been out for four hours, when found, and was simply frozen hard. Wonderful to relate, although after great exertion and attention, he was brought to, and is now alive, but out of the country. The miners got up a subscription and sent him away. I myself got my face, hands and legs frostbitten, but not seriously. I immediately changed and looked after myself.
Q: Would you advise anyone to go to Klondyke?
Don: Candidly I would not unless he has something to go to there or is an old-timer returning. There is nothing in it, for as I said at first, most of the claims have been taken up.

Donald answered many more questions from the curious reporter, and concluded by saying that he would make the return journey via London, but would be home for Christmas.

The other bonus for the year was that Donald's sister, Jessie, and husband Jim had their first son, Ronald Edwin.

1900–1905

Don picked up two partners while in England; Messrs Newton and Cobham. When they travelled from England back to the Klondyke, they carried with them a complete saw-milling plant to cut timber for the shafts. They were now also using a steam thawing plant in order to continue mining through the winter months. They had eight or nine claims between them and were bringing out some exceptionally good gold.

Don sent a photo home of himself fully rigged out in winter gear complete with luxurious fur hat with ear flaps.

Through his son and daughter-in-law and good friend, William, Edwin kept abreast of Donald's activities, although letters home to William were few and far between from his son.

Donald Fraser at Klondyke
Photo: courtesy Rockhampton Regional Library History Centre

Edwin sued August Eisman who had defaulted on payments on a property purchased from Edwin. It was a mixed outcome.

'I would rather have the money, Jane, than this title deed,' Edwin said, waving the papers in the air. 'It was a hollow victory.'

Jane had watched Edwin's financial struggle over the past years. She wasn't sure if his newly-developed cantankerous nature was because his assets were diminishing, or because he was sixty-five and his rheumatism was playing havoc with him. They were resident at Coorooman, and the brewery was languishing through lack of support. Part of the property had been sold, although a large chunk remained. The sawmill struggled but kept afloat.

There was a knock on the door. One of the employees reported to Edwin that Jack Albert, a South Sea Islander fisherman living along Coorooman Creek, about seven miles away, had died. Edwin learnt that he'd recently been admitted to hospital in Rockhampton, but had been discharged. Jack lived with his partner Ida and had been complaining of pains in both his head and stomach.

Edwin sent a telegram to the Police Magistrate, who sent Constable Deevey to investigate. The constable, hearing the information, decided the death was natural, so he buried Jack's body near his camp, above the flood line.

When 1901 rolled around, while Edwin watched and heard the Federation celebrations, he said to Jane, 'There goes the Separation movement for all time. With all the country's colonies forming the Federation, they've become States in their own right. Our efforts have been for nought.' He took of swig of scotch and plonked the glass down.

She hated to see him like this.

The next piece of bad news came when they heard that a

swagman who'd been camping on the old stage in the abandoned Cremorne Gardens fell through a hole and received serious injuries.

'That trapdoor should have had a cover over it, Jane. Just because the place is closed doesn't mean you forget things like that.'

A short time later, one of Edwin's employees, Charlie, ran amok. He stripped naked, walked into the Coorooman kitchen, and smashed crockery. Neither Jane nor Edwin were home at the time, but staff were terrified. Charlie then wandered around the neighbourhood armed with a knife and a large sapling, threatening anyone he came across. Finally, Mr Ingham of Inghamstown, with some help, captured him and tied him up before calling the Emu Park police.

'He's in hospital, Jane. Maybe it was something he drank? Who knows?'

Before long, Edwin was advised that a case was being brought against him by Medland Mitchell for employing an Islander boy named Charlie Santo, without indentures, which Edwin denied. This was a different Charlie from the one who ran amok.

His good friend, Rees R Jones defended him in court.

Edwin arrived home at Coorooman from the court case, seeming satisfied, but all he would say was that he had the best solicitor in town. Jane waited for the newspaper to be delivered via the train, to read about it for herself. The paper, she'd learnt, was more thorough and more objective than Edwin.

Medland Mitchell, the paper said, was an Inspector of Pacific Islanders and the first witness. He was also the plaintiff. The prosecutor was Mr Pattison.

Mr Jones (Edwin's solicitor, to Mr Mitchell): You are a common informer, then.

> M. Pattison (The plaintiff's solicitor): Come, don't have any of that. (To the witness) Do you know Mr. Macaree?
> Witness (Mr Mitchell): I do.
> Mr. Macaree: More than I do. I don't know him, and I don't want to.
> Mr Jones: You keep quiet.

Jane paused in her reading, sipped her tea, and thought it extraordinary that Edwin's own solicitor, Mr Rees Jones, had to ask him to be quiet. She read on:

> Witness said he knew a Kanaka named Charlie Santo. On the 26th of June he was on the defendant's property at Coorooman Creek. The Kanaka was sawing wood. Witness had made a search of the Divisional Board's Office and also at the Lands Office. The portion upon which the Kanaka was working tallied with that occupied by Mr Jaggard. The Kanaka told witness for whom he was working. Mr. Logan, a sugar farmer at Yeppoon was with witness at the time. There was about half a cord of firewood where the defendant was at work.
> Mr Jones: When did you become a common informer?
> Witness: When did I become a common informer?
> Mr Jones: Yes. My question was plain enough.
> Witness: What do you mean by a common informer?
> Mr Jones: You are going about seeking to lay informations, are you not?
> Witness: Is there anything dishonourable in that?
> Mr Jones: Are you doing it?
> Witness: Yes. Is there anything unlawful in it?
> Mr Jones: Not unlawful; but it is disgraceful.
> Witness: Is it? That may be your opinion.
> Mr Jones: Where do you come from?
> Witness: The Mackay district.

> Mr Jones: And what do you call yourself?
> Witness: A labour agent
> Mr Jones: A labour agent of what?
> Witness: I have been three years in the Government service as a recruiting agent.
> Mr Jones: And you say you saw this Kanaka on Mr Jaggard's land.
> Witness: Yes.
> Edward Percival Logan said he was in sugar farming residing at Yeppoon. He knew Charlie Santo. On the 20th of June he was with Mr Mitchell at the defendant's place between a quarter and a half mile from the sawmill. The Kanaka was cutting firewood.
> Mr Jones: I suppose you know it was Mr Jaggard's land he was on?
> Witness: I did not know and I did not care, Mr Jones.

Dr F H V Voss, Inspector of Pacific Islanders and Assistant Immigration Agent at Rockhampton, stated he knew the defendant who owned the Coorooman sawmill and brewery. Charlie Santo had not entered an agreement to work for Mr Macaree nor into any agreement.

Charlie Santo who was sworn on the Bible said he was a native of Samoa. He saw Mr Mitchell at the Yeppoon plantation and also Mr Logan. He also saw them at Coorooman Creek. He was cutting wood there. He said it was for himself.

> Mr Macaree: Nothing of the sort.
> Mr Jones: He said "for himself."
> Mr Pattison: Nothing of the sort. That is not what he means. I shall have to deal with that man as a hostile witness.
> Mr Jones: He is not a hostile witness.
> Mr Pattison: You can never get these Kanakas to give these

shows away. I ask the Bench under the 16th Section of the Evidence Discovery Act to allow me to treat him as a hostile witness. Then I will show what he told Mr Mitchell and Mr Logan. The witness has made a false statement, and I shall have to contradict it.

(To the witness) Did you tell Mr Mitchell and Mr Logan that you were working for Mr Macaree?

Witness (Charlie Santos): No. I no say such a thing.

Mr Pattison: Do you mean to say that you did not tell them that?

Witness: No I work for myself

Mr Pattison: Then I shall put Mr Mitchell and Mr Logan back into the box.

Mr Jones: You cannot do that. In the first place the man was not on Mr Macaree's land.

Mr Macaree: I never saw the man in my life before.

Mr Pattison: That is all very well. I ask the Bench, under section 10 of the Evidence Discovery Act that I be allowed to call these witnesses again.

Mr Jones: Suppose he did call these two witnesses, how does that further the case one bit? What the man might have said in his absence does not affect Mr Macaree. It is neither law, justice, nor equity to admit such evidence.

Mr Pattison: The man made a statement to both Mr Mitchell and Mr Logan, and now he goes back it.

Mr Jones: Who would believe, Mr Mitchell?

Mr Pattison: I have very good reason for believing that the Kanaka is saying differently from what he did for a very good reason.

Mr. Jones: You have no right to say that.

Mr Pattison: What this man is saying this morning he has been frightened into.

Mr Mackean (Magistrate): The evidence will be allowed.

Mr. Mitchell was then recalled.

Mr Pattison: I ask that it be noted that this witness is being called by permission of the Bench.
Mr Jones: And I object to his being called by permission of the Bench, because the Bench has no right to allow such a thing.
Mr. Pattison: He is being called by the permission of the Bench to prove that the Kanaka made a statement at some other time inconsistent with his present depositions.
Mr. Mitchell, examined by Mr. Pattison, said that on the 20th of June he saw the Kanaka and spoke to him.
Mr. Jones: Was Mr. Macaree present?
Mr. Pattison: Never mind about that. I have leave to examine this witness.
Mr. Jones: You are not going to foist this evidence upon the Bench in this way. I will not sit here tamely and allow such a thing to be done.
Witness (Mr Mitchell): It was not necessary for me to see Mr Macaree at all.
Mr. Jones: You hold your tongue, sir, or I will ask the Bench to deal with you Do I understand the Bench to say that it will admit as evidence anything that was said behind Mr. Macaree's back? It is contrary to one of the first principles of justice.

Jane paused again. She understood why Edwin was so appreciative of his solicitor. She was in awe that the court reporter could keep up with the statements being made. Her head hurt, but she was determined to finish.

Mr. Pattison: I have evidence to show that the Kanaka contradicted himself and gave a statement inconsistent with his present testimony. The Act we are dealing with does not say whether the defendant is to be present or not. (To the witness) What did he tell you?

Mr Jones: I object. This is one of the most extraordinary things I ever heard of in my life.

Mr. Mackean (to the Deposition Clerk) Take a note of Mr Jones's objection, and let the witness answer the question.

Witness: In the course of conversation Santo told me that he was cutting wood for Mr. Macaree on contract and that Mr Macaree paid him.

Mr. Jones: Did he volunteer that statement?

Witness: He did. Of course I asked him.

Mr. Jones: You wouldn't be a common informer if you didn't.

Mr. Pattison: Oh, I say, don't let us have any more of that.

Mr. Mackean (to Mr. Jones): It does no good. This is not a vindictive action. The man is simply doing his duty.

Mr. Jones: We will see all about that. (To the witness) Have you ever been in Rockhampton before?

Witness: Yes, four years ago last May. I think a few of them know me.

M. Jones: Did you get any money on that occasion?

Witness: Yes.

Mr Jones: Did you get any from Mr Johnson, who was keeping the Royal Hotel then?

Witness: Yes.

M. Jones: And it has never been paid?

Witness: No, not yet.

Mr. Jones: You are in the habit of giving dishonoured cheques?

Witness: No, but this has nothing to do with this case.

Mr Jones: Never you mind whether it has or whether it has not. It was never paid?

Witness: No: but that was no fault of mine.

M Jones: You gave a cheque, and you had no funds in the bank to meet it?

Witness: Not at the time it was presented.

Mr Pattison: How long was it held?

Witness: Four years before it was presented. I asked them not to present it for a little while, and they sent it up by the next boat.

Mr Jones: It was dishonoured?

Witness: There were not sufficient funds to meet it. There was only £3 then, but there was plenty of money afterwards.

Mr Mackean: I do not see what this has to do with the case.

Mr Jones: I am going to object to this man's evidence, and I shall keep on objecting.

Mr Mackean: You have no authority under the Government to prosecute?

Witness: No, sir.

Mr. Pattison: It is not necessary.

Mr Mackean: And you are a Polynesian labour agent dealing with the employers of Polynesians?

Witness: Yes. We have heavy crops up north, and we want all the labour we can get.

Mr. Jones: What's the meaning of all this? I object to all this padding.

Mr Pattison: The Bench asked the question and the witness has a right to reply.

Mr Jones: The Bench ought not to do anything of the sort.

Mr Mackean: I have a perfect right to ask the question I asked, and I do not think you yourself will say I have not, Mr Jones. I asked him whether he had authority from the Government to act as he is doing.

Mr Jones: It is most irregular. What does it matter to us what they want up north?

Mr Mackean: I am not going to put my hand over his mouth.

Mr Jones: I do not object to that: but I do object to these statements being made by a common informer.

Mr Logan was then recalled.

> Mr Jones: I must again object to all this evidence being given. It is very clear that this is altogether irregular. It is laid down very clearly in the "Queensland Magistrate" that conversations which take place out of the hearing of the persons charged cannot be given in evidence.
> Mr Pattison: Under certain circumstances they can.
> Mr Jones: Not at all.
> Mr Pattison: If I can show that the witness has made a statement inconsistent with what he had said previously I can give it.
> Mr Jones: Of course you cannot. It is one of the most elementary privileges that a man who is charged shall not have things given in evidence against him which have been said outside his hearing.

Yet again Jane took a break. She placed the paper on the table and rubbed her temples. The law was certainly complicated. With determination, she resumed her task of finishing this article hoping for more clarity.

> Mr Mackean (reading from the "Queensland Magistrate"): What is the meaning of this? The evidence of an accomplice is admissible, although it cannot be fully relied on?
> Mr Jones: That is not what I was referring to. It is further on.
> Mr. Mackean: We will hear the evidence.
> Mr Jones: Take a note of my objection. This will have to go further. I will go for a prohibition.
> Mr Pattison: Very well. Do what you can and give us a rest.
> Mr. Logan, re-examined by Mr. Pattison said that when he saw Charlie Santo on the 20th of June he said he was cutting wood for Mr. Macaree.
> Mr Jones: Now is that what he said? Give us the exact words.

Witness (Mr Logan): He said "Me cut 'im wood along old man."

Mr Jones: And then you have the audacity to swear deliberately that he said he was cutting wood for M. Macaree?

Witness: Yes.

Mr Jones: Don't you know that that is a lie?

Witness: It is not a lie.

M. Jones: Haven't you sworn that he said he was cutting wood "along old man" and before that you said he told you he was cutting wood for Mr. Macaree? Isn't that a lie?

Witness: I have told no lie at all.

Mr Jones: I will not bandy words with you. Kindly tell the Bench the exact words he said, and the Deposition Clerk will take down just what they were, and no more.

Mr Pattison: Who did he mean by the old man?

Mr Jones: He has no right to say.

Witness: I had a conversation with Mr Macaree before this. Shall I give it to you?

Mr Jones: You had no right to ask Mr Macaree a single question. Were you paid by the government to do this?

Witness: No. certainly not.

Mr Jones: Oh! you volunteered?

Witness: I went round to get boys for myself.

Mr Jones: Then you are an interested party?

Witness: Yes, because I want the boys to work in the cane.

Mr Jones: This Kanaka boy did not say any more than what you have told us?

Witness: No.

Mr Jones: Then when Mr. Mitchell said the boy mentioned Mr Macaree's name that was a lie?

Witness: I do not know. I certainly did not hear him say Mr Macaree.

Mr Pattison: You say you were there the previous

Thursday?

Mr Jones: I object to anything that took place the previous Thursday.

M. Pattison: It is re-examination. Mr Logan can explain why he knows "the old man" means Mr. Macaree.

Mr. Jones: That was days before.

Mr Mackean: The remark that he has just made about the boy saying he was working for Mr Macaree was only witness's own interpretation.

M. Pattison: Did you speak to Mr Macaree before this?

Witness: I did.

M. Pattison: What did you say?

Mr. Jones: Don't answer the question. I object most decidedly. What took place beforehand has nothing to do with this. You have this witness's evidence of what took place at this interview with the Kanaka and you can't have anything else.

Mr Pattison: That is the case for the prosecution.

Mr Jones: I submit there is no evidence to show that Mr Macaree had anything to do with this man. His name was not mentioned: The Kanaka was not even working on his land.

Mr Mackean: We will hear the other cases first.

Mr Pattison: I think the Bench must give its decisions as it goes along. I don't want my friend to take any advantage afterwards.

Mr Mackean: We want to hear what Mr. Macaree has to say.

Mr Pattison: Mr. Macaree is not game to go into the witness-box.

Mr Macaree: Isn't he? I will go into the witness-box at any time.

Mr Jones: The boy says himself he was not employed by Mr. Macaree and his name was not mentioned by Mr. Logan.

> *M. Mackean: Did not one witness say he was on Mr Macaree's premises?*
> *Mr Jones: It was Mr Jaggard's.*
> *Mr Pattison: Let Mr Macaree go into the box.*
> *Mr Mackean: In this case it should have been proved that he was in the employ of Mr Macaree.*
> *Mr Jones: That would have been another matter. I ask that the case be dismissed with professional costs.*
> *Mr Mackean: The case is dismissed, with £2.2s professional costs and cost of Court.*
> *Mr Jones: And there are Mr Macaree's expenses. (To Mr Macaree) What was your railway fare?*
> *M. Macaree: Five pounds. (Laughter.)*
> *Mr Jones: I mean your railway fare from Coorooman Creek?*
> *Mr Macaree: Five pounds would not cover the time I've lost. There is railway fare and cab fare.*

The Bench allowed 4s 2d. railway fare and 5s for Mr Macaree's attendance.

Mr Pattison said there were three other cases against Mr Macaree, but on the previous decision he would withdraw them.

> *Mr Jones: I will not ask for professional costs in these cases.*
> *Mr Pattison: They should leave their Kanakas alone when they are summoned.*
> *Mr Jones: What can you do when a man comes here and passes dishonoured cheques?*
> *Mr Pattison: That has been your strongest point in this case, I think.*

With relief, Jane dropped the paper onto the table. She'd read enough. More than enough. She was still a tad confused. When Edwin returned, she asked for clarification.

'They are so desperate for cheap labour in the cane fields that they try to claim any unregistered Islander they come across. Or should I say, any they hear about.'

'And is Charlie yours, Edwin?'

'There'll be more charges. But not against me. And did you read where our very first friend in this colony has been admitted to the Benevolent Asylum in Dunwich in Brisbane?'

Jane looked puzzled.

'Barrington Jenkyns. He's 91.'

'He was a gracious man.' Edwin handed her the newspaper.

William Fraser had purchased a sawmill near Nerimbera. He converted it into a tannery that employed twenty-five men who treated up to 300 hides per week.

And yet another bonus arrived for grandparents, William and Annie, and Edwin and Jane, when they were blessed with their third grandchild, Dorothy Hilda.

Still in the Klondyke, Donald tried to raise £500 and form a company. His father continued to be a tough teacher and wouldn't participate. Don couldn't believe how much gold there was to be had. While he was absent from the leases trying to convince others to invest in the business, he lost his quartz mine to a claim jumper and to add to the misery, he was unsuccessful in raising the funds. He didn't make a fortune after all but returned home to Rockhampton in 1903 with his passion for mining unabated, and a least some capital to begin the next phase.

Yet again, Edwin found himself in court, defending a charge of employing a Pacific Islander, Dhoorie, without the proper paperwork.

This time Mr J Pattison defended Edwin. Dr Vivian Voss

was still the Inspector of Pacific Islanders and Assistant Immigration Agent at Rockhampton, and had earlier received a letter from Edwin stating there were a number of Kanakas camped at Coorooman Creek and he was requesting of the Inspector that they move.

Matthew Bryan, an immigration inspector, and main witness for the prosecution, along with Charles Moyce, a butcher and an informer, cycled to Coorooman. Bryan had planned to round some Kanakas up and claimed he saw Dhoorie working at the sawmill. He said Dhoorie was shifting chains that were used to fastening logs onto railway trucks.

In evidence, Bryan said he remarked: 'I see, Mr Macaree, you have some of your black brethren working again.'

Bryan claimed Edwin replied, 'Oh, yes. There are some here and I shall not put them away. They do not do any harm about here. As I told you before, Dr Voss knows they are here and I will not send them away. I'll go to gaol first.'

Bryan said Edwin then gave instructions to the men about loading logs and Dhoorie helped.

Bryan saw Edwin give directions to two men; one was James Macaree and the other was called Bill. Dhoorie was not present then. James asked his father if they should go on loading the trucks and Edwin said, 'Yes. Be careful and get the thick end of the girder up first otherwise you will get it jammed.' It was then, said Bryan, they used the chains that Dhoorie has been moving earlier.

Bryan said it was on Edwin's land, and he had seen Kanakas working inside the mill in the past.

Moyce corroborated Bryan's claim. He then said he heard Edwin say, 'I don't employ that man. I let the work by contract.' Dhoorie was the only Kanaka there. He took the chains from the truck to the sheds. Moyce did not see Kanakas working with logs – only with the chains.

Dhoorie was seen by Bryan, so Bryan claimed, to carry the chains 15 feet further in.

When Bryan was leaving, Edwin is purported to have said, 'Well, you'll make it as light as you can for me.'

Edwin's solicitor, Mr Pattison, in defence, said Bryan knew there were a number of Kanakas camped there and he didn't ask Edwin if Dhoorie was working for him. Bryan didn't see Kanakas working the logs. The contract was with the teamsters from stumps to loading the logs, and the teamsters employed whoever they wanted.

The reason Jim Macaree and Bill Fenson were loading was because the teamsters were off bringing in another load. Edwin recalled Bryan coming to his office months earlier asking if he employed Kanakas. He told him he did not.

Edwin did not order Dhoorie to move chains, nor did he see him. The chains in question belonged to the Government and were fixtures on the railway truck so neither Dhoorie nor anyone else could carry them away.

Edwin said he did not pay his son regular wages. He credited him in the books with amounts varying from £1 10s to £2 per week. Bill Fenson was an engine driver who worked for Edwin.

There was a private siding running on to his land. The truck was about a chain in distance from the siding. The Government put the skids there, and they were for general usage. Edwin said he told the men to load the trucks about eleven or twelve o'clock. Bryan arrived there about ten or half-past ten o'clock. Edwin said he deducted 7s 6d from what was due to the teamsters for loading the truck that day. He saw Dhoorie in the late afternoon or early evening that day. He swore he did not see him at the truck. He told Bryan he did not know he was there. The Kanaka was camped on Edwin's land, and Edwin had known him for about twelve months. He had not employed an Islanders since the 1st of October, 1901, and Islanders had not, to his knowledge, been employed on his premises.

A letter was produced in evidence in Edwin's handwriting:

> 'Coorooman, 18/12/1902.
>
> Mr Fenson, please tell all the other men, Thomas Hamilton Green and the Islanders that I do not want them to get any more until the weather changes. You and Jim and the boys must break down the logs, for I cannot pay wages. The expenses are too heavy for me.
>
> Yours truly,
>
> E Macaree.
>
> PS If Motley comes back tell him to put the harness out of the wet to dry then we can grease it. EM.'

Edwin's solicitor said that if Edwin had been guilty of employing a Kanaka he would not have had his own men loading the logs while the informer and the inspector were present. The reason Edwin's men were working that day was to get the truck away on the afternoon train.

The case against Edwin was dismissed.

Jane couldn't believe it when, in 1904, Edwin told her he was putting his name forward to the Livingstone Shire Council to fill a casual vacancy as an alderman. The Gogango Divisional Board had, by then, been divided up into two council areas where Coorooman and Emu Park were part of the Livingstone Shire.

'Edwin, haven't you had enough?'

'When you can't beat them, Jane, you become one of them.' And so he did, at the age of 69, gaining more votes than his competitor, Henry Beak.

But his next battle became one with the Rockhampton Council in 1905 when the property valuations, according to their valuer, had dropped from the previous year. The Council over-rode that advice and increased valuations. Protests were heard in the Valuation Appeal Court with a Police Magistrate on the Bench. Edwin was in the esteemed company of such defendants as the Queensland National Bank, Walter Reid and Company, and Rees Rutland Jones himself.

Not one of Edwin's property valuations were reduced.

Location	Council Valuation	Valuer Valuation	Bench Decision
Alma Street	£234	£208	£234
Archer Street	£70	£70	£70
Agnes Street	£40	£40	£40
Gracemere Road	£30	£30	£30
Bolsover Street	£396	£300	£396
East Street	£120	£100	£100

And a final property the Bench found in favour of the Council valuation of £170, £70 more than the valuer had valued it.

Outside the Courtroom, there were many unhappy complainants. 'Thank goodness the North Rockhampton Council are more just,' Edwin said to Rees Jones. Edwin still owned Cremorne, although not much was happening there.

In June, at Coorooman, the family celebrated the wedding of Emma, Edwin and Jane's only daughter to Brisbane based Lionel Ball, the Assistant Government Geologist.

A few months later, Jim and Jessie produced their second

son, their fourth child, James William Kenneth, whom Jessie insisted on calling Kenneth. Everyone else, though, called him Ken.

James and Jessie Macaree's four Children.
Standing: Muriel and Ron, Seated, Ken and Dorothy

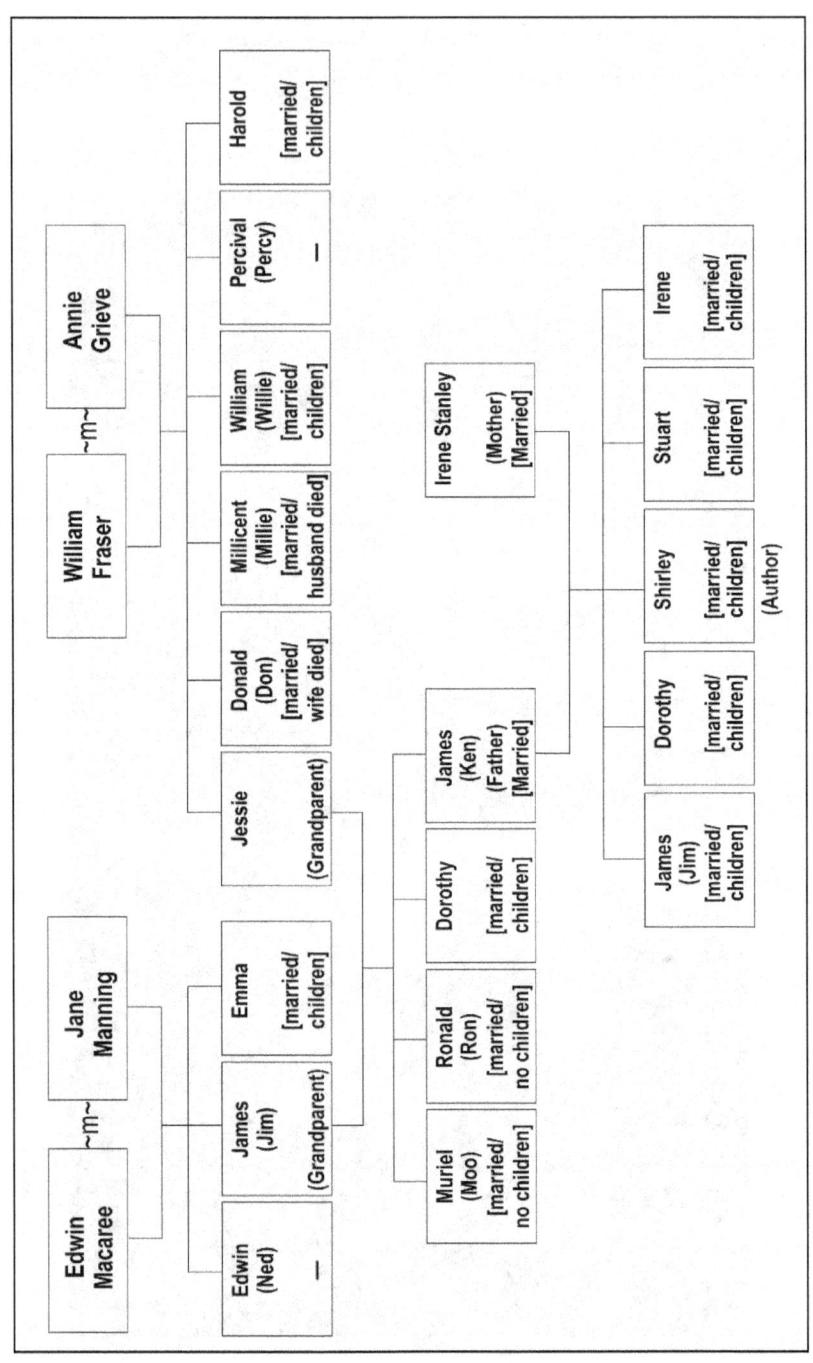

Macaree Fraser Family Tree

Life for Edwin at Coorooman became more difficult as his body became frailer. He and Jessie moved to Emu Park for comfort and for the fresh sea air and kinder temperatures.

Jim carried on the business, and also supplied his father-in-law's tanning business at Nerimbera with bark, collected around Coorooman.

Stripping bark at Coorooman for Wm Fraser's tannery

Edwin sold 3857 acres of his Coorooman Estate in early 1910 to Messrs Cumming and May. The land included the brewery, sawmill, buildings and plant, and all but one of the houses. The sawmill still employed seven men and was profitable. Mr Cumming cleared the land and planted crops. He started a dairy with about seventy cows. He repaired the residences on the hill for staff, and his own family lived in the two-story home near the brewery.

A small portion of land remained in Edwin's hands with a small residence. While he could no longer work physically, his brain was still as sharp as new razor, and his letter writing continued unabated.

In September, 1910, he penned a letter of protest against the

Livingstone Shire, from which he'd retired a few years prior, to the Editor of the Morning Bulletin.

> *Sir,*
>
> *It seems as if the Livingstone Shire Council is endeavouring to ride roughshod over the ratepayers of Emu Park. At one meeting it decided to raise the rates 3d. in the £. The next month, it sent out accounts for two years' rates and what it was pleased to call a separate rate of 3d. in the £. There is no common sense in this. To my mind the ratepayers themselves should have a voice in the matter. The man who proposed the motion to impose this special rate has no rates to pay. I am of opinion that this special rate cannot be lawfully demanded on the notice, there being no right of appeal.*
>
> *I am, &c, E. MACAREE. Emu Park, 19th September, 1910.*

Three days after he penned this letter, Edwin Macaree died peacefully in his sleep at the age of 75.

Post Edwin Macaree

Jane died three years after Edwin, and their son Ned died of a pulmonary disease in 1917 at the age of 56, on his property.

Jessie Macaree, the eldest of the Frasers, was busy with her young family of four children, and moved to Cremorne after the sale of most of Coorooman, although her husband, Jim, moved back and forth, as had Edwin. The hotel was eventually converted into a significant luxurious residence and became the family hub.

Jim sold some of his father's properties and involved himself in new ventures, but stayed well out of public life.

Jessie's father, William, as half of the Fraser and Craig partnership, forged ahead with his mining investments, including the Hunter Gold Mines at Cawarral.

Young Will Fraser with his older brother, Don, formed Fraser & Co. They acquired mining leases. The gold leases at Black Ridge at Clermont were surrounded by controversy. At a meeting of the Miners' Association in 1905, the following motion was carried, much to the disappointment of people of Clermont.

> "That in the opinion of this meeting the introduction of the leasehold principle in alluvial mining on the Clermont goldfield would be prejudicial to the best interests of the field and

would greatly retard its development, and that the gold-mining regulations, apart from leasing, allow of sufficient ground to be taken up by any person or company to enable them to recoup themselves for any expenditure that is likely to be necessary in any ground that has yet been discovered on the Clermont goldfield."

Don put forth the following amendment:

"That the miners of Black Ridge have a strong objection to the system of leasing being applied to alluvial workings on the Clermont goldfield; but being aware that the wet ground at the Wild Cat lead is too expensive for the individual alluvial miner or party of miners to work, will not oppose the granting of a lease for the ground provided always that it shall not be claimed as a precedent for leasing alluvial country on other parts of the Clermont goldfields and that the labour conditions of the lease shall be strictly enforced.'"

But it was defeated.

The Clermont Council and the Progress Association passed resolutions in favour of granting the lease for the good of the town. It was claimed that local miners couldn't get the gold out because of the difficulty of mining, but were resentful of letting anyone else try.

Fortunately for Don and Will, existing leases were exempt and the following month they put 200 tons of rock through their own battery which pounded and crushed the rocks. This battery had been moved from their father's mine at Cawarral when the ore there diminished. They milled rocks for other exempt miners as well. They were getting two ounces to the ton at times.

A year later miners met to discuss Don's proposal of allowing larger claims for reasons of economy, so machinery could be used. He was willing to buy up other claims, or allow shares in his company in lieu. Most were in favour, but a few held out. The Star of Hope Syndicate was formed and managed by Don. Their True Blue claim produced 111 ounces of gold.

Two years later, controversy was again raised at a public meeting at Black Ridge.

Two of the motions put were in relation to Will's large Homeward Bounder lease which had been abandoned years before he acquired it:

"That this meeting requests The Minister for Mines (The Hon J W Blair) to order an inquiry into the actions of Mr. D. M. Jones, Warden, Clermont, with regard to the method of conducting mining business on the Clermont goldfield, more especially with regard to his action in granting registration to William Fraser, jnr., of an excessive area of ground, under section 47 of the Mining Act, without obtaining sworn evidence in the Warden's Court in Clermont."

"That the foregoing resolution is forwarded by the Chairman to the Minister for Mines coupled with a request that such inquiry shall be held at the Black Ridge."

There was a third motion responding to a three-month exemption that had been granted to Will because of excessive water issues. It seemed unfair since a Government pumping plant was available for lease at 20s per week.

All three motions were passed, and Will duly rented the pump and had his employees back to work. Over time, though, the excessive water problem could not be solved. Water needed for the Fraser Battery was short, so the issue was resolved between the two with the Homeward Bounder shaft being sunk to supply the water.

The Warden's authority, though, stood.

Coal was another commodity the Frasers delved into. William senior was a member of the original syndicate that opened the Dunstan colliery at Baralaba. He had also held a lease at Blair Athol. Persistently astute, William disposed of his assets when he considered them at their peak.

Don took on the lease of the old Mammoth coal mine. The Mines Department showed sympathy in Don's experiment with this project by transporting 300 tons of the coal to be tested by the British Admiralty free of charge. However, despite favourable assessment, no order was placed.

Mammoth Coal Mine ca 1905. Photo: courtesy Qld State Library. Photographer, L C Ball, husband of Emma Macaree and later Government Geologist.

The Mount Morgan Gold-mining Company performed tests on the coal from Frenchman's Plains, which was Don's property. The difficulty was the amount of water that needed to be pumped out.

Don struggled to work a lease at the Limestone quarry at Mount Etna.

Just after the death of his good friend, Edwin, William had surgery on one of his eyes. It was a failure, resulting in the loss of the eye. The sight in the other eye wasn't good either. With mutual agreement, William went ahead and dissolved his partnership with Daniel Craig. He and Annie retired to The Pines at Emu Park. Don purchased a property there as well.

1914–1918

Jessie and Millie's four brothers enlisted after World War I was declared. In order of birth, Jessie, married to Jim Macaree, was the eldest. Then there was Donald, Millie, Willie, Percy and finally Harold.

Donald Lovat Fraser, who was 29, six feet tall and very fit, signed up in October 1914. He was British by birth and was a metallurgist. He formed part of the 5th Light Horse Regiment and trained at Enoggera as a private.

Don Fraser (centre) at Enoggera, 1914

Within a couple of days, he was elevated to Corporal. Just before Christmas, he was shipped out on the *Persic* and in May 1915 he landed at Gallipoli, where he was again promoted; this time to sergeant. He spent a few months in Gallipoli and when he could, he wrote home. He wrote to his elder sister, Jessie. No stamp was required because he was at the front.

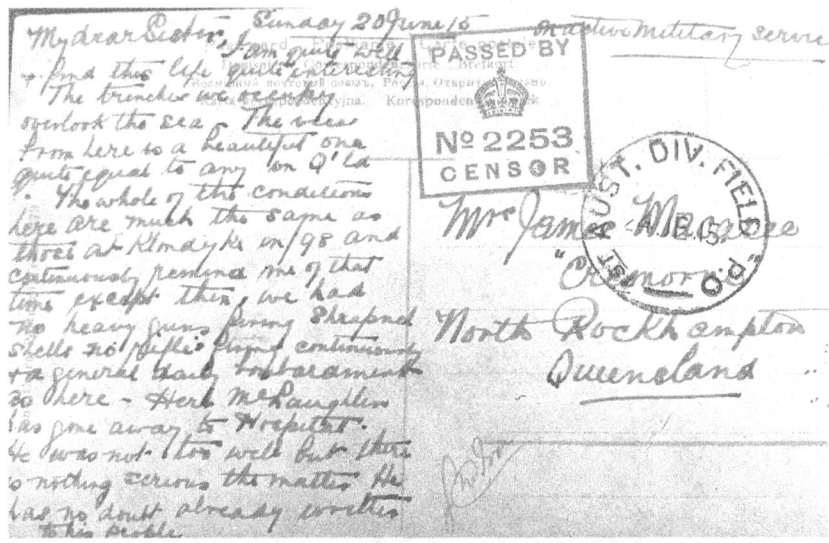

Don Fraser's postcard from Gallipoli to his sister, Jessie, at Cremorne

Sunday 20 June 15 On active military service
Mrs James Macaree
"Cremorne"
North Rockhampton
Queensland

My dear Sister,

I am quite well and find this life quite interesting. The trenches we occupy overlook the sea. The view from here is a beautiful one quite equal to any in Q'ld.

The whole of the conditions here are much the same as those at Klondyke in '98 and continuously remind me of that time except then we had no heavy guns firing shrapnel shells no rifles firing continuously to a general daily bombardment as here. Herb

McLaughlin has gone away to Hospital.

He was not too well but there is nothing serious the matter. He has no doubt already written.

I will write more fully as soon as we are permitted to do so. I called home last week telling them I was well. No news from Harold yet. He's probably in Cairo or Alexandria.

From Donald Fraser

Don Fraser's ANZAC book, 1915

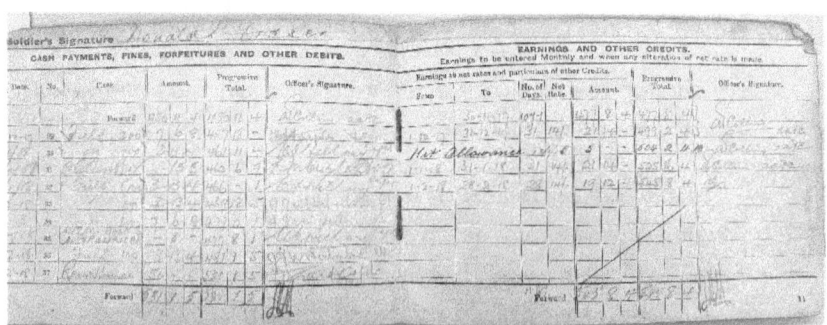

Don Fraser's Army Pay Book

In July of 1915, suffering serious diarrhea, (he had both dysentery and enteric fever) he was shipped off to a hospital at Mudros on the Greek Island of Lemnos. From there he was moved to St Andrew's Hospital in Malta. Still very ill, he was admitted to a hospital in Portsmouth in England, where he finally recovered. In November he became an NCO in the 42nd Battalion and was sent to Edinburgh where he underwent officer training.

From there, in 1916, he was transferred to the 2nd Light Horse Regiment and sent to France and Belgium.

By 1917 he'd been promoted to a provisional lieutenant and was later that year seconded to the 11th Brigade as in Intelligence Officer where he was a fully fledged lieutenant.

In 1918, on April 21st, he wrote the following report after witnessing the shooting down of the German air ace, Manfred von Richthofen, alias the Red Baron. Von Richthofen was known to have shot down eighty allied aircraft, and was greatly esteemed for his abilities by both sides.

> *Australian infantry Brigade.*
> *Reference Sheet, Corbie, 1/20.000.*
> *Description of the shooting down of Cavalry Captain Baron von Richthofen, the famous German aviator, at 10.45 on 21st April. 1918:*
> *At about 10.45 a.m., 21st instant, I was in the wood at J.19 75.63 and saw two aeroplanes approaching, flying westward, directly towards the wood, at a height of about 400 ft. above level of River Somme over which they were flying. I had noticed that the leading machine had British markings, just as it reached edge of wood and immediately afterwards I heard a strong burst of M.G. fire coming from direction of south-east corner of the wood.*
> *Immediately afterwards the red painted enemy machine*

appeared overhead, flying very low and unsteadily, and probably not more than 200 ft. from the ground.

I lost sight of the British machine, as my attention was concentrated on the enemy plane, which was flying as if not under complete control, being wobbly and irregular in flight. It swerved north, then eastwards, rocking a great deal and suddenly dived out of my sight, the engine still running full open.

I ran out of the wood and over to where it had fallen, about 200 yards away alongside Bray-Corbie road. About six men reached the wrecked plane before me.

I immediately undid the airman's safety belt and got assistance to pull him from the wreckage, but he was quite dead, and was considerably cut about the face, and was apparently shot through the chest and body.

As a large number of men were collecting, I requested Captain Adams, 4th Battalion, A.I.F., to place a guard over the plane to prevent looting, and to disperse the crowd, as the spot was open to enemy observation and I feared we would be shelled. A guard was duly placed over the machine and the crowd dispersed.

I searched the dead airman, taking his papers and personal effects, which consisted of a few papers, a silver watch, gold chain with medallion attached, and a pair of fur-lined gloves. I gave them to Captain Hillary, of 11th Brigade Staff, who took them down to our German speaker, Corporal Peters, who, on investigation, gave the identification of the famous German airman, Baron von Richthofen.

I reported this to General Cannan and Third Australian Division promptly.

On General Cannan's direction I went out to get particulars of the machine gunners who had brought the plane down, and found Sergeant Popkin, of 24th Australian MG.

Company, at his anti-aircraft M.G. location.

At this time I was not aware that any other M.G. had been firing at this plane. I congratulated Sergeant Popkin on his successful shoot, but afterwards found out that two A.A. Lewis gunners belonging to the 53rd Battery A.F.A. had also fired at this plane when it was directly over my head, but the noise of engine prevented my hearing the shooting. The 53rd Battery Lewis gunners probably assisted in sealing the fate of this airman, as he apparently flew right into their line of fire. However, I am strongly of the opinion that he was first hit by Sergeant Popkin's shooting, as he was unsteady from the moment at that first burst of fire.

The airman's body was afterwards taken in charge by officers of the AFC and the wrecked plane salvaged by them after dark.

A funeral was held for the enemy pilot with a guard of honour and a three-gun salute. The event was filmed, such was their respect for him. (That film is still available to watch online.)

Donald had souvenired von Richthofen's scarf at the time, and kept it. In later years he showed it to his mates at the Rockhampton Club, but when he flew to Germany decades later, his conscience compelled him to return it to von Richthofen's family.

Later in 1918, Donald was sent to England, ill again. He rejoined his Battalion a couple of weeks later, and in December of 1918 he sailed to Australia for a 75 day leave pass, returning in March of 1919.

In August of 1919 the *Anchises* took him home permanently to Australia where he returned to his mining career.

Percival Victor Fraser, who was Percy to his family, was already overseas and working for the British Navy.

He had sailed from Rockhampton to London as a crew member in 1906, was discharged, and found another ship, another then another. He came back to Australia occasionally. In 1911 he attained his Certificate of Competency as an engineer. He had been the Marine Chief Engineer on the *SS Patella* for three years when the war broke out.

Percy Fraser in the Naval uniform

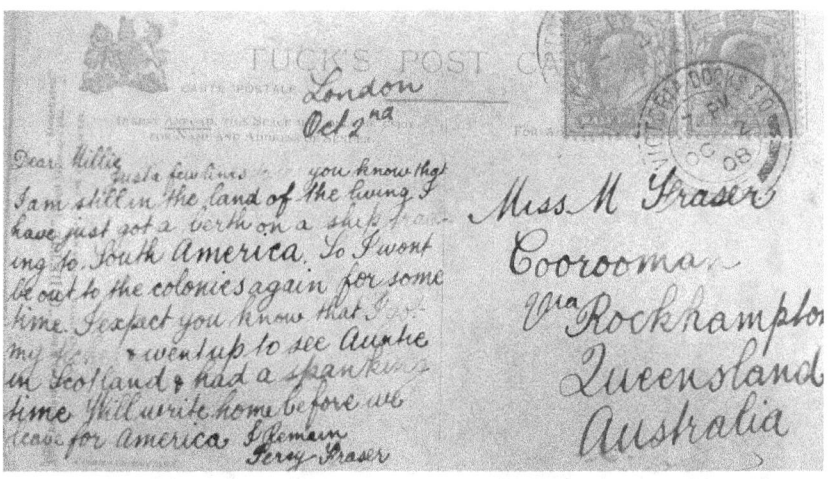

Percy Fraser's postcard to his sister, Millie, 1908

London, Oct 2nd.
Dear Millie,
Just a few lines to let you know that I am still in the land of the living. I have just got a berth on a ship trading to South America. So I won't be out to the colonies again for some time. I expect you know that I got my ticket and went up to see Auntie in Scotland & had a spanking time. Will write home before we leave for America. I remain Percy Fraser.

He enlisted in the Eastbourne unit of the Royal Flying Corps on 25th November, 1914 as a wireless operator. He was promoted to Warrant Officer, and undertook training as a pilot with the Royal Naval Air Service.

In one of his letters home in 1915 he said:

I am still in London, but hope shortly to get away. I have been to an aviation school, and taken my pilot's certificate (No.1230). I have been before a selection committee at the Admiralty, and they offered me a warrant officer's job. I took my ticket on a Beatty-Wright biplane. It's grand sport, and is quite as safe as any other sport.

Percy Fraser, flying instructor, in plane, 1915

Donald and Percy happened to find each other in England at the same time and were able to travel to Scotland to visit their aunt, much to the delight of their parents.

Donald (standing) and Percy Fraser with their Aunt in Scotland

Donald typed a letter home on 1st December in 1915, from his friend, Henry Cobham's home at The Knapp, Haslemere, in Sussex. (Cobham had been a partner to Don in Klondyke.)

Dear Mother, Father, and Sister,
You will be pleased to hear that I am having a splendid holiday. I have been staying with my friend Cobham at the above address for some time now and last weekend I went down to Eastbourne to stay with Percy – Mr and Mrs Cobham also went down and stayed at an hotel. Mrs Cobham has not been well for some time and she will stay there for a few weeks.

I returned here on Monday. I found Percy looking very well and in very comfortable quarters. He has a bedroom and a sitting room in a house close to the Aerodrome and the people with whom he is boarding like him very much and he is much liked by everyone.

He is a wonderful airman and is said to be one of the very best of instructors.

The Sub Lieutenants whom he is teaching told me that he is the gamest of airmen, and speak very highly of him. I found that I got quite a lot of "reflected glory" by being his brother.

On Sunday morning Percy got permission from the Commanding Officer to take me up in the Air although it was a very cold morning registering well below freezing point. I enjoyed the experience immensely.

I had absolute confidence in Percy's ability to handle the machine and so had no fear – I was sitting just behind him in a seat he usually occupies when instructing with a strap around my waist. He was also strapped into his seat.

Within about 50 yards of the point at which he started the engine, we took to the Air and then rapidly mounted high up until we reached an altitude of 1500 feet. A very strong wind was blowing (over 30 miles per hour) and we could only make 10 miles per hour against it, but the speed to me seemed terrific. The sensation was quite pleasant until we struck "bumps" in the air that threw our machine about, but Percy soon got it steady again and we continued out over the beach to the Sea when he turned back. When turning it is necessary to what is called "Bank" the machine, that is turn it from the level to an inclined position to prevent it from side slipping. The feeling of this "Banking" is a horrible one to the inexperienced flier as it feels as if the machine is turning over and this thought is not a pleasant one 1500 feet above a hard cold earth – I know I gripped the spreaders of the machine very very tightly and had a very cold feeling in my stomach when he banked, but soon recovered my confidence when we got on an even keel again – we had about a 20 mile flight, and then he started to descend. This an almost worse experience than banking as the machine dives down to the earth from 1500 feet at a rate of 70 miles per hour and at a very steep angle – I thought for a moment or two that Percy had lost possession or control of the machine, but he was sitting so quietly and coolly in his seat that he quickly re-established my confidence – and we landed quite safely and so gently that I hardly knew I was again on Terra Firma.

The air was very rough the day I was up and the whole experience was a very pleasant one for me particularly as it was my brother who took me up. The earth seems to be rushing towards you when descending and it makes you grip the standards very tightly.

I have no ambition to "loop the loop" yet as some aeronauts have done but this desire may follow supreme confidence in the Air – anyhow I will let you know before I make any attempt.

Percy has lent me several suits of his clothing and necessary shirts etc., also a suitcase, and I am now parading the neighbourhood in Mufti.

I now weigh 12 stone 12 lbs and Percy's clothes are just a little too small for me, but they are quite all right and I am glad to get out of uniform – I will get my 6 weeks furlough this weekend. Most of my letters have gone astray, and I have not heard from you for some time. Harold had not written either or perhaps his have also been returned as were several that Cobham wrote to me in Malta and Gallipoli. They came back to him through the dead letter office while I was staying with him. Beta Joe and Mars Richardson have been very kind to both Percy and I. They are living in London and I often talk to them on the 'phone. Percy and I had dinner with the Cobhams *at their Hotel at Eastbourne last Sunday.*

Well, my dear Mother and Father & Millie I often wonder how you all are and wish that I were able to come and see you – Xmas will be past before you will get this, but I am going to send you a cable about that time wishing you happiness etc.

You will have heard of the severe criticism the English people are making … (paper eaten away) bad administration of the Dardenelles Operations. Sir Ian Hamilton has of course been recalled and is now in England. I have not anything definitely fixed regarding my future movements but I will try and get a commission in a flying corps. I have already been offered a commission in Kitcheners' army but I do not want them. I am sure to get a commission directly I return. With very fondest love to you all.

I am, Your son, Donald.

Percy continued his instruction of student pilots. On 10th January, 1916, less than one month after Donald's flight, a student pilot, G Duke crashed the plane, with his instructor, Percy, into a field near Hampden Park, and Percy and Duke both met their death after being pinned under the wreckage.

Donald, who was still living locally, was devastated. He was able to be involved in the funeral. He wrote a long explanation to his parents, William and Annie, and attached the newspaper report of the inquest.

He then wrote to his little sister, Millie.

My dear sister,

You will have had particulars of the sad sad news of our dear brother Percy's death some time now as I wrote immediately after the accident giving all the facts as far as I could learn them.

This dear old fellow's face looked very fine, strong and brave in death with a half smile.

We had become quite attached to one another after the many years of separation and I admired him and his strong resolute character, this great ability that commanded every one's respect.

He had been recommended for promotion the day before this accident occurred and it was his intention after that promotion to get a commission and apply to be sent to the fighting front which would not have been nearly as dangerous work as training new pupils daily.

I had advised him to do this as I feared an accident sooner or later as lots of these new men have no nerve for flying after they get into the air and they do the most extraordinarily silly things when first taken up.

I am afraid dear old Percy could not have lived through this war as he was too courageous and adventuresome. He would no doubt have earned much distinction had he got to the front but he was full of self confidence and would always take more than his share of risks. It was always he who went up, every morning to test the air or find out whether it was safe for flying in windy gusty days.

He would have done great things had he lived to get to the front, I am sure. His C.O. said he was such an excellent instructor that he wanted to keep him with him.

He was so full of nerve that he could allow pupils who made mistakes correct them themselves without taking control from them as every other instructor did.

I am enclosing your last letter read by him and which he had in his pocket when the accident occurred as I thought you might like it, Millie.

I am also enclosing a newspaper cutting of the Inquest. I feel sure the accident occurred owing to the elevator controls becoming jammed and in addition having a passenger pupil who lost his head. Percy was said to be quite cool and fighting for control of the machine right up to the last moment. People on the ground could hear him directing the passenger right up to the last moment. I sincerely hope my darling mother and dear father are bearing up bravely over this great blow. Thousands and hundreds of thousands of mothers have lost their sons in this great war. Dear old Percy had more than done his share in training 70 or 80 men until they got their pilot's air certificates. He had trained more men than any other in England or elsewhere during the time he was instructor.

With my fondest love to you all,

I am your affectionate brother, Donald.
ps I have to report for duty on Feb 1 next.
I am having a stone placed over Percy's grave.

Harold Livingstone Fraser, 23, the youngest in the family, and an apprentice architect, enlisted in January 1915. He was sent to Blackall for training with the 5th Light Horse Brigade with the AIF. He was just over six feet tall. He had, earlier, broken his left collar bone.

Harold Livingstone Fraser in uniform

Within a few months he was elevated to Corporal, and by June he was at Gallipoli where he spent four months. In October 1915, he was sent to the Sinai Campaign as a Light Horseman where he saw action, which led to his being shot in the right shoulder at the Battle of Romani in August 1916, where he was evacuated to Katia, and later to Mazar and finally to Ismailia. He was promoted to Sergeant and in September he rejoined his unit.

The Australian Light Horsemen, at ease on horses, physically fitter and of high character, were considered "bushies" but renowned for being quick-thinking and having fast reflexes. They were often selected for pilot training because of these attributes. Harold was no exception. He was detached from his unit in January 1917 and reported to the Royal Flying Corps in Egypt as a cadet.

By April, after training at the School of Acrobatics, he transferred to the 21st Reserve Squadron in Abbassia, just outside Cairo.

In June he was graded as a flying officer with the rank of Lieutenant with the Australian Flying Corps.

He played a significant role in the Palestine and Sinai Campaigns, mostly over enemy lines, in reconnaissance, photography, and bombing. He was involved in fights over the next ten months and was in the air over 250 hours in all.

In January 1918 he was awarded The Military Cross for 'Gallantry during active operations against the enemy.'

Annie Fraser, his mother, was his Next of Kin because at this stage William Senior was almost blind, and unable to read. Annie received the following letter:

Mrs A Fraser
Emu Park
ROCKHAMPTON. Q'LD

Dear Madam,

I have much pleasure in forwarding hereunder copy of extract from Fourth Supplement No. 30624 to the London Gazette dated 9th April, 1918 relating to the conspicuous services rendered by your son, Lieutenant H. L. Fraser, No 1 Squadron Australian Flying Corps., late AIF.

AWARDED THE MILITARY CROSS

"HIS MAJESTY THE KING has been graciously pleased to approve of the above-mentioned reward for distinguished services in the field in connection with military operations, culminating in the capture of Jerusalem." Dated 1st January, 1918.

Lieutenant HAROLD LIVINGSTONE FRASER

The above has been promulgated in Commonwealth of Australia Gazette, No. 137, dated 30th August, 1918.

Yours faithfully,

.......................Captain.

Harold flew through the first half of 1918 on the Palestine front until he was so traumatised from what he did and what he saw that he could fly no more. He was admitted to hospital suffering a general breakdown. He had nervous insomnia, headaches, and was unable to carry on. After a stay in hospital, where he didn't make a recovery, the Medical Board assembled in Port Said to investigate his case. He was favourably discharged on 30th July 1918 following extensive reports where his disability was listed as 'Debility' and a full pension was recommended. And so Harold returned home just a few months before the war ended.

William Wakefield Fraser, or Willie as he was known, had been rejected initially when he tried to enlist. His eyesight was tested at 6/36, meaning he was legally blind, although he wore glasses and worked as a clerk. His second enlistment attempt in October 1916 was successful. Willie was then 32 years old, 5 feet 10 inches tall, and the little toe on his left foot was missing.

He trained as a gunner as part of the Field Artillery Reinforcements at Liverpool before being sent to the front where he spent 332 days. For his efforts, he was exposed to mustard gas. This gas reacted with fluid in the airways and formed into hydrochloric acid causing suffocation by blistering. Willie survived but carried permanent injuries to his lungs and throat.

He was declared medically unfit after that shocking exposure, and so in September 1917, he was honourably discharged.

Post War Years with Jim and Jessie Macaree

Jim and Jessie Macaree, my grandparents, welcomed their oldest son, Ronald, home from the First World War. He later married Jessie Rodgers. They had no children. An engineer, he eventually became manager of the Rockhampton Gas and Coke Company.

In 1919 Muriel, my Aunty Moo, the eldest Macaree child, became engaged to Arthur Deacon. After their marriage, they made their home at 55 Edward Street in North Rockhampton. They too had no children of their own.

Dorothy Macaree married Ulan Coxon of Elwell, a sheep property near Longreach. The reception took place at Cremorne, and after the bride and groom left, the party continued into the night, much to Jessie's delight.

Dorothy and Ulan, over the ensuing years, had six children, four girls and two boys.

Ken Macaree, my father, the youngest child of Jim and Jessie, on turning 21 in 1926, took out a life assurance policy. Before filling in the form, he went to his mother.

'Mother, I have names other than Ken, don't I?'

'Yes, you've also got James and William, Kenneth,' she replied.

And so he wrote Kenneth James William. But it was James William Kenneth.

A large portion of the Cremorne land was sold off, leaving the main residence, which had once been the hotel, as well as relevant outbuildings including maid quarters, laundry and workroom. The home was quite magnificent as was its decor and Ken grew up surrounded by luxury and servants. A considerable sized garden still remained.

Ken took up a position as a stockman on Elwell where his sister, Dorothy and her husband Ulan lived and worked. But Ken was forced to return home when he suffered badly from an allergy to horses. He went into partnership with his father Jim at Coorooman in 1931 when he was in his mid-twenties.

The Coorooman Eucalyptus Products Company advertised as being owned by James Macaree and Son. It employed about thirty people who collected leaves locally grown. The pure oil was bottled for medicinal purposes, and also shipped off to use in the preparation of Lyptus Jubes.

James Macaree & Son Eucalyptus extraction plant, Coorooman

A couple of years later Ken Macaree experienced his first court appearance when he pleaded guilty to cutting down timber near the water tanks at Tungamull without a licence. In defence he said he believed his father had a permit to take timber from the area for commercial purposes.

He later discovered that his father did, in fact, have a permit, and wrote to the Department explaining that the trees were taken for commercial purposes, and asked for a remission of the fine.

Jessie preferred the comforts of Cremorne to Coorooman. Her husband, Jim, travelled back and forth on the train. He was always seen carrying his Gladstone bag, and in later years, on arrival at North Rockhampton Station, he would pass it out the window to his grandson, my brother, Jim.

James Macaree (Snr) Gladstone bag

Young Jim, my brother, would watch his grandmother, Jessie unpack. The bag always held old Jim's dirty washing.

'You dirty old man,' grandmother said to her husband one day as she tipped out the contents. 'You've been using my good tea-towels as cleaning rags again.' Young Jim noticed oil stains on them.

Another time when young Jim was visiting Cremorne, he heard his grandmother call from the kitchen door to his grandfather, Jim, 'You dirty old man, you're not at Coorooman now.'

When young Jim looked, old Jim was peeing in grandmother's treasured rose garden out in the courtyard.

Old Jim was a competent engineer and could invent, repair or build just about anything. Young Jim (no longer young) called him a tinker. Old Jim built solar panels outside the Cremorne bathroom in an era they were almost unheard of. They supplied continuous hot water to the bathroom.

Both Macaree grandsons of Jim and Jessie, James Donald (young Jim) and Stuart Kenneth, inherited the same skillset.

The Macarees' and the Frasers' lives continued to be intertwined, and the centre of that relationship was Cremorne.

On Don Fraser's return from the war, he took up where he'd left off. His mining ventures into all kinds of minerals over the next four decades were many, varied, highly colourful, sometimes litigious, and mostly profitable.

He said to a family member, 'There's a fine line between making large profits and ending up in jail.'

Will Fraser's health was poor after his exposure during the war to mustard gas, but he was able to take over part of his father's business. He was an auctioneer and commission agent and went into partnership with G Baglow. They expanded by picking up the agency for Colonial Mutual. Will took an active interest in returned soldiers through the Returned Sailors' Soldiers' and Airmen's Imperial League, (an early form of the RSL). He involved himself in Diggers' Day. He was outspoken on and supportive of the provision of war service homes. Willie went into partnership with James Macaree senior in the Balmoral Woolscour, but that shut in 1923.

For his own needs, Will purchased five acres of land and hired a hand to milk a few cows he purchased. He was of the belief that fresh milk was good for his health. In later years, when Will wasn't capable, my older brother Jim said, 'Dad would pop me into the basket of his bike, and he'd ride to Wandal, I think it was, and milk his Uncle Will's cow.'

Harold initially involved himself in the family businesses after returning home from the war, but eventually followed his passion and began flying again. He married in 1922 and began a family. Their oldest child was named Harold. In 1929 Harold Snr (known as Captain Harold Fraser), rented a paddock in Rockhampton, owned by G Connor. Harold formed, with his friend Robert Cousins, a Company known as the Rockhampton Aerial Services. They also formed an Aero Club.

The history of Harold's flying businesses has been well documented in Glenn Cousins' book, *Men of Vision over Capricorn – A story of Aviation History in Central Queensland*. Glenn was the son of Robert Cousins, Harold's friend.

Ken Macaree's family, including my four siblings and me, grew up in Wheatcroft Street, near the Boys' Grammar School where our home created a dead-end to Marris Street. A few doors away, in Marris Street, lived Glenn Cousins, and his wife, Shirley, together with their two children Noelene and Ian. Such is the interwoven history of Rockhampton that I was in and out of their home as we children played, unaware of these strong connections. My connection with Noelene is maintained.

During the Fraser/Cousins partnership, which had been built on friendship, Robert Cousins' father held the position of Mayor of Rockhampton.

The Rockhampton Aerodrome, Connor Park was opened in March of 1930 where the first official passenger airliner arrived from Brisbane.

Harold entertained by stunt flying his Bluebird for the expectant crowd below.

Harold Fraser MC. Plaque at Connor Park

Miss May Bradford, an accomplished equestrian who had already attained her A-Class Pilot's Licence, was trained to become a commercial pilot by Harold. She was heralded as being, at the time, the only woman in Australia to hold a ground engineer's licence.

Still in 1931, Harold responded by searching for a lost plane and pilot.

The Morning Bulletin reported on page 7 on the 27th August in 1931, the following:

> *Broadbent Found Safe and Sound Awaiting Rescue.*
> WET AND MUDDY LONG WALK IN SWAMP AEROPLANE BOGGED WITHOUT SLEEP FOR 66 HOURS
> *(By the "Bulletin's" Special Representative with Captain Fraser)*

Wearing a tweed suit, a scarf wrapped round his neck, and a pleased smile on his face, Broadbent, the young Sydney aviator who had been lost since Monday, was found yesterday by Captain Harold Fraser, standing beside his machine, stranded on a mud island in Broadsound, at the mouth of the Styx River.

The time was precisely 8.15 a.m. when the Rockhampton Aerial Services Genairco plane, flown under instructions from the Shell Oil Co., circled over Broadbent's royal blue Avro-Avian.

The wheels of Broadbent's machine were sunk deep in the mud, but the machine was undamaged and the flier appeared to be in the best of health.

A ground party was directed to the spot where the 'plane lay, and with the assistance of these men, Broadbent and his machine were soon in the air again.

Captain Fraser, a mechanic and a "Bulletin" reporter left Connor Park at 7.25 a.m. The visibility was good, but mists surrounded the mountains to the north. At 7.40 the pilot picked up the railway line, and followed it until the Styx River came in sight.

Near its mouth the Styx widens considerably and there are immense banks of mud. From the air the ground looks solid, and its inviting appearance undoubtedly was the cause of Broadbent's unfortunate landing.

At 8 o'clock Captain Fraser sent over his first message to the land party.

MR. BROADBENT. "See if you can see him in the mud flats to the right," the note read.

The 'plane circled the mud flats a few miles from the mouth of the river, but there was no sign of the missing 'plane there.

"Keep a lookout for fires" was the second message.

After hugging the mud flats for 10 minutes the plane

headed for the open sea.
(A photo then appears in the newspaper with the plane visible.)
A difference in flying conditions was immediately noticeable. From Rockhampton to the river the 'plane had flown perfectly, but over the water it bucked considerably.
The 'plane circled over a small island, timbered at the shore. In the centre was an open space.
"There he is!" Captain Fraser was the first to see Broadbent. In less than a minute, the Genairco was circling over the stranded Avro-Avian. Leaning against the wing was Broadbent, wearing a tweed suit, with a scarf around his neck. He was bare-headed, and appeared to be uninjured. He waved to the rescuing 'plane and motioned not to land.
A paper bag containing half a dozen oranges was thrown to Broadbent, and Captain Fraser flew back to Styx for more food. Two tins of meal, two packets of biscuits, two packets of cigarettes and two boxes of wooden matches were purchased and once more the 'plane headed for the island of mud. Two bottles of water were also carried.
Broadbent was not wearing his coat when Captain Fraser returned, and the sleeves of his khaki shirt were rolled up.
The sugar bag containing the food and cigarettes was thrown over and the bottles of water followed. Broadbent picked them up, signalled that all was well and made for the nearest shade to eat his first substantial meal for a few days.
At Hartley the news of Broadbent's safety was welcomed by the population, but as no news had been received of the search party which had left the previous afternoon some anxiety was felt on their account.
On the return journey the rescue party was located on the bank of the river on the mainland. Captain Fraser landed in an ideal field nearby, and the ground party came up.

> "Have you seen him?" "Where is he?" "Is he safe?" Question after question was fired at the fliers from members of the excited group.
>
> Expressions of relief were heard on all sides when the news was given out that Broadbent was safe. ...
>
> After the ground party had been two hours on its journey to Broadbent Captain Fraser went aloft, and, leaving the mainland, circled over the bogged machine, indicating its position. When the rescuers were within 200 yards of the 'plane Captain Fraser turned his machine back towards Rockhampton, and in less than an hour he landed at Connor Park. ...

A few years later, Harold suffered his own crisis. He'd been returning from a commercial run for the Aerial Service to Clermont where he'd dropped four passengers, when, at a height 4000 feet, the engine fell out of the plane.

He was 12 miles from Capella at the time. At 3000 feet, the plane went into a spin. At 1000 feet, Harold reckoned he had no chance. But he played with the controls, and, through a series of dives and stalls, he somehow managed to steady the plane.

Although he was in a heavily wooded area, he also managed to find a small clearing, about 45 by 50 feet, where, miraculously, he landed. Undaunted, Harold then walked 10 miles into Capella to raise the alarm.

Dick Gilpin, the licensee of the Capella hotel, (who later ran the corner store on the corner of Talford and Archer Streets) was heard to say, 'If he can fly a plane like he can drink scotch, I'm not surprised he landed without an engine.'

The propeller and engine were found later some 350 yards from the landing.

Harold Fraser's wrecked plane, minus the engine, near Capella

The 1930s

The 1930s were kind, neither to the Macaree Family nor to the Fraser Family. The deaths occurred, first of Annie Fraser in 1932, and the following year of William.

In 1933, Ulan, the husband of Dorothy Coxon, (Jim and Jessie's second daughter), was on his sheep station of Elwell, near Muttaburra checking a fox trap about half a mile from the homestead. As Ulan dismounted, his horse pulled him onto the wire. It exploded the weapon, and entered Ulan's left foot, smashing it to pulp.

Ulan managed to tourniquet his leg while workers, who heard the explosion, rushed to his aid and called the ambulance.

Dr Arrata of the Muttaburra Hospital was forced to amputate the leg below the knee, but Ulan's condition worsened and Dr Arrata sent an urgent message to Rockhampton for serum. Leaving by plane at 6 am on Sunday, Harold Fraser rushed the serum to the hospital. He had Jessie Macaree, who was not only Dorothy's mother, and also his own sister, with him.

The mercy flight was to no avail. Ulan died from his injuries, leaving his wife Dorothy a widow with five children. They'd lost Eric, a few years prior to Diphtheria.

Just two years later, Dorothy herself died from a chest illness.

The oldest girl went to live with Moo (Muriel), Dorothy's older sister, who had no children. Dorothy's mother, Jessie, after raising four children of her own, took two of the girls and raised them at Cremorne, while another went to live with one of the Coxon family and the oldest boy stayed locally.

Don married in the 1930s but tragically, his wife and child both died during childbirth a few years later.

Ken Macaree, my father, married in the 1930s. He suffered the same tragedy as Don, losing his wife and child, although the child lived with severe cerebral palsy for a while. Instead of bringing Don and my father Ken closer through their losses, it seemed to do the opposite, when my father told Don to go and live and love again. But Don never remarried whereas in the late 1930s my father married my mother, Irene Stanley.

More Fraser and Macaree deaths occurred over the following decades, including old Jim Macaree, Jessie Macaree, and Willie Fraser. Most of them were related to conditions of aging, but the one tragic death was that of Harold when he was 60.

By 1950, Harold had become a successful grazier and resided on his homestead near Kingaroy. His family were away on holidays, when, one night, he awoke to flames throughout the place.

Workmen were woken by his screams, and saw him fall from a window, alight. He was rushed to Kingaroy Hospital, but succumbed to the burns some 15 hours later.

Now only Donald and Millie were left.

Cremorne, the Hub.

*Jessie Stuart Macaree (nee Fraser)
on the steps of Cremorne.*

My childhood memories of Cremorne were ones of always arriving wearing a dress, (whereas normally I'd be clad in play-clothes). I'd receive a warm kiss from grandmother, Jessie. Grandpa Jim could be found in his squatter's chair by my grandma's rose garden, beer in hand. If I came close he'd hook me with his walking stick. It was our game.

The playing of piano, or cards or any other game was

forbidden on Sundays – our most common day for visits. If I sat on my father's lap in the lounge room, I became distressed as I stared at a picture of Simpson and his Donkey on opposite wall. The painting from World War I shows Simpson ushering the donkey, carrying a dead or wounded body around a cliff path. The image haunts me to this day. The back yard was much more inviting and fortunately I was often relegated to the outdoors.

The smooth, curved, worn figurehead of the *Deutschland* in the yard frustrated me as I battled to make it stand upright in order to play with it. The task was an impossible one. I tap-danced on an old, large blue and white tin sign that said *White Horse Inn*. The other side of it had been used to mix concrete.

The outdoor cubby-house with a concrete floor, domed by thorny bougainvillea, which probably sat over the original rotunda, was so dark it scared me, even though it had miniature furniture within. I ventured down to the railway line where the jujube tree grew, but after trying to eat one, I gave that up too.

Out on the front veranda was my father's rocking-horse from his childhood. When I tired of this, I went further along to my older cousins' cubby house.

Our holidays, when we lived in Wheatcroft Street, were mainly to Coorooman. My memories there are of a dusty, bumpy, old dirt road to Emu Park. Often, though, we'd catch the train from Archer Street Station to Coorooman. We didn't have a car. To pack up, Dad laid an old army blanket on the floor and placed all the bedding and clothes on top. With the ends tucked in, he rolled it up tightly and place straps around it. He then threw the bundle over his shoulder. Mum carried food in baskets. We helped. We all traipsed the kilometre or so to the station full of excitement. Such fun. At least for us.

There was no electricity. Dad lit a carbide lamp at night. It stunk badly. The beds were canvas stretchers. The accommodation was a primitive hut. It must have been hard for Mum. The perishable food was kept in a Coolgardie safe hung out under the awning at the back. The butter was always runny.

We replenished supplies of fresh food from the Tookers who still lived across the creek and grew crops as they'd done for a couple of generations.

Coorooman Hut, all that was left

My older brother Jim was the first of our generation to live there, with his wife Carol. Jim worked night shifts at the Bulletin Office as a compositor. They had a German shepherd, and Jim shot kangaroos for dog meat. In true Macaree style, he wasted none of it, and skinned and tanned the hides. It was during this time that he taught me to handle a rifle – the family .22 calibre – and to shoot.

I felt very brave walking across the railway bridge, which was still in use, as it was a huge drop to the creek below.

Next, my brother Stuart, with his partner Marlene, knocked down the old hut and built a timber home there. Stuart worked up the road in his mate Bevan's sawmill, and was paid in timber. Stuart and Marlene married in the back yard of Coorooman surrounded by sunflowers. Stuart discovered a plant growing that he initially couldn't identify, but which turned out to be tobacco and must have dated back to Edwin's days.

It was during 1960, '61 and '62 that we moved from Wheatcroft Street to Cremorne to support Don Fraser, now in his eighties, and his long-widowed sister Millie who was just a tad younger. Don was blind, as his father had been, but knew the layout well. Every morning he walked to his office in Quay Street. He had to navigate about ten metres of deep gravel outside Cremorne before crossing Bridge Street and proceeding along Reaney Street to the bridge. One morning, he tripped in the gravel and fell to his knees.

'You okay, pop?' a bike-rider said, dismounting to help.

'Don't you pop me!' an angry Don replied, getting himself up.

At dinner time it was my role to set the table with strict measurements around Don's place at the head of the table. His own pepper and salt were to be placed six inches from the top of his knife. My mother was the only one he allowed to help him. My father and Don held a quiet truce. My younger brother, Stuart, had the toughest time, as Don's only access to the rest of Cremorne from his bedroom at the front was through Stuart's bedroom. At six every morning, Don made his way to the bathroom. With his walking stick he prodded the then eight or nine-year-old sleeping Stuart, saying, 'Get up boy. The sun will burn a hole in you.'

He asked Stuart one day, 'Can you pour me a nip of Scotch?' Stuart received a quick lesson in what was to become his daily chore.

If four-year-old Irene said good-morning, she received sixpence from Uncle Don.

Old Aunty Millie, in the early stages of dementia, tootled around the house, often with a red and white striped humbug in her mouth, taken from her glass jar on the shelf of the bookcase.

I worked my way through the novels in the bookcase, which included P G Wodehouse's *Jeeves* series, and Arthur Conan Doyle's *Sherlock Holmes* series.

On the wall of my bedroom hung a large photo of Uncle Percy's tombstone. I got permission from my mother to take it down.

With my room only two away from Millie's, I'd often hear a crash through the night. Dad would rush by to pick her up from the floor and put her back in bed. The falls became so regular that Don took the major step of placing her in care at his expense in the glorious, bright, front room of Tannachy Hospital, overlooking the river. I visited, but she never knew who I was.

The room next to Millie's at Cremorne was full of ancient objects. Standing in the doorway, I saw a cylinder record player among the items, but, because no electricity was connected, I was reluctant to enter and explore. My brother told me later that it held relics collected by Don during WWI.

I was the oldest child still living at home, and I rode my bike across Moore's Creek Bridge, along Glenmore Road, over the Alexandra Bridge (where the planks clattered the whole way) and up the road till I reached the just-opened Rockhampton High School at Wandal.

One day, while we were all home, a telegram arrived for Mum. We stood about in anticipation. She read: *arriving with fiancé tomorrow. Love Dorothy.* Dorothy was my older sister.

Don immediately asked my mother, 'Have you met him?'

Mum replied in the negative.

'Good God, woman,' he said. 'He could be black. Or worse still, he could be a Catholic.'

Silence reigned.

After a couple of years, Don took the courageous step of travelling to Switzerland to have his eyes operated on.

He sailed with his long-serving secretary, but, halfway there, he fell and was badly injured. He was flown back to Brisbane but died at the age of 87.

The beneficiaries of his will were many, including his favourite charities and us.

We moved back to our home in Wheatcroft Street and Cremorne was left sitting vacant. My father retrieved many of the family records of letters, diaries, and ledgers, and lodged them with the Rockhampton Library.

The huge gold gilt mirror was sold to a menswear store in East Street. Whilst most furniture was moved out, that room of treasures sat there undisturbed while the homeless made themselves comfortable in the abandoned premises.

And then came the fire. Another one. Cremorne was razed to the ground; probably by accident when the trespassers tried to warm themselves.

The Cremorne gates, all that remained, were donated to the Rockhampton Show Grounds where they still stand, although considerably modified.

The Gates from Cremorne.
Later relocated to the Rockhampton Show Grounds

Truly, the fire heralded the end of an era spanning four generations of Rockhamptonites.

*****

Bibliography and References

McDonald, Lorna, *Rockhampton, A history of Rockhampton and District*, 1981, UQ Press.

Ed L Huf, L McDonald and D Myers, *Sin, Sweat and Sorrow, The Making of Capricornia Queensland 1840s – 1940s*, 1993 CQU Press.

Glenn S Cousins, *Men of Vision over Capricorn, A story of Aviation History in Central Queensland*, 1994. Boorarong Publications.

Bird, J, History of Rockhampton, 1904, The Morning Bulletin.

Rockhampton Municipal Library: Macaree/Fraser collection. (Donated by JWK Macaree)

Rockhampton Bulletin, and Morning Bulletin, via National Library of Australia: https://trove.nla.gov.au/newspaper (unless otherwise notated, all quotes from newspapers are from these two newspapers.)

The Northern Argus Newspaper, via National Library of Australia: via https://trove.nla.gov.au/newspaper

The Capricornian Newspaper, via National Library of Australia: via https://trove.nla.gov.au/newspaper

National Archives of Australia, War records: http://www.naa.gov.au/collection/explore/defence/service-records/army-wwi.aspx

Queensland Government Records of Births and Deaths: https://www.qld.gov.au/law/births-deaths-marriages-and-divorces/family-history-research

Rockhampton Regional Council Cemetery Records: https://www.rockhamptonregion.qld.gov.au/Council-Services/Cemeteries/Burial-Indexes

Acknowledgements

First and foremost, I must acknowledge my family's contribution.

To my husband, Barry, who puts up with my passion for writing, even encouraging me, thank you!

And to my siblings: Big brother, Jim, thanks for the stories and sending me so much. Stuart, thanks for remembering and relating your stories too. The males seem to be carriers of many tales. Dorothy, thanks for your enthusiasm and wisdom, and Irene thanks for your great map, chart and photo talents and the many hours you slaved to make them work.

To our long-deceased and warmly-remembered father, Ken Macaree, thanks for your foresight in retrieving all the Macaree/Fraser papers from Cremorne and donating them to the History Centre at The Rockhampton Regional Library.

To Leanne and Cheryl who work at the History Centre, and to Ann-Maree at the Library, thanks for your support.

To John Fletcher, the walking, breathing encyclopedia on early Rockhampton, who, through his association with the Rockhampton Historical Society, shared many stories of Edwin with me, thank you. (And Erica, too.)

To Ann Gaskell, administrator of the Facebook page, Rockhampton Pioneers, thanks for the almost-daily history lessons that keep us informed.

To Helen Iles, the 'Rock' and my hero at Linellen Press, for whom nothing is impossible, thank you for your constant guidance and support.

About the Author

Shirley moved from her home town of Rockhampton at the age of 21. She has since moved house more than 25 times, accompanying her mining industry husband, before finally settling in Western Australia.

Shirley has worked in the welfare sector for over 35 years including seven years with Lifeline WA, where, with her background in psychology, she trained counsellors, and volunteered as one herself. She travelled the State, disseminating suicide intervention strategies, after which she wrote **'Twenty-Four Seven'** and its sequel, **'Georgie-Girl'**, fictionalising her experiences.

Prior to this, she wrote **'The Rocky Girl'**, which chronicled life during the 1950s and '60s in Queensland. This was the forerunner to the true crime story, **'Mima – A case of abduction, rape and murder'**, which was published in 2016. Mima was a work colleague of Shirley's in Rockhampton in the 1960s and was murdered while working for the electricity authority.

'Edwin – Flamboyant Australian Pioneer', a work of historical fiction, is a venture into a new genre for Shirley.

www.ingramcontent.com/pod-product-compliance
Lightning Source LLC
Chambersburg PA
CBHW071726080526
44588CB00013B/1913